Dowland

COMPOSER ACROSS CULTURES
Formerly The Master Musicians

Bach • Malcolm Boyd
Bach • David Schulenberg
Berg • Bryan R. Simms and Charlotte Erwin
Berlioz • Hugh Macdonald
Beethoven • Barry Cooper
Brahms • Malcolm MacDonald
Byrd • Kerry McCarthy
Carter • David Schiff
Chopin • Jim Samson
Debussy • Eric Frederick Jensen
Dowland • K. Dawn Grapes
Handel • Donald Burrows
Liszt • Derek Watson
MacDowell • E. Douglas Bomberger
Mahler • Michael Kennedy
Mendelssohn • Philip Radcliffe
Monteverdi • Denis Arnold
Mozart • Julian Rushton
Musorgsky • David Brown
Puccini • Julian Budden
Rossini • Richard Osborne
Schoenberg • Malcolm MacDonald
Schumann • Eric Frederick Jensen
Strauss • Laurenz Lütteken
Tallis • Kerry McCarthy
Tchaikovsky • Edward Garden
Tchaikovsky • Roland John Wiley
Vaughan Williams • Eric Saylor
Verdi • Julian Budden
Vivaldi • Michael Talbot

Dowland

K. DAWN GRAPES

OXFORD
UNIVERSITY PRESS

Oxford University Press is a department of the University of Oxford.
It furthers the University's objective of excellence in research, scholarship,
and education by publishing worldwide. Oxford is a registered trade mark of
Oxford University Press in the UK and in certain other countries.

Published in the United States of America by Oxford University Press
198 Madison Avenue, New York, NY 10016, United States of America.

© Oxford University Press 2024

All rights reserved. No part of this publication may be reproduced, stored in
a retrieval system, or transmitted, in any form or by any means, without the prior
permission in writing of Oxford University Press, or as expressly permitted
by law, by license or under terms agreed with the appropriate reprographics
rights organization. Inquiries concerning reproduction outside the scope of the
above should be sent to the Rights Department, Oxford University Press, at the
address above.

You must not circulate this work in any other form
and you must impose this same condition on any acquirer

Library of Congress Cataloging-in-Publication Data
Names: Grapes, K. Dawn, author.
Title: Dowland / K. Dawn Grapes.
Description: [1.] | New York : Oxford University Press, 2024. |
Series: Composers across cultures |
Includes bibliographical references and index.
Identifiers: LCCN 2024013112 (print) | LCCN 2024013113 (ebook) |
ISBN 9780197558850 (hardback) | ISBN 9780197558881 |
ISBN 9780197558867 | ISBN 9780197558874 (epub)
Subjects: LCSH: Dowland, John, 1563?-1626. | Composers—England—Biography. |
Lutenists—England—Biography. | Dowland, John, 1563?-1626—Criticism
and interpretation. | Dowland, John, 1563?-1626—Travel. |
Music—England—16th century—History and criticism. |
Music—England—17th century—History and criticism.
Classification: LCC ML410.D808 G73 2024 (print) | LCC ML410.D808 (ebook) |
DDC 780.92 [B]—dc23/eng/20240322
LC record available at https://lccn.loc.gov/2024013112
LC ebook record available at https://lccn.loc.gov/2024013113

DOI: 10.1093/9780197558881.001.0001

The manufacturer's authorised representative in the EU for product safety is
Oxford University Press España S.A. of El Parque Empresarial San Fernando
de Henares, Avenida de Castilla, 2 – 28830 Madrid (www.oup.es/en or
product.safety@oup.com). OUP España S.A. also acts as importer into Spain
of products made by the manufacturer.

Contents

Composers Across Cultures	vii
Preface	ix
Acknowledgments	xiii
Guide to Abbreviations and Editorial Methods	xv

BECOMING DOWLAND

1. "Musicke, which from my childhoode I haue euer aymed at" (England, 1563–c. 1579)	3
2. "I trauelled the chiefest parts of France" (France, c. 1579–c. 1583)	9
3. "Enfranchisd in the ingenuous profession of Musicke" (England, c. 1584–1594)	19
4. Music for Lute	30

NAVIGATING THE CONTINENT

5. "A man to serve any prince in the world" (German Lands, 1594–1595)	45
6. "I founde the Cities furnisht with all good Artes" (Italy, 1595)	55
7. "You shall not neede to doubt of satisfaction here" (German Lands, 1595–1597) — *Dowland's Psalmes*	68
8. *The First Booke of Songes or Ayres* (1597)	83

SERVING TWO NATIONS

9. "Personal Lutenist to the King" (Denmark, 1598–1602)	107
10. *The Second Booke of Songs or Ayres* (1600) and *The Third and Last Booke of Songs or Aires* (1603)	120
11. *Lachrimae* (1604)	138

12. "Frozen in a colde and forreine country"
    (Denmark, 1602–1606) 151

RETURNING HOME

13. "Old frend, thy yeares have made thee white"
    (England, 1609–1612) — *Micrologus* 163

14. *Varietie of Lute-Lessons* and *A Musicall Banquet* (1610) 176

15. *A Pilgrimes Solace* (1612) 188

16. "Maister Doctor Dowland" (England, 1612–1626) 201

Epilogue 211
Appendix A: John Dowland, Letter to Robert Cecil, 10 November 1595 213
Appendix B: Calendar 217
Appendix C: Select List of Works 219
Appendix D: Personalia 225
Notes 229
Select Bibliography 253
General Index 257
Index of Dowland's Works 261

Composers across Cultures

One hundred twenty-five years ago, when J. M. Dent & Sons published Charles A. Lidgey's *Wagner* (1899), much of the European musical world was in the grips of the phenomenon known as Wagnerism, reason enough to inaugurate *The Master Musicians* with Wagner. Over much of the twentieth century dozens of volumes, many under the editorship of Eric Blom, expanded the series to represent figures deemed critical to understanding the eighteenth and nineteenth centuries, and modern times, the exception being Denis Arnold's venture back to the seventeenth century with *Monteverdi*. In 1994 OUP acquired the series, now renamed Master Musicians, and under the editorship of Stanley Sadie continued to broaden its representation and update previously treated subjects. More recently, the series has expanded its treatment of English composers, including Byrd, Tallis, and Vaughan Williams, and American composers, including MacDowell and Carter, while not neglecting European figures such as J. S. Bach or Bizet.

Now, we embrace the next stage of the series, re-envisioned as Composers Across Cultures. This series renews the commitment to publishing the most authoritative scholarship about major historical composers of influence, and to that end inaugurates Composers Across Cultures with K. Dawn Grapes's *Dowland*. We are also expanding the purview of the series to include significant figures less vigorously explored in scholarship, whether they align with the traditional canon of Western art music or engage with jazz, popular, and non-Western musical traditions. Thus, our second volume, Michael Cooper's *Margaret Bonds*, offers a compelling account of a neglected African American composer whose music is now being recognized for her contributions to American music history and culture. In response to the increasing globalization of music, Composers Across Cultures seeks to explore the inexhaustible diversity of music, and its common links to our shared humanity.

—R. Larry Todd
General Editor

"The applause of them that judge, is the encouragement of those that write."

    John Dowland, *Third and Last Booke of Songs or Aires* (1603)

Preface

By all accounts, early modern musician John Dowland was a successful man. Well-educated, sought after by numerous European courts, and highly paid, he and his achievements shine. As a lutenist first and foremost, he could never hope to obtain one of the choice English church appointments of his age, nor would he be considered for the position of *kapellmeister* in any European court. Yet he was still included in lists of the greatest English musicians of the era, mentioned in the same breath as Tallis, Byrd, Morley, and Bull. His *First Booke of Songes or Ayres* proved to be the most popular English songbook of its time, with four reprints. Three other volumes of his songs gained public favor. He translated a treatise on music theory, and his *Lachrimae* collection of instrumental consort music features the first English multi-movement, cyclic set of variations. In spite of these marked accomplishments, Dowland's writings, many of his chosen lyrics, and his self-created artistic persona and developed musical style weave a tale of wistful nostalgia, one of a man always seeking more. This juxtaposition of great success and implied discontent lays the foundation for the story of one of music history's most compelling figures. If Dowland's fame and success, supported by the quality of his music, provided him an ongoing artistic legacy, it was his humanity, expressed through the tenor of his music, that keeps him relevant and interesting today.

Comparatively, we know much more about Dowland's life than many of his contemporaries, and yet, as will become abundantly clear in the pages that follow, there are still many questions left unanswered. Thus, it seems appropriate to grace the cover of this biography with an image of an unknown figure, simply titled, "Man Playing a Lute." This chalk rendering by Matteo Rosselli (1578–1650) is one of many drawings and paintings from the time featuring some unnamed person playing the most popular instrument of the day. The use of this image is in no way intended to suggest that the figure portrayed is John Dowland. In fact, there are no known images of Dowland to show us what the musician looked like. Rosselli's sketch is appealing, precisely because the subject's facial features cannot be distinguished. The Florentine artist may never have heard the name John Dowland, but our English lutenist likely donned attire similar to that of Rosselli's subject when he performed in Florence for Grand Duke Ferdinando I de' Medici in 1595. We may never know for sure.

What can be ascertained about Dowland is mostly pieced together through his own writings. An extended 1595 letter to Robert Cecil stands as the only piece of correspondence surviving in the lutenist's hand. It reveals more about the first half of his life than does any other source. Two other letters written to him and later copied into an unidentified letterbook (currently held in the Folger Shakespeare Library in Washington, DC), as well as one additional dispatch sent to Dowland in Denmark (now preserved in the Royal Danish Library), complete his surviving personal correspondence. Most of the rest of what we know about Dowland is found in the prefatory material preceding the composer's five published music anthologies. Together, these primary sources provide a solid outline for Dowland's life, as is reflected in this current monograph. Many details filling in this outline are the result of work produced by previous scholars. Twentieth-century lutenist-scholar Diana Poulton created the first full-length biography of the composer in 1972, an impressive feat during an era when technological development had not yet opened up lines of communication and research opportunities we take for granted today. Her scholarly competition with John M. Ward helped solidify now-commonly-accepted measures of Dowland's life and music, and her transcriptions with Basil Lam of Dowland's lute solos provided a collection for studying his instrumental selections in modern notation.

A great deal of important scholarship has taken place in the forty years since Poulton's second edition of *John Dowland* was published. Acquisition and identification of manuscript sources containing Dowland's music can be credited to Robert Spencer and other lutenist-scholars of his generation who advocated for continued interest in the musician. In 2000, David Greer provided modern editions of Dowland's lute songs in the *Musica Britannica* series. More recently, scholars such as Peter Hauge, Sigrid Wirth, and Arne Spohr have been invaluable in providing new archival discoveries illuminating Dowland's years in Denmark and the German lands. Equally important are examinations of Dowland's music, the texts he set, and considerations of his political and religious stances, such as those taken on by Peter Holman, Kirsten Gibson, Matthew Spring, Anthony Rooley, Ian Payne, David Pinto, and others. My appreciation for these researchers cannot be left unspoken.

As part of Oxford University Press's Composers Across Cultures series (formerly The Master Musicians), *Dowland* synthesizes the invaluable work of these scholars while simultaneously contextualizing Dowland's life and music in a new, cohesive overview that also offers alternate perspectives on the composer's life. This modern kind of biography, one that illustrates how musicians of the late-sixteenth and early-seventeenth centuries moved among different, and at times overlapping, social, diplomatic, aristocratic, artistic, and mercantile circles, reveals Dowland as much more than "just" a musician. I hope this book will serve as a valuable resource for music scholars, students, and performers, as well as for those in fields such as history, literature, political science, and religious studies. If the resulting narrative also piques the interest of readers outside of academia, introducing the great John Dowland and his music to those who do not already know his name, my fondest wish will be realized.

Fort Collins, Colorado
28 April 2023

Acknowledgments

Many individuals deserve credit for bringing *Dowland* to life. My sincerest appreciation goes to Oxford University Press editor Norman Hirschy and Composers Across Cultures series editor R. Larry Todd for their unfailing encouragement and confidence, and to Eric Saylor and Kerry McCarthy, whose outstanding biographies in the series served as exemplary models for my work. Cristi MacWaters, Maggie Cummings, and Janet Rombach stand as part of the best Interlibrary Loan division anywhere—without you I would be lost. The Colorado State University College of Liberal Arts and its School of Music, Theatre, and Dance offered funds for travel and time for sabbatical, but more importantly, a reliable cheering section. This project was also endowed by the Renaissance Society of America's Claude V. Palisca Fellowship in Musicology, the Royal Musical Association's Margarita M. Hanson Award, and the Martin Picker Fund of the American Musicological Society, supported in part by the National Endowment for the Humanities and the Andrew W. Mellon Foundation. Special thanks to all of my NABMSA, RSA, and AMS colleagues for listening to endless papers related to Dowland as I formulated a plan. Especially heartfelt gratitude goes to Jeremy L. Smith, Katharyn Benessa, and Barbara R. Davis for insights and suggestions related to early drafts. And to David Grapes, I offer my appreciation for, well, just about everything. *Nil sine numine.*

Guide to Abbreviations and Editorial Methods

Oft-cited sources by or about Dowland referenced in this book are abbreviated as follows (full citations are available in the bibliography):

Primary sources

- *CL*   Letter, John Dowland to Robert Cecil
- *FB*   John Dowland, *First Booke of Songes or Ayres*
- *LST*   John Dowland, *Lachrimae, or Seaven Teares*
- *MB*   Robert Dowland, *A Musicall Banquet*
- *PS*   John Dowland, *A Pilgrimes Solace*
- *SB*   John Dowland, *Second Booke of Songs or Ayres*
- *TB*   John Dowland, *Third and Last Booke of Songs or Aires*
- *VLL*   Robert Dowland, *Varietie of Lute-Lessons*

Secondary sources

- *CLM*   Diana Poulton and Basil Lam, *Collected Lute Music of John Dowland*
- *DM*   John M. Ward, "A Dowland Miscellany"
- *JD*   Diana Poulton, *John Dowland*
- *LB*   Matthew Spring, *The Lute in Britain*
- *NI*   Sigrid Wirth, *Weil es ein Zierlich vnd lieblich ja Nobilitiert Instrument ist*
- *RG*   K. Dawn Grapes, *John Dowland: A Research and Information Guide*

Regularly cited archives and journals are abbreviated as follows

- BL   London, British Library
- CUL   Cambridge University Library
- DNA   Copenhagen, National Archives
- *EM*   *Early Music*

EMH   *Early Music History*
FSL   Washington, Folger Shakespeare Library
JLS   *The Lute: Journal of the Lute Society* (UK)
JLSA *Journal of the Lute Society of America*
LMA   London, Metropolitan Archives
LN   *Lute News: The Lute Society Magazine*
ML   *Music & Letters*
MT   *Musical Times*
NA   Kew, National Archives

During Dowland's lifetime, England had not yet adopted the Gregorian calendar, still adhering to the Julian calendar. Thus, original English primary source documents dated 1 January through 24 March indicate the previous year, some ten days off. All years are updated in this volume to reflect modern dating.

Primary-source spellings and punctuations are modernized for greater readability where appropriate, except for chapter title quotations, printed primary-source volume titles, and, in some cases, names within the context of a quotation.

John Dowland's Europe

BECOMING DOWLAND

1
"Musicke, which from my childhoode I haue euer aymed at"
(England, 1563–c. 1579)

"For myself was born but thirty years after Hans Gerle's book was printed." Lutenist John Dowland wrote these words in his son's 1610 *Varietie of Lute-Lessons*, providing the first clue to his date of birth: 1563. Two years later, he confirmed the information in his final songbook, *A Pilgrimes Solace*, asserting "being I am now entered into the fiftieth year of mine age."[1] By that time, Dowland was the most internationally renowned English musician of his age, having traveled and worked in England, France, Denmark, and the German and Italian lands. Over the course of his lifetime, he produced four songbooks, a collection of instrumental consort music, and a translated theoretical treatise. His music was also included in hundreds of volumes copied and printed by others. Best known for his incredible skills as a professional lutenist, he was also a savvy businessman and advisor. But Dowland's path was not always a smooth one. He faced disappointments and at times found himself in compromising positions. In 1563, however, no one could have anticipated the role this newborn child would play in the history of English music.

The year 1563 was legacy creating beyond the birth of this remarkable musician. John Foxe's *Actes and Monuments* was first printed, memorializing Protestant martyrs of the previous decade. The Canterbury Convocation codified the Forty-two Articles of Religion, a doctrinal statement of the Church of England that formally juxtaposed Protestant doctrine with elements of Catholic liturgical practice, thus defining accepted practice in England's houses of worship. The Treason Act of 1563, which twenty years later would serve as the basis for Catholic executions, was first enacted. William Byrd, the most revered composer of his generation, began his earliest-known professional appointment at Lincoln Cathedral, embarking upon a career that produced some of the most marvelous sacred music of the era.

In 1563, Elizabeth I was less than halfway into the first decade of her forty-four-year reign as Queen of England. The monarch faced a few political and personal setbacks, such as the loss of Le Havre in France and a concerning bout of smallpox, but the year was little different from those surrounding it in the lives of most Englanders. Economic, religious, military, and succession-related questions continued as they had since Elizabeth's accession, but many English subjects, regardless of their support for or against the monarch, found themselves easing into social and political stabilities as the queen solidified her administration, soothing the uncertainty of her first years on the throne. Amidst this setting, Dowland was not the only important figure born in 1563. Robert Cecil, destined to become Queen Elizabeth I's chief advisor many years later and a man who held significant sway over Dowland's career, also entered the world.

No christening record has been found to document Dowland's birth and so we take the composer at his word as to his birth year. The year 1563 saw one of the worst plague years in London's history. Although estimates vary, some 20,000 people in the city and surrounding parishes died, accounting for approximately twenty-four percent of London's population.[2] Those with means left the city in droves, attempting to escape and wait out the illness that pervaded the city's more populated sections. Church registers are full of burial listings, and overwhelmed or sick clergy had difficulty maintaining accurate records. Londoners traveling outside the city postponed christenings or found willing local parishes in which to dedicate their children. And although parishes had been enjoined to keep records of baptisms, marriages, and burials since the time of Henry VIII, this regulation was not rigidly enforced. Even where the practice was more conscientiously followed, information was not always complete. Further, while some surviving parish christening records are written in beautiful, legible hands, many are barely decipherable due to poor penmanship or copy condition. Spelling irregularities were the norm rather than the exception. It was not until 1597 that the Elizabethan government re-codified recording requirements with additional safeguards to preserve statistical data. Thus, it is unfortunate, but not surprising, that notice of Dowland's birth has eluded discovery. Hence, the musician's place of birth remains ripe for speculation.

In the mid-seventeenth century, Thomas Fuller, one of Dowland's earliest biographers, indicated that the lutenist was a product of Westminster. Still, the historian admitted he did not know for sure, noting, "as I have most cause to believe."[3] It was there that the matter stood until some two hundred fifty years later, when Irish historian W. H. Grattan Flood argued that Dowland was born near Dublin and later moved to England.[4] His cited evidence, however, was circumstantial and has never been substantiated. Most musicologists have since deemed Flood's assertions unlikely, especially when considering Dowland's own words to Robert Cecil that he was "born under her highness" and his manuscript declaration that a group of his psalm settings were composed by "an unhappy Englishman."[5] Other instances in which he describes himself as a native Englander are found elsewhere, such as in the prefatory material of his *First Booke of Songes or Ayres* (1597) and his *A Pilgrimes Solace* (1612). So while Dowland likely came from somewhere in England, his entrance into the world remains a matter of conjecture, much like his childhood circumstances.

Branches of families with the Dowland surname lived throughout England during John Dowland's life, but none have been tied definitively to the musician. These lines fall mostly within a working class of tradesmen. Twentieth-century Dowland biographer Diana Poulton lists the professions of mason, printer, fisherman, and tailor, as evidenced in wills of sixteenth-century persons with similar last names.[6] To require a will indicates these working-class figures owned enough personal property to bequeath to future generations. Given Dowland's later successes with music publishing, one especially intriguing figure is a Robert Dowland who was apprenticed to a Stationer's Company printer in 1556.[7] Unfortunately, there is little additional information on the man or his activities. Might he have been a relative, perhaps even John's father? There is no way to tell. Indeed, as far as documentation goes, nothing is known of Dowland's life until he reached his late teens, when he worked for Sir Henry Cobham, England's ambassador in Paris. Still, the types of circumstances in which Dowland was raised can be contextualized through an examination of customs of his day. Certainly the musician had assistance in establishing the foundations of a career from which he emerged as the leading instrumentalist of his time. Although we do not know who helped him on his path to greatness, we can imagine the steps he may have taken.

Dowland made just one public statement about his early years, when he informed the reader in his *First Booke of Songes or Ayres* (1597) that he was always destined for "the ingenuous profession of Music, which from my childhood I have ever aimed at, sundry times leaving my native country, the better to attain so excellent a science." Musical training for children of the period was achieved through several methods. In a family with more means, students received some musical training in public schools, or in especially wealthy families through private tutors. The lute was heralded for many years as an instrument to be mastered in a well-rounded education. Humphrey Gilbert's design for "the erection of an academy in London for education of her majesty's wards, and others of the youth of nobility and gentlemen" (1564) called for "one teacher of music, and to play on the lute, the bandora, and cittern."[8] Dowland more likely came from a lower station. Throughout his career, he was quite concerned with his public regard and certainly would have revealed an elite legacy had his family descended from a higher rank.

The two most common sources of comprehensive musical training for children of more humble beginnings were found at cathedral choir schools and through apprenticeship. Since 1560, Westminster statutes codified that choristers, who were always boys, be "of tender age with clear voices, able to sing."[9] They were to "learn the art of music and to play on musical instruments." The art of music they practiced included not only singing and playing, but also theory and basic compositional skills. A typical day consisted of singing an early morning service, courses in Latin, music lessons in singing and instruments, choir rehearsals for services and plays, and music theory instruction.[10] This was the path taken by most musicians ultimately employed in cathedrals as choirmasters and organists, such as William Byrd, Thomas Morley, and Thomas Weelkes. Dowland certainly demonstrated his knowledge of theoretical practices through his writings and compositions and he was highly literate. His education seems comparable to that of students of the choir schools. Yet while most of his printed anthologies feature voices, he himself was never described or recorded as a singer during his lifetime. Even though choristers trained on both lutes and viols, the more likely path for Dowland's musical education, resulting in a specialized instrumental career, was through apprenticeship with a learned master.[11]

In the year of Dowland's birth, a governmental act was passed requiring anyone who wished to enter a trade to complete an apprenticeship.[12] This included musicians, most specifically instrumentalists who wished to join the ranks of town waits. These performers often played multiple wind instruments and served cities in a variety of ways. Apprenticeship was also the common method for training those hoping to work in noble households. Apprenticeship not only afforded youngsters the opportunity to learn a trade, but also positioned those so motivated to make professional connections that might aid them later in their careers. The 1563 act codified the previously understood minimum length of apprenticeship at seven years. If Dowland completed an apprenticeship before he left for France in his late teens, he must have begun service at least by the age of ten. While this may seem young by modern standards, it was not unusual at the time, especially for musicians. Most apprentices in varied occupations commenced service in their teens, but the tradition of boy choristers seems to have embedded the idea of early training for all types of musicians. Additionally, children of vagrants or those who were orphaned were apprenticed in a variety of trades as part of poor laws that aimed to combat poverty.[13]

While no extant documents related to a Dowland apprenticeship are known, descriptions of several musical apprenticeships from this time period survive. In 1579, Dowland's contemporary Daniel Bacheler, son of a laborer, was sent to be apprenticed in his uncle's house at seven years of age. The relative, Thomas Cardell, was a lutenist and dancing master within the Elizabethan court. Seven years later, Bacheler's apprenticeship, which was set at a wearisome sixteen years, was transferred to one of the most powerful men in Elizabethan England: Sir Francis Walsingham.[14] Bacheler went on to serve other equally important figures, such as the Earl of Essex and James I's consort, Queen Anna. Fellow lutenist Robert Johnson was apprenticed in 1596 at around age thirteen in the household of Dowland's *First Booke* dedicatee, George Carey, Baron Hunsdon.[15]

In many ways, a domestic apprenticeship was an appealing prospect for its security and potential for raising one's social stature. An apprentice was not paid, but could expect board, lodging, and clothing to be provided by the family holding the indenture. An apprentice might receive occasional gifts as well. A professional in the family's service or a contracted outsider provided instruction in a specified craft. This teacher was also often tasked with managing other details of the apprentice's care.[16] Musical instruction sometimes took place one on one but might also occur alongside children of the manor if the apprentice's master taught them as well. A music apprentice could expect to learn not only their primary instrument, but also singing, secondary instruments, theory, and composition. In return, the apprentice was expected to represent the family well with devoted service and to maintain an upright character. Doing so helped to build a reputation that might allow a musician to move into paid service in the same residence, or subsequently to an equally or even more prestigious household, or perhaps into court service once their indenture was complete.

While most of Dowland's training would have taken place through demonstrated instruction with an established lutenist, an important lute instruction book was available in England in the 1570s, a translation of the French master Adrian Le Roy's *A briefe and plaine Instruction to set all Musicke of eight diuers tunes in Tableture for the Lute* (1574). From this volume, Dowland could reinforce his training in left- and right-hand technique and tablature conventions related to reading the notational system specifically created for the instrument.[17] As is featured in this book, Dowland most likely learned to play on a classic six-course lute, that is, one with six sets of strings, the most standard lute in England at that time.[18] Later in his life, he moved on to favor the seven-course Elizabethan instrument, which added a string set a fourth below the lowest six-course configuration. In some cases, Dowland later composed for the nine-course lute, indicating he played on multiple types of instruments throughout his career.[19]

The lute was an especially popular instrument in England in the mid-sixteenth century. Those in the upper echelons of society saw musical proficiency as a desired trait in a well-rounded gentleman or lady. Thus, elite households sought out instrumental tutors to serve their educational needs. Not only are lutes found listed among wills as valuable items to be distributed to heirs, but a number of portraits of the time show figures playing, holding, or standing near the instrument. The gentry and mercantile classes also took to the lute, learning the instrument through private instruction or printed tutorials. Large numbers of lutes were imported into the country, and the instrument is mentioned in multiple texts of the era.[20] The lute was also heard in incidental music provided for theatrical productions and included in consorts of instrumentalists providing courtly entertainment. Talented lutenists made their living by teaching in domestic settings, performing at court or university functions, or working in the theatres. A skilled musician might find subsistence through all three endeavors. This is the life for which Dowland's early musical training prepared him. The youngster's education set him on a course that led him into the service of an important Elizabethan diplomat, Sir Henry Cobham. Around the year 1579, a young John Dowland took his early-acquired skills to France.

2
"I trauelled the chiefest parts of France"
(France, c. 1579–c. 1583)

"Fifteen years since, I was in France, servant to Sir Henry Cobham who was Ambassador for the Queen's Majesty."[1] John Dowland wrote these words to Robert Cecil on 10 November 1595, providing the earliest time and place in which the English musician can be placed: Paris in the early 1580s. The long, dense letter to Cecil supplies more information related to Dowland's life than any other extant source, beginning with the reference to his early French sojourn. Although still in his teens, Dowland had probably already completed an internship with an established lutenist in England by 1579. An opportunity to journey to Paris, in any capacity, was surely alluring. Travel as an educational extension had long been established in England and by the final decades of the sixteenth century was no longer encouraged only for sons of noblemen. Artisans, tradesmen, merchants, or anyone who hoped to expand upon future prospects could look upon a trip with a noted upper-class statesman as a way to increase his own social prestige while preparing for service within a society that valued connections and loyalty.[2]

For Dowland, time in France not only allowed him to learn or polish his command of the French language and develop international social skills but also provided him with an introduction to Continental musicians. The French court employed highly skilled lutenists, such as Charles and Jacques Edinton, Estienne Dugué, and both of the King's royal printers, Adrian Le Roy and Robert Ballard, from whom Dowland could consider what a courtly position for a skilled lutenist involved.[3] In travels outside of Paris, when the ambassador followed French King Henri III to his country palaces, in the summer of 1580 when plague raged in the city, or when Dowland took excursions on his own, the musician must have studied the sonic landscape of the countryside. His memories of the nation never left him, as declared in the dedication of his 1597 *First Booke of Songes or Ayres*: "I traveled the chiefest parts of France, a nation furnished with great variety of Music."[4]

Whether Dowland traveled with Ambassador Cobham from England to France in 1579 when the diplomat assumed the ambassadorship or if he joined him there subsequently remains unconfirmed, although the first seems more likely. There is also no indication of Dowland's role in Cobham's entourage. He may have been engaged as a household musician or as a music tutor for the ambassador's wife or young children, who also resided in Paris. Perhaps he served as a secretary or was simply a household servant. Cobham was not known as an active supporter of the arts. In fact, in correspondence to Elizabeth I's Secretary Francis Walsingham, he complained more than once of the French Court parties and entertainments that took up much of his time.[5] Dowland was likely expected to participate in non-musical tasks, even if he was concurrently looked upon for his musical talents. Cobham's wife, Anne, whose presence and influence in relations with the French court are often overlooked, may have held a greater appreciation for Dowland's artistry than did her husband. Regardless, the young musician's experiences with the ambassador, who oversaw England's only permanent embassy at the time, undoubtedly helped prepare him for roles and expectations in the international courts in which he found himself later in his career.

Dowland's employer, Sir Henry Cobham, was a career diplomat of noble heritage who maintained a long relationship with Queen Elizabeth.[6] During Mary I's reign, he served in the then-princess's household. After his mistress ascended the throne, he assumed the role of Gentleman Pensioner, as part of the group whose main directive was protecting the queen. He was knighted by his monarch at the Earl of Leicester's 1575 Kenilworth entertainments and was sent on multiple diplomatic missions to Paris, Spain, Vienna, and the Low Countries before his appointment as French Ambassador in 1579, a post in which he remained through most of 1583.[7] The French king seems to have enjoyed Cobham's presence, which proved mutually beneficial for both England and France. The ambassador was middle-aged at the time, as well as reportedly cold and aloof, and his standing as part of a noble family likely separated him even further from the still-teenaged Dowland. Yet the young musician had much to learn under Cobham's care.

Cobham was sent to Paris with certain primary goals: cooperation in a campaign to install Don Antonio as rightful heir to the Portuguese throne; the establishment of reparations for English subjects whose property was seized by French ships; and continued marriage negotiations between Queen Elizabeth and King Henri's younger brother, Francis, Duke of Anjou and Alençon.[8] The real value of ambassadors, however, in which Cobham did not disappoint, was the capacity to communicate information and news related to their foreign post back to Elizabeth, her Privy Council, and, most especially, Elizabeth's spymaster Walsingham, who had occupied the French ambassadorship himself in the early 1570s. Cobham also kept tabs upon and relayed information about English Catholic exiles in Paris and served as an advocate for those who showed loyalty to the Crown and wanted to return to England.[9] Not much could happen in France that did not filter through Cobham's residence, and news from England was regularly received and assessed. The ambassador's company included about twenty men who served in a variety of roles, from secretaries to couriers to household servants.

The English embassy in Paris occupied a building rented from Madame de Selve, presumably Renée de Montmirail, widow of Odet de Selve, himself an ambassador for France to England, Vienna, and Rome.[10] The residence lay in an enviable location for keeping up with the continuously fluctuating mood of Paris, near the left bank of the Seine and directly across from Notre Dame, where the wealthiest resided. Close by were cloistered abbeys and the Place Maubert, around which neighborhoods teamed with merchants.[11] Traditionally a market area, the Place Maubert also provided a park-like setting used as a gathering place for speakers and demonstrators, a site of book burnings of Huguenot tracts and pamphlets, and a public space for sporadic, but important, executions, most often featuring Protestants burned at the stake. The embassy was also not far away from the route that one of Henri's fraternities marched from L'Eglise des Grands Augustins to Notre Dame in 1583, hooded in white robes and accompanied by singers from the king's chapel.[12] In this location, the English embassy must have seemed like a Protestant oasis in the middle of a Catholic desert.

Cobham's residence was also less than a mile from the house of Jean-Antoine Baïf, founder of the Académie de poésie et de musique, a society of musicians (both singers and instrumentalists), poets, and patrons, who, like the Florentine Camerata in Italy, sought to revive classical poetry, but in vernacular French.[13] This group was especially interested in *musique mensurée*, or using specific meters to set modern poetry, which then found its way into court airs that followed. The academy was founded in 1570 during the reign of Charles IX, after which a similar academy, the Académie du Palais, convened during Henri III's tenure that included many of the same members. The king attended their concerts at the Louvre and possibly some house concerts at the home of Baïf.

Paris, the largest city in Europe at the time, was the center of a wide variety of musical activities, of which Baïf's academy was but one outlet. The vibrancy of the Parisian musical scene, led by those associated with the French court, must have influenced Dowland's personal musical style and subsequent compositional activity. Music was valued by all of the Valois royalty, and their outstanding musicians became a means for the French Court to advertise its stature.[14] The court attracted and maintained a substantial number of musicians. Between 1575 and 1580, Henri regularly employed at least seventeen instrumentalists and seventeen singers in his chamber, although the number was reduced in 1584.[15] In addition to Henri's regular instrumentalists, musicians most often promoted to the position of valet—a servant included in the king's most intimate circle—were lutenists and lutenist-singers.[16] In 1575, Henri advanced three lutenists and a violinist to this elite group, followed by two lutenists in 1580. The households of other royal family members also retained their own musicians.

Official functions routinely included musical activities, and there may have been times when Dowland accompanied Cobham on court visits, thus experiencing French courtly music firsthand. The ambassador informed Walsingham:

> [King Henri] ordered that every Sunday, Tuesday, and Thursday after dinner there should be dancing openly in the queen's chamber, and after supper in the great hall, commanding that all his gentlemen, being "in quarter," should "apparel themselves those days for to be present, and such as list, to dance."[17]

A more detailed report of one specific occasion describes how the king himself took part:

> In the first ball or dance the tabors and fifes do sound a pavan where the king leadeth the young queen by the hand and danceth with her, being followed with a number of his greatest princes and princesses and other ladies of the court.
> In the second dance the said tabors and fifes do sound an almain . . .
> In the third dance the violons sound the branles in the which because it is danced round in form of a ring, there can be no great order observed in it . . .

In the fourth dance the violons sound the corrantes, where commonly the queen giveth over, but the king continueth and danceth with the ladies and maids of honor at his pleasure.

In the fifth dance the violons sound la volta, in the which the king taketh his greatest pleasure, will always dance the same with the queen mother's maids of honor.

In the end and sixth dance the cornets together with the violons sound a galliard, but then the king leaveth and sitteth down between his queen and the queen mother, giving the looking on to his young princes and ladies, and after retireth himself into his cabinet, having first given the goodnight to the queens and all the company.[18]

The types of dances represented are worth noting, especially the important opening pavan and closing galliard, as well as the almain, for these are the dances that made up the bulk of Dowland's instrumental compositions and that also influenced the formal elements of many of his songs. Although lutes are not specified in the dancing example above, they were included in royal events. In February 1580, Cobham described a private banquet for the king, to which he had been invited by the queen mother. He notes that one section of this particular entertainment opened with "six musician maskers, playing on their lutes." Later "two boys sang a French song to the lute." For the final dances, "there entered a dozen maskers playing on lutes."[19]

In Paris in 1581, royal favorite Duc de Joyeuse married Mademoiselle de Vaudémont, the sister of Queen Louise. The two weeks of festivities surrounding the nuptials were quite the occasion. Pierre de Ronsard, whose poetry had been celebrated in French chansons for decades, and Baïf, who was patronized by the Duc, collaborated with composer Claude le Jeune and choreographer Jean Antoine de Baïf on a commission to provide choreographed songs for *mascarades*—entertainments manifested in procession. The songs used were *airs de couer*, strophic songs presented in the fashionable French style that may have influenced Dowland's later lute song compositions.[20]

The highlight of the festival, however, was a five-and-a-half hour production entitled *Le Balet comique de la Royne*, more commonly known as *Circé*. This extravagant performance, presented at the Louvre, is now considered by many dance historians to be the first true, full-length court ballet. The spectacle featured poetic invocations of mythological creatures, singing, and instrumental music, as well as dancing. Up to forty singers and forty instrumentalists were utilized and French royals and guests participated in featured and chorus roles. Dowland might or might not have witnessed the entertainment firsthand, but Cobham attended the event.[21] Creator Balthasar de Beaujoyeulx's libretto with commentary, enhanced by set and costume design engravings and printed instrumental music, dances, and solo and multi-part songs, appeared in print in Paris the following year, providing notation of the dramatic music and showing the importance and value given to solo song to anyone with access to the book, including aspiring musicians.[22] Cobham purchased a copy.

Another printed music collection that appeared in Paris during Dowland's stay was Guillaume Tessier's 1582 *Premier Livre d'Airs tant François, Italien, qu'Espaignol*. Dowland likely had met, or at least knew of, Tessier. As a Huguenot in Paris, his religion caused him difficulties procuring a job in the French court. Tessier approached Cobham in 1580, requesting permission for himself and his family to travel to England in search of work. Cobham's report back to Walsingham indicates he discouraged the Frenchman:

> And now there is an old musician named Guillaume Tessier, borne in Brittany, with his two sons, and a daughter which pretend to pass into England, whom I have persuaded for that the times are full of troubles, and all courts occupied in the consideration of the events thereof, that he would rather defer his journey. But the sickness in Paris, and the lack of rewards here will force him (as he says) to seek countries.[23]

Not long after his song collection was produced, the "old musician" traveled to London anyway, and then on to Scotland.[24] One of Tessier's aforementioned sons was likely Charles Tessier, a lutenist like Dowland, and the two may have shared common Parisian acquaintances.[25] This was not the last time these men would cross the same circles.

Guillaume Tessier's songs, or *airs*, manifested as a traditional set of partbooks for four to five voices that was notable for its international flavor. Some of the songs included are found in earlier manuscripts as lute songs for solo voice and lute accompaniment. Especially compelling is the print's dedication and its opening song praising Queen Elizabeth. The anthology was one of ten volumes of strophic songs printed in France between 1579 and 1583 during Dowland's residence.[26] Half of these publications use the word *air* in the title to describe their contents, as Dowland did in his later songbooks. The French royal privilege for music printing at the time was held by Ballard and his cousin Le Roy, whose lute tutorial first appeared in English translation during Dowland's formative years.[27]

Le Roy was the first person to use the term *airs de couer* in print, in his own *Airs de cour miz sur le luth* of 1571. Scholar Jeanice Brooks argues that Le Roy's label, freely exchangeable with the terms *chanson* and *voix de ville*, shifts the focus of these strophic songs to the royal court as vehicles for courtly poetry, decorum, and grace, traits that later defined the songs in Dowland's *First Booke*.[28] Whether Dowland knew of Le Roy's songbook is uncertain, but it was the last book of lute songs printed in France until 1608. Its presentation, with lute tablature on one page and a featured vocal part on the page facing, is evocative of Dowland's own first songbook published in 1597. Certainly the decades between the two publications, Dowland's wide-ranging experiences in other countries and at home in the interim, and new trends and English conventions had a greater impact on musical choices made in his later anthology, but the influence of early impressions upon a young musician's creative mind should not be underestimated.

When Cobham and Dowland arrived in Paris, France was still entrenched in the aftereffects of years of religious wars between the Catholic state and Protestant Huguenots. Conflicts began in earnest in the 1560s, and many Parisians still had vivid memories of the 1572 St. Bartholomew Day Massacre, as did Walsingham, who as French ambassador at the time harbored Protestants seeking shelter in his Parisian home. In 1580, Henri III signed the Treaty of Fleix, which brought the wars of religion to an uneasy truce, but tensions never completely subsided during his reign. While the accord restored some rights to Protestants, the state's official religion and power structures remained Catholic. In many ways, France provided a theological mirror image of the early portion of Elizabeth's reign. Thus, the young Dowland left one state that insisted upon Protestantism for another that insisted upon Catholicism.

When Elizabeth assumed the English throne after the death of her Catholic sister, Mary I, in 1558, loyalty to her Protestant Church of England was expected from subjects, but conformity was not rigidly enforced. After issuance of a papal bull in 1570, the landing of the first English-born, Continental-trained Jesuit missionaries in 1580, and discovery of a series of plots to replace Elizabeth on the throne, new laws and stricter enforcement of harsh penalties were put in place for recusancy, Catholic practice, and harboring priests. During Dowland's Parisian stay, the English Parliament approved the 1581 "Act of Persuasions," formally titled "An act to retain the queen's majesty's subjects in their due obedience," which declared that anyone who chose the Catholic church over the queen's church was guilty of treason. Anyone with knowledge of noncompliant acts by others who did not report them was deemed guilty of the same.

Excessive fines were established for non-church attendance, fees so high that only the very wealthy could pay their way out of regular church attendance. The alternative was prison, or worse. Practicing priests could expect torture and death if discovered. That same year, Jesuit priest Edmund Campion, a leader in the underground Catholic community, was captured, arrested, tortured, and publicly hanged, drawn, and quartered. The English press issued materials and defenses from both sides, and martyrologies and anti-martyrologies appeared. In the spring of 1582, a royal proclamation "To denounce Jesuit traitors" emphasized the state claim that priests were not really there for religious purposes, but for treasonous ones, an act that set the stage for future prosecutions.

France—already the destination for many English subjects who sought a Catholic education, were called to join religious orders, or who chose exile to freely practice their chosen religion—saw a new influx of English Catholics. It is unlikely that any English subject in Paris in the 1580s could have avoided the constant news of ongoing religious tensions in England as disseminated by exiles in a city that embraced their religion. As a member of the English ambassador's household, Dowland no doubt was privy to some of the official versions of news as it arrived from London court officials. Cobham was a staunch Protestant and devotee of the queen, but he also relied upon English exiles and other Catholic informants to gather state intelligence. It is little wonder then that the young John Dowland came into contact with Catholics who led him to consider conversion.

By 1582, Dowland must have been quite comfortable in his French habitat. That year, he made acquaintance with a group of English Catholics, including "one Smith a priest, and one Morgan sometimes of her majesty's Chapel, one Verstigan who brake out of England being apprehended and one Morris a Welshman that was our porter, who is at Rome."[29] He recalled that "men thrust many idle toys into my head of religion, saying that the papists' was the truth and ours in England all false, and I being but young their fair words overreached me and I believed with them." Richard Verstegan was perhaps the most well known of these figures. He covertly published a book about Catholic martyr Edmund Campion in London in 1582 but was discovered, requiring his escape to France.[30] At least two of the men Dowland listed, Morgan and Morris, were probably musicians, facilitating closer access to the young lutenist. Nicholas Morgan, a gentleman of the Chapel Royal since 1567, fled England in the summer of 1582 and is subsequently recorded as working in Sainte-Chapelle, Paris from 1583 to 1586, likely returning to England by 1591.[31] He later settled in Antwerp, where he became one of the largest producers of recusant literature. Morris is the last name of Gentleman of the Chapel Richard Morris who, according to the 1583 chapel checkbook, "fled beyond the seas." Morris might also refer to Thomas Morris, a musician noted at the English College in Douay who was destined for Rome in the summer of 1582, but who may have been delayed, necessitating a longer stay in Paris.[32] That Dowland lists him as one "who was our porter" suggests that the man also worked for Cobham, so perhaps this was a different Morris altogether.

Cobham, who surely encouraged or even required his servants to bring him intelligence, would not have looked favorably upon Dowland's conversion. Removal from his duties would surely follow, had the statesman believed Dowland was seriously involved with someone like Verstegan. Dowland, however, does not show up on any extant lists of known papists sent back to England, indicating that either Cobham did not know about his employee's conversion, did not think Dowland important enough to report, or did not want Elizabeth informed that one of his own subordinates was associating with those of questionable loyalties. Perhaps Dowland never outwardly showed signs of commitment to the faith.

At some time during his Parisian stay, Dowland was sent on behalf of an English ambassador to check on a group of English merchants being held in a French prison. Their representative William Wardour wrote afterwards, appealing again for help. His letter states the ambassador previously sent "favorable charity by your servant John Dowland."[33] The document, however, bears no specified recipient name, for it is addressed only to "The right honorable, the Ambassador of England." When the correspondence was cataloged in the British calendar of state papers in the early twentieth century, it was dated 1584, even though no year is penned on the original document.[34] Aligned with this estimated date, incoming ambassador Edward Stafford is then listed in the calendar as recipient. Scholars have since used the calendar and the later added marking of 1584 to conclude Dowland was either retained or rehired by Stafford, remaining in France when Cobham returned to England in late 1583. The new ambassador was much more amenable to association with Catholics as a means to gather information and was rumored in some circles to be an outright sympathizer. Yet it is possible that Dowland visited the prisoners on behalf of Cobham and that their reply arrived after Stafford assumed office or was left behind at the embassy.[35] Whenever Dowland returned to England, either with Cobham or later, he seems to have encountered no issues, indicating that his Paris Catholic connections, if they bore any significant weight, were not well recognized by the state.

Dowland's time in France also provided him an opportunity to network with a number of influential English figures who passed through Paris during his stay. In 1580, poet and translator Thomas Watson arrived in the company of Thomas Walsingham, the secretary's cousin. Francis Walsingham himself arrived for a short stay in 1581 to discuss marriage negotiations between Elizabeth and Anjou. Perhaps most intriguingly, two men, both also born in 1563 and who would later figure prominently in Dowland's life, visited Paris around this time. First to arrive was a young Robert Sidney, brother to the famous statesman and poet Philip Sidney. Cobham wrote to Walsingham in October 1581 that "Mr. Sidney has come hitherto from Germany. He is a proper gentleman, and methinks like his elder brother."[36] Robert later served as godfather to Dowland's son and he eventually became one of the most important political figures in England. Several years later, another Robert, Robert Cecil, arrived in Paris in 1584.[37] Cecil, whom Dowland approached a decade later for permission to travel to the German lands, is especially important because of the aforementioned letter Dowland penned to him in 1595, the first primary source that places Dowland in France in the 1580s. Did Dowland meet either of these men during this period? If so, it may have provided him with connections who played significant roles in his future endeavors. Any new contacts, as well as his daily experiences in France, surely affected his music, his future prospects, and his state of mind upon returning to England, where he built a reputation as the finest lutenist in the land.

3
"Enfranchisd in the ingenuous profession of Musicke"

(England, c. 1584–1594)

When Dowland returned to England from France in the mid-1580s, his clearest path forward as an instrumentalist was employment in one or more influential households, teaching the lute to family members, making music with others associated with the same patron circles, and providing entertainment for special occasions. His music was already known upon his homecoming, or else he entered the public consciousness fairly quickly, as evidenced by an entry in Anthony Munday's book *A Banquet of Daintie Conceits*. Munday's volume of song lyrics was entered into the Stationers' register, the official log of prints to be produced by members of the publishing trade guild, in 1584. The anthology, however, was not printed until 1588. No notated music is included with any of the poems in the book, but Munday's title page suggests that each work is to be sung "either to the lute, bandora, virginals, or any other instrument." Each entry is then labeled with the typical broadside-ballad directive that matches text with a specific well-known melody. The seventeenth entry in Munday's volume instructs the reader to sing a six-verse "ditty" to the tune of "Dowland's Galliard."[1] Which galliard tune the printer intended for performance remains open for speculation, but that Dowland's music was referenced at all indicates that at least some of his compositions were already well known.

In July 1588, Dowland reached an especially important milestone when he received a Bachelor of Music degree from Christ Church, Oxford, an accomplishment he touted often throughout his career. For example, his *First Booke of Songes or Ayres* (1597) proudly announces that the anthology was "composed by John Dowland, Lutenist and Bachelor of Music." He subsequently appended the degree to his name in every one of his other publications, leaning on the convention that earning a university credential was one of a limited number of ways in which those born outside the upper classes could work toward upward social mobility in early modern England.

The nation's social hierarchy had long been established. At the top of the social stratum was the nobility, with royalty ranking highest, followed by peers with the titles duke, marquess, earl, viscount, and baron. Ranking slightly lower was the gentry—landowning families who often descended from lesser noble lines. The yeomanry served as a middle class of workers, comprised of merchants, artisans, and those who were employed by the upper classes. At the bottom were the poor, those unfortunate individuals who had no means of regular income and relied upon "Poor Laws" for survival.[2] Within this general structure, one means of moving up from the yeoman class to the level of gentleman was through education. Professional ranks such as barrister or physician were afforded gentlemanly status, offering careers and financial security for non-firstborn sons of the elite. They also provided a way to earn respectability for those born further down the social ladder. Dowland's Bachelor of Music designation, bestowed by one of the oldest and most prestigious institutions in Europe, added credibility to his resume.

Music baccalaureate degrees were offered in England as far back as the early sixteenth century but were not always earned in the same way as other degrees.[3] Bachelor of Arts students were required to attend music lectures, but requirements for the Bachelor of Music seem to have been much more flexible. Some recipients read in residence, with requirements to complete some sort of project to confirm their suitability. Others were granted degrees as a reflection of their past professional accomplishments, often prompted by recommendation of an important patron.[4] This path did not necessitate any long-term presence on campus. Those admitted to the degree often had already established themselves as accomplished musicians. Dowland was just twenty-five years old, and thus, his achievement seems impressive. Surviving records indicate that fewer than ten individuals were admitted as Bachelors of Music at Oxford in the 1580s. Most were church musicians, often closely linked to the Elizabethan court. This profile, of course, does not fit Dowland, thus meriting special notice and enhancing the importance of whoever may have served as his sponsor. While it is impossible to determine who this might have been, a number of people with direct ties to the musician were also associated with Christ Church. For example, Robert Sidney, whom Dowland may have met in France, attended the school in the 1570s and 1580s.

Dowland was not the only musician named Bachelor of Music at Oxford in July 1588. Thomas Morley was awarded the same degree, marking the first of several parallel events in the two musicians' lives.[5] In addition to being named in the official Oxford registry, the two are recorded together as Oxford graduates on an inserted slip of paper found in composer Thomas Whythorne's manuscript biography, now housed at the Bodleian Library.[6] Whythorne was an Oxford man himself. Although his manuscript was completed in 1575, the paper insertion has been dated to between 1592 and 1595, placing it chronologically closer to the 1588 degrees.

Intriguingly, several others who received honorary Oxford degrees the same year are named in titles of Dowland instrumental works. In April 1588, Robert Devereaux, second Earl of Essex, whom Dowland approached in 1594 for permission to travel to the Continent, received a Master of Arts degree, incorporated from his Cambridge honor. Taking part in this distinction, a number of other gentlemen were created Masters of Arts as well, including two sons of Henry Norris, and Robert Sidney. Sidney and Essex, as well as someone named Mrs. Norris, are all honored in the titles of Dowland dances.[7] The lutenist's Oxford music degree also aided his quest for larger public recognition as he presented himself as a learned and credentialed musician with skills above all others. His new status as an Oxford man linked him to renowned scholars, writers, and professionals of the period and surely granted him access to academic circles outside those he had previously encountered, including the Inns of Court, England's legal learning institutions that supported artists through both patronage and sponsorship of theatrical works.

At the same time, Dowland established himself beyond academic circles, associating with persons holding important positions in the Elizabethan court, such as George Carey, dedicatee of Dowland's *First Booke* (1597), and Robert Cecil, both of whom would follow their fathers into roles as Queen Elizabeth's Lord Chamberlain and Secretary of State, respectively. In the 1590s, Dowland also participated in or contributed artistically to several events directly related to the queen and her courtiers. One such occasion is commemorated in a trilogy of Dowland songs related to a special Accession Day display. Each year, this anniversary of Queen Elizabeth's reign was celebrated with grand festivities, including ceremonial tilts featuring Elizabeth's most favored courtiers. These highly theatrical tournaments featured jousting in costume and ultimately served to exalt the queen.

On 17 November 1590, Sir Henry Lee officially stepped down from his title of "Knight of the Crown," an honorific he held while representing the monarch in the annual ceremonial tilts for two decades.[8] Lee's retirement must have been especially heartfelt, for he had long maintained a special relationship with Elizabeth. For years, Lee was responsible for putting together entertainments that helped establish and sustain the monarch's fabled persona as the ageless "Virgin Queen." Tribute was afforded as Lee and his "Knight of the Crown" successor, George Clifford, third Earl of Cumberland, approached Elizabeth following their rides that momentous day. William Segar documented:

> Her majesty beholding these armed knights coming toward her, did suddenly hear a music so sweet and secret, as everyone thereat greatly marveled. And harkening to that excellent melody, the earth as it were opening, there appeared a pavilion ... The music aforesaid, was accompanied with these verses, pronounced and sung by Mr. *Hales,* her majesty's servant, a gentleman in that art excellent, and for his voice both commendable and admirable.[9]

"His golden locks time hath to silver turned," the song lyrics that followed, later appear as the eighteenth song in Dowland's *First Booke* (1597).[10] The words were preserved not only in Segar's recollection but were also recorded in George Peele's *Polyhymnia* (1590).

> His golden locks, Time hath to silver turned,
> O Time too swift, o swiftness never ceasing:
> His youth 'gainst Time and Age hath ever spurned
> But spurned in vain, Youth waneth by increasing.
>   Beauty, Strength, Youth, are flowers, but fading seen,
>   Duty, Faith, Love are roots, and ever green.
>
> His helmet now, shall make a hive for bees,
> And lovers' sonnets, turned to holy psalms:
> A man at arms must now serve on his knees,
> And feed on prayers, which are Age his alms.
>   But though from court to cottage he depart,
>   His Saint is sure of his unspotted heart.

And when he saddest sits in homely cell,
He'll teach his swains this carol for a song.
Blest be the hearts that wish my sovereign well.
Cursed be the souls that think her any wrong.
   Goddess, allow this aged man his right,
   To be your beadsman now, that was your knight.[11]

As neither Segar's nor Peele's verse representations include musical notation, there is no way to know for certain that the music used to accompany singer Robert Hales was, in fact, Dowland's setting. Yet no other musical versions of the text survive.[12]

A second Dowland song provides additional connections to the same day's activities. "Time's eldest son," printed in his *Second Booke of Songs* (1600), sets a text found in Wells Cathedral musician John Lilliat's manuscript commonplace book. Lilliat's copy indicates the poem was a proclamation of Lee "in yielding up his tilt staff," surely referring to his final joust.[13] The lyrics and music mirror "His golden locks" both topically and stylistically, with six-line stanzas accentuated by final couplets, and themes that move from the pursuits of youth to those of spiritual meditation reflecting the onset of age.

Time's eldest son, old age the heir of ease,
Strength's foe, loves woe, and foster to devotion,
Bids gallant youth in martial prowess please,
As for himself, he hath no earthly motion.
   But thinks, sighs, tears, vows, prayers, and sacrifices,
   As good as shows, masques, jousts, or tilt devices.

Then sit thee down, and say thy *Nunc dimittis*,
With *De profundis, Credo,* and *Te Deum.*
Chant *Miserere*, for what is now so fit this,
As that, or this, *Paratum est cor meum,*
   O that thy Saint would take in worth thy heart,
   Thou canst not please her with a better part.

When others sings *Venite exultemus,*
Stand by and turn to *Noli emulari,*
For *quare fremuntum* use *oramus*
Vivat Eliza, For an *Ave Mari.*

> And teach those swains that live about thy cell,
> To say *Amen* when thou dost pray so well.[14]

For a final verse in his miscellany, Lilliat appends the last stanza of "His golden locks" ("And when thou sadly sit'st in homely cell...") onto the poem and marks the entry *quod Henry Leigh*, leaving little doubt as to authorship of the two poems.

Many years later in Robert Dowland's *A Musicall Banquet* (1610), the Dowland-Lee trilogy is made complete with the John Dowland song "Far from triumphing court." Its lyrics are again attributed to "Sir Henry Lea."

> Far from triumphing court and wonted glory,
> He dwelt in shady unfrequented places.
> Time's prisoner now, he made his pastime story,
> Gladly forgets court's erst-afforded graces.
>   That goddess whom he served to heav'n is gone,
>   And he on earth, in darkness left to moan.
>
> But lo, a glorious light from his dark rest,
> Shone from the place where erst this goddess dwelt.
> A light whose beams the world with fruit hath blest,
> Blest was the knight while he that light beheld:
>   Since then a star fixed on his head hath shined,
>   And a Saint's image in his heart is 'shrined.
>
> Ravished with joy so graced by such a Saint,
> He quite forgot his cell and self denied.
> He thought it shame in thankfulness to faint,
> Debts due to Princes must be duly paid:
>   Nothing so hateful to a noble mind,
>   As finding kindness for to prove unkind.
>
> But ah, poor knight though thus in dream he ranged,
> Hoping to serve this Saint in sort most mete.
> Time with his golden locks to silver changed,
> Hath with age-fetters bound him hands and feet.
>   Aye me, he cries, goddess my limbs grow faint,
>   Though I time's prisoner be, be you my Saint.[15]

The song serves as a sort of conclusion to the previous two, with the final stanza line "Time with his golden locks to silver changed" conflating the other opening texts and concretely linking the three. This last poem is written from the perspective of an aged "poor knight," time removed from the one who at midlife stepped down from serving his queen. In these lyrics, Lee's "saint," "that Goddess whom he served to heav'n is gone," dates the text between Elizabeth's 1603 death and his own in 1611.[16] The song's placement in *Musicall Banquet* then serves as a final tribute not only to Elizabeth, but also to Lee himself. Printing the songs in three separate anthologies over the course of fifteen years is an example of just one way that Dowland successfully maintained his association with the same courtly circle throughout his career.

Dowland's name, or at least what seems to be a shortened version of it, also appears in the description of an entertainment given at Sudeley Palace in 1592.[17] Queen Elizabeth regularly left London to tour her realm. These trips were termed "progresses." Nobles in the areas to which she sojourned were expected to house the queen's entourage, an endeavor often complicated and always expensive. Artistic productions featuring verse, music, dancing, and elaborate staging became a favorite way to honor Elizabeth. In 1592, after being regaled at Bisham Abbey, home of the Lady Russell for whom Dowland titled a lute solo, the court moved onto Sudeley Castle, residence of Giles Bridges, third Lord Chandos.[18] In a Sunday production titled *Daphne and Apollo*, "her majesty saw Apollo with the tree, *having on the one side one that sung, on the other one that played*, and the song is 'My heart and tongue were twins, at once conceived'" (emphasis added).[19] A lute song would be very appropriate in this outdoor performance. The song mentioned, "My heart and tongue were twins," later appears in Dowland's *A Pilgrimes Solace* (1612), in a version potentially close to what the queen heard so many years earlier.

Dowland may have participated in these 1592 events, first as "the one that played" in *Daphne and Apollo*, and then with the intention of performing in a scheduled drama the following day. This second staging, however, was canceled because of inclement weather. In the script for the halted production, the character Nisa insists that someone named Cutter sing. The bit of dialogue includes a previously unspecified character with two lines, who is signified with the abbreviation "Do." and revealed as one who also plays.

NIS. Then sing, and you sir, a question, or commandment?
DO. A commandment I, and glad that I am?

NIS. Then play:
DO. I have played so long with my fingers that I have beaten out of play all my good fortunes.[20]

A song, "Herbs, words, and stones, all maladies have cured," was to have followed. At the time, Dowland had already established himself as a master lutenist, and certainly could have filled the role of "Do.," had the production taken place. The final line that "Do." speaks implies a sort of melancholy that became associated with him, while the song following proposes a salve. An opportunity for Dowland to play before the queen would have been irresistible. The cancellation of the event could only have brought disappointment to whoever was scheduled to appear.

Other events of note in the later years of the 1580s and early 1590s involve Dowland's home life. No records survive with details of his marriage or the birth of his children, but Dowland's son Robert indicated in his 1626 marriage allegation that he was born in or around 1591, listing his age as "about thirty-five years."[21] Thus, we might assume father John was married some time before that date. Who Dowland's wife was remains a mystery. John mentions her in his 1595 letter to Robert Cecil, stating that the Landgrave of Hesse "sent a ring into England to my wife valued at 20£ sterling," and he later instructs the statesman to send word, if so desired, "by my poor wife."[22] Mrs. Dowland was also involved in business dealings related to at least one of her husband's song collections, for in 1600, "Mistress Dowland" appears in the background of litigation files involving a dispute between the publisher and printer of Dowland's *Second Booke of Songs*.[23] Yet no evidence exists that Mrs. Dowland or any of their children ever traveled to the Continent with Dowland on his journeys. Further, no genealogical connections have been discovered related to any children other than Robert, although in the same letter to Cecil the musician refers to his offspring in the plural.

Son Robert, however, draws together John Dowland and Robert Sidney, whom Dowland may have encountered in France. Sidney was the dedicatee of Robert Dowland's 1610 musical anthology *A Musicall Banquet*, in which he is revealed as the younger man's godfather:

> Since my best ability is not able in the least manner to countervail that duty I owe unto your Lordship, for two great respects: the one in regard (your Lordship undertaking for me) I was made a member of the Church of Christ, and withal received from you my name; the other the love that you

bear to all excellency and good learning (which seemeth hereditary above others to the noble family of the *Sidneys*), and especially to this excellent science of music, a skill from all antiquity entertained with the most noble and generous dispositions.[24]

Sidney may have been in attendance for Robert Dowland's christening into the Church of England, depending on its date. If 1591 was truly the year of Robert's birth, someone else, such as Sidney's agent Rowland Whyte, may have stood proxy for the courtier, for the statesman was stationed as Governor in Flushing in the low countries that year. Still, that Sidney served as godfather for Dowland's son provides confirmation of several things: that Dowland had connections within the influential Sidney-Essex circle with all its artistic influence, and that the lutenist, at least by 1591, had moved away from his Catholic associations.

Dowland, even if not practicing outwardly, had returned from France to England with sympathies for the Catholic cause. In 1595, he wrote to Cecil that "within two years after [meeting papists in France] I came into England where I saw men of that faction condemned and executed, which I thought was great injustice, taking religion for the only cause, and when my best friends would persuade me, I would not believe them."[25] These well-meaning friends who tried to dissuade Dowland from defense of Catholic practice were certainly Protestant, providing some clue as to the circles in which he moved after his return. The Sidney family was staunchly Protestant. Yet there is also evidence that the family, so devoted to the nation's Protestant standing, also reached out to those on the other side of religious debate. For instance, Robert's brother Philip had an unusual relationship with Edmund Campion, the Jesuit priest executed at Tyburn for treason in 1581.[26] Robert Sidney, however, would never knowingly have stood as godfather to a child who might be raised in the Catholic faith. Thus, it is quite certain that by this time Dowland was willing to present himself as a member of the Church of England, regardless of what his inner beliefs might be. Clearly, this was not a new stance for him. In order to receive his 1588 degree from Oxford, he would have been required to sign the Oath of Supremacy.[27] Not long afterward, Dowland's first musical contributions to appear in print were six harmonizations of metrical psalms he composed for Thomas East's 1592 musically expanded *Whole Booke of Psalmes*.[28] This collection was used by those with various Christian denominational preferences but was foremost the primary hymnal of the English Reformation.

Dowland, however, maintained that he was unjustly condemned for his earlier Catholic dalliance by those who mattered most. When a lute position opened up in Elizabeth's court upon the death of John Johnson in 1594, Dowland believed he was not granted the post because the queen labeled him "a man to serve any prince in the world, but ... an obstinate papist."[29] He explained to Cecil:

> Then in time passing one Mr. Johnson died and I became an humble suitor for his place (thinking myself most worthiest), wherein I found many good and honorable friends that spake for me, but I saw that I was like to go without it, and that any might have preferment but I, whereby I began to sound the cause, and guessed that my religion was my hindrance.

Dowland's own stance toward Catholics may have contributed to the perception, and as late as 1595, his own words suggest he may have considered himself as Catholic, although he also claims that he never attended any mass in England, nor understood the rite. Perhaps charges originated from his former employer Cobham or from other court musicians who disliked Dowland and were intimidated by his skill. Other reasons that he was not offered the job seem more credible—a different, unrecognized offense or even a simple clash of personality that Dowland chose not to acknowledge. Elizabeth, after all, in spite of increasing tensions with Catholics, had shown herself appreciative of exceptional artists, without regard to religion. Thomas Tallis and William Byrd, to whom she granted the valuable music printing monopoly, Sebastian Westcote, master of the Children of St. Paul's, and Thomas Morley, Dowland's Oxford colleague, are notable examples of Catholics in her employ.[30]

Dowland was clearly frustrated as fellow musicians rose in the queen's estimation while he was unable to persuade her of his own loyalty and value. In the six years immediately after he received his Oxford baccalaureate, thirteen men were sworn in as Gentlemen of the Chapel Royal, the official royal liturgical music organization. Four were inducted in the year 1592 alone; Morley was one of those so raised.[31] Such an appointment granted respectability in the immediate addition of the title "gentleman."[32] Although Dowland was not a practicing church musician as these men were, and therefore not suited to the group, his lute skills were reputably unmatched, and the opening among the lutenists in the "Queen's Music" seemed tailor-made for him.

Some thirty instrumentalists served the queen at the time, including five or six lutenists.[33] John Johnson had received his post in 1579, alongside Mathias Mason, as part of a three-lute consort. Robert Hales, who sang at Lee's retirement, was added to the payroll in 1582, filling multiple roles as singer and lutenist. While Dowland may have expected Johnson's position to be filled immediately upon his 1594 death, it was not unusual for such a post to remain vacant for years, which proved true in this case.[34] Dowland's self-assessment of his qualifications for the job was no doubt accurate, as evidenced by his Oxford degree, his connections to members of the circle surrounding Elizabeth, and his musical presence in manuscripts and prints. He was even directly linked with Johnson in several places, including Munday's lyric book, a John Case treatise defending music, and a manuscript of lute pieces containing pieces in both men's hands.[35] But ultimately, only the queen's opinion mattered. Regardless of the accuracy of Dowland's assertion that his perceived religious status was the reason for his non-advancement, he was not hired to serve in Elizabeth's court. He petitioned for the job and even had support from his courtier friends and patrons, but to no avail. A year later, the job was not yet filled. When an offer to travel to the German lands arrived, Dowland, with a seemingly wounded sense of pride, could only move onward.

4
Music for Lute

In early modern times, the role of composer was not so neatly separated from that of performer as it is today. Although Dowland became well known for his songs and his consort music for instrumental ensemble through their dissemination in print, he was, in fact, first and foremost a lutenist. All of the music he composed utilizes the instrument in a prominent role. His earliest compositions were understandably those for lute solo, created for his own performance. Dowland no doubt could read and play from lute tablature, but early in his career, he had no need to write out his music. He certainly had the ability to perform both his own and others' pieces by ear and from memory, embellishing *ad libitum* to demonstrate his virtuosic capabilities. Thus, it was not until after he returned to England from France that his lute music began to appear in English manuscripts in tablature, copied by professional scribes as well as lute students and amateur players.

Most of Dowland's lute solos fit into standard instrumental categories of the day: improvisatory-sounding pieces, instrumental settings of popular songs and ballads, and, most especially, dances.[1] Improvisatory keyboard pieces in the late Renaissance and early Baroque eras often took names such as *preludium* and *toccata*. Lutenists favored the titles *fantasia* and *fancy*, which are tied closely to the style of the imitative Italian *recercare*, a sort of predecessor to the Baroque fugue. These compositions typically did not follow a set form and were created to sound as if players were improvising their parts in the manner done by professional performers. Once notated on paper, the solos preserved a virtuosic artist's efforts for later replication by others, while also providing a model for those who were not so highly skilled in improvisation. Dowland's improvisatory-sounding pieces represent some of his most difficult works, attesting to the lutenist's absolute mastery of his instrument.

Dowland's fantasias and fancies open with imitative treatment of a short thematic motive and often become increasingly difficult as they progress. One of Dowland's signed fantasias, titled "Farewell," clearly demonstrates aspects of the lutenist's technique.[2] The composition is notable for its chromatic nature, presenting a distinctive ascending chromatic fourth movement at the start that might be heard as a filled-in inversion of Dowland's famous "Lachrimae" tear motive. As if in response, "Forlorn Hope Fancy," copied into a different manuscript about five years later, reverses this opening ascent (Ex. 4.1).[3] It is not coincidental that Dowland's improvisatory-sounding pieces are generally found in fewer manuscripts than are many of his dances, for most amateurs would not have mastered the skills required for such complicated contrapuntal music.

Dowland also wrote a number of compositions based on ballad tunes such as "Fortune my foe," "Loth to depart," and "The George aloe." As was often the case in instrumental versions of these well-known tunes, several of Dowland's intabulations progress through a series of variations on the

Ex. 4.1 "Farewell" and "Forlorn hope fancy," chromatic opening comparison

main theme, providing additional evidence of his exceptional technique and ability to improvise. One spectacular example is Dowland's "Walsingham."[4] The original Walsingham tune, sometimes referred to as "As I went to Walsingham," was quite popular and shows up in hundreds of versions by many different composers.[5] The Dowland variations set, found in a manuscript copied around 1600 by Mathew Holmes, includes a first section introducing the "Walsingham" tune, lasting the equivalent of twelve bars in modern barred notation.[6] This main theme is followed by six variations of the same length that explore the primary material by varying compositional texture, moving the melody into lower contrapuntal lines, altering the metrical feel, and embellishing the theme with fast-moving scalar passages.

More than half of Dowland's surviving lute solos were inspired by dance forms, most especially the pavan, the galliard, and the almain, although the lutenist also composed other dance types, such as jigs. These specific dances were not unique to Dowland and are found in the catalogs of most English instrumental composers of the day. Anthony Holborne's 1599 printed consort music collection is even titled *Pavans, Galliards, Almains, and other short Æires both graue and light*. Dancing was still practiced in courtly circles throughout Dowland's lifetime and the composer may have had occasion to play for events in which dancing took place. Dances followed specific forms, often with repeated strains, in order to accommodate dancers' expectations of meter, numbers of counts, and regularity of phrases. By the sixteenth century, the slower pavan was commonly paired with a sprightly galliard, often matching melodic material, but Dowland and his colleagues did not necessarily follow this practice. Many late-sixteenth- and early-seventeenth-century composed pavans and galliards stood on their own, intended for performance rather than dancing.[7]

The pavan was a very stately dance in duple meter, usually composed of three repeated strains and performed by couples as a processional. In his 1589 treatise on dance, Thoinot Arbeau described the courtly nature of the form:

> A cavalier may dance the pavan wearing his cloak and sword, and others, such as you, dressed in your long gowns, walking with decorum and measured gravity. And the damsels with demure mien, their eyes lowered save to cast an occasional glance of virginal modesty at the onlookers. On solemn feast days the pavan is employed by kings, princes and great noblemen to display themselves in their fine mantles and ceremonial robes. They are

accompanied by queens, princesses and great ladies, the long trains of their dresses loosened and sweeping behind them, sometimes borne by damsels ... Pavans are also used in masquerades to herald the entrance of the gods and goddesses in their triumphal chariots or emperors and kings in full majesty.[8]

Dowland's compositions were generally much more complicated than expected standard formulas and were clearly intended to demonstrate the capabilities of his instrument rather than serve as dance accompaniment. Although always stately, Dowland's pavans vary quite a bit in feeling, from the pleasant "Dr. Case's pavan" to the wistful "Sir John Langton's pavan." Dowland's most famous work, "Lachrimae," features an iconic melodic opening based on a descending tetrachord and is structured as a pavan. Its slow, steady dance outline enhances the mournful mood indicated by its title.

In previous instrumental ensemble prints found on the continent, such as Tielman Susato's 1551 collection *Danserye*, multi-part dances were most often notated with repeat signs at the end of each simple strain. In practice, performing musicians might use the repeat to create improvised divisions, all the while retaining the necessary structure for dancing. Music in tablature by Dowland and his contemporaries often featured no repeat signs. Double strains were written out completely, in order to specify elaborations that would have previously been improvised the second time through. Thus, rather than having three repeated strains, Dowland's pavans often appear with six non-repeated sections, each ending with a double bar. It quickly becomes apparent to the listener that the implied second, fourth, and sixth strains are really embellishments of the one proceeding (Ex. 4.2). Robert Dowland's *Varietie of Lute-Lessons* (1610), which features ten of his father's compositions, omits the double-barred strain markings altogether, visually creating the look of a completely through-composed piece.

Of all the dances, Dowland was most fond of the galliard. More than two dozen distinctive galliards credited to Dowland survive in prints and manuscripts, equaling all other dance forms combined. The triple-meter galliard upon which Dowland's music was based was marked in practice by athletic jumps and kicks. Arbeau humorously stated,

> The galliard is so called because one must by gay and nimble to dance it, as even when performed reasonably slowly, the movements are light-hearted. As it needs must be slower for a man of large stature than for a small man,

Ex. 4.2 "Lachrimae" strains 1 and 2 comparison, CUL Dd.5.78.3

inasmuch as the tall one takes longer to execute his steps and in moving his feet backwards and forwards than the short one.[9]

Queen Elizabeth especially favored the dance throughout her lifetime. In 1589, when she was in her fifties, John Stanhope, gentleman of the privy chamber, wrote to Lord Talbot, "My Lord, the queen is so well. I assure you six or seven galliards in a morning, besides music and singing, is her ordinary exercise."[10] Almost ten years later, she was still participating. In 1597, an ambassador from France testified, "She takes great pleasure in dancing and music," and in 1599, a Spanish ambassador witnessed "the head of the Church of England and Ireland . . . in her old age dancing three or four galliards."[11]

One of Dowland's galliards, appearing in *Varietie of Lute-Lessons* in 1610 as "The Most Sacred *Queen Elizabeth*, her galliard," commemorates the queen's activity.[12] This title, however, seems to have been added posthumously to a recycled piece, for the composition appears much earlier in the 1580s or 1590s as "K. Darcy's galliard," as well as without title in a set of mixed-consort manuscripts from about the same time.[13] A second galliard in the same source, with similar opening material, is later titled "The Queen's galliard" in Margaret Board's lute book, dated to the 1620s and 1630s.[14] The question of which queen the piece refers to in this particular version is muddled, for not only had Elizabeth been dead since 1603, but James I's wife, Anna, had also recently died in 1619.

Dowland's galliards are often notated in the same way as his pavans, with embellished strains written out rather than indicated with repeat signs. At times, Dowland's galliards channel tunes written in other forms. For example, his "Galliard to Lachrimae" utilizes the "Lachrimae" pavan melody, set as a galliard. Another galliard uses the ballad tune "As I went to Walsingham" for inspiration, separate from the version he set in variations.[15] Dowland even composed a "A galliard by Mr. Dowland, Bachelor of Music, DB," the DB crediting his colleague Daniel Bacheler while bringing further attention to his own credentials. Thus, the work stands as a galliard based upon the galliard of Daniel Bacheler, attesting to the common practice of composers borrowing material, acknowledging each other's work, and at times, trying to best one another.[16]

The almain, referred to as the *allemande* in French because of its origin as a German dance, was another couples dance performed in procession.[17] Arbeau defined the almain as "a simple, rather sedate dance . . . You can dance it in company, because when you have joined hands with a damsel several others may fall into line behind you, each with his partner."[18] French lutenist Adrian Le Roy, whose lute treatise was issued in English translation in 1568 and 1574, included pavans, galliards, and allemandes among other dances in his earlier *Premier Livre de Tabulature de Luth* of 1551. Several pavans and galliards are also found in the 1568 English version of his lute treatise.[19] Dowland's pavans and galliards, although varied in affect, tend toward what today would be considered the minor mode. In his almains, however, the musician favored the more open-sounding major mode, composing pleasant quadruple-meter dance-inspired pieces reminiscent of the sort he heard during his time in France. With few exceptions, Dowland's almains tend to be simpler for the player than do his other forms.[20]

Dowland fitted a number of his lute dance tunes, originally intended for lute solo, with words.[21] The most famous was his lute tune, "Lachrimae," which became "Flow my tears" in the *Second Booke of Songs*, reset for voice with lute accompaniment. Others included "Can she excuse" (transformed from a galliard later associated with the Earl of Essex), "My thoughts are winged with hopes" (Souch's galliard), "Now, O now I needs must part" (Frog galliard), "If my complaints could passions move" (Piper's galliard), "Awake sweet love" (Darcy's galliard), and "Shall I strive with words to move" (set both as Mignarda and Noel's galliard). All of these pieces appeared as lute solos in a manuscript copied by Oxford man Mathew Holmes, before being revealed in their song form in later Dowland printed volumes.

Many manuscripts provide no titles or attributions for the lute pieces they contain. Where Dowland's music is titled, the labels are intriguing. Some are simply named according to their form ("galliard" or "fantasia"), but many of Dowland's dance titles reveal the circles he followed, naming public figures and others the musician either knew personally, or at least knew of. For example, "The Lady Russell's pavan," "Captain Candish, his galliard," and "Smith's almain" are just three of almost three dozen unique compositions for lute or instrumental consort that are dedicated to specific individuals. Some certainly reflect the original label applied by the composer; some were so named only in later manuscripts or prints, indicating reuse of earlier material not originally intended to represent the individual designated; and others became the basis of songs with newly added texts and titles. There were times that Dowland reversed this process, taking a song and rearranging it for instruments as he had done with ballad tunes, although this seems to be the less common scenario. The individuals Dowland recalls in his titles reflect a wide spectrum of social, economic, religious, and political interests. From royalty to nobility to gentry to common man, Dowland was not exclusive.

Dowland's named works also reach beyond gender lines. More than a dozen women are represented in the titles of eighteen surviving Dowland works. Katherine Darcy Clifton, Bridget Fleetwood, Lady Hunsdon, Lady Laiton, Lady Mildmay, Mrs. Norrish, Lady Rich, Lady Russell, Mrs. Vaux, Mrs. White, Mrs. Winter, and, as mentioned previously, even Queen Elizabeth each find mention in Dowland dance titles, suggesting that women played a large and important part in the era's musical culture. At the very least, the titles serve as a reminder that young women often learned to play the lute in pursuit of artistic well-roundedness.[22] Some of the most important manuscripts containing Dowland's music were owned and used by women such as Margaret Board, Jane Pickering, and Elisabeth, daughter of Moritz, the Landgrave of Hesse.[23] Dowland was not the only composer to dedicate his pieces to people he knew. Naming compositions for individuals seems to have been a standard practice. Other lutenist-composers such as John Danyel, Francis Cutting, Francis Pilkington, John Johnson, and Robert Johnson all composed similarly titled pieces, although rarely naming them for women. As with so many aspects of the lute repertoire, Dowland's output surpasses them all.

Dowland's lute solos and duos survive in at least eighteen prints of the sixteenth and seventeenth centuries and in more than sixty manuscripts from the same time. Only a very small number of these were likely "authorized" by the composer. Three of Dowland's songbooks include either a lute duo (*First Booke*, 1597), a lute-bass viol duo (*Second Booke*, 1600), or a lute solo (*Pilgrimes Solace*, 1612). Robert Dowland's *Varietie of Lute-Lessons* (1610) features ten John Dowland lute solos, and *A Musicall Banquet* (1610) opens with one. A handful of manuscript pieces survive in Dowland's own hand, or are signed with his name, but these are exceptions.[24] Thus, it is difficult to ascertain how closely the music found in manuscripts matches Dowland's original intention. The farther removed geographically and chronologically from Dowland's own experience, the less confident we can be as to an accurate portrayal of the lutenist's musical ideas within these artifacts. In many cases, pieces attributed to Dowland more closely reflect the needs of a particular copyist than Dowland's or are arrangements of pieces originally composed by him. Even those copied by Dowland himself represent a single moment in time, for it is unlikely the lutenist played his music exactly the same way in any two performances.

Dowland's music was circulating in manuscript by the late 1580s and 1590s, early in his career in England. More than twenty manuscript collections from the time period contain arrangements of his pieces. While the majority of these consist of lute solos in tablature, consort and vocal music appear as well (see Table 4.1). One of the most important manuscript sources of Dowland compositions is a series of four volumes of lute music copied between 1585 and 1615 by precentor and singer Mathew Holmes of Christ Church, Oxford.[25] Collectively, the four volumes contain over 700 lute works, including more than 100 individual pieces by Dowland, the most-represented composer by far. Whether Holmes was collecting lute music in an official or unofficial capacity remains unclear.[26] Holmes's first volume was compiled from about 1585 to 1595, during the years Dowland was establishing himself in England. It includes some forty-five lute works by Dowland or based upon his music, with a few settings for the bandora, another plucked stringed instrument of the time. The second volume was begun in 1595 but not completed until around 1600. About half of the Dowland works in Holmes's first volume include titles. Eighteen Dowland pieces, titled or untitled, are clearly attributed with the composer's name or initials. While this number may seem small, that any of the pieces include attribution

Table 4.1 Selected manuscripts containing John Dowland music, c. 1583–1595

Manuscript(s)	Archive	Medium	# Dowland works	Year(s) created
Siena	NL-DHnmi	lute	1	c. 1580–1590
Dallis	IRL-Dtc	voice w/lute	1	c. 1583–1585
Holmes 1 and 2	GB-Cu	lute	50+	c. 1588–1600
Cambridge consort books	GB-Cu	consort	4–10	c. 1590
Wurstisen	CH-Bu	lute	1	c. 1591–1594
Richard	PL-Kj	lute	4	c. 1594/1601
Marsh	IRL-Dm	lute	4	c. 1595
Wickhambrook	US-NH	lute	5	c. 1595
Trumbull	GB-Cu	lute	3	c. 1595
Hirsch	GB-Lbl	lute	7	c. 1595
Euing	GB-Ge	lute	29	c. 1595–1600
Folger	US-Ws	lute	16	c. 1590s
MS 4° mus 125	D-Kl	consort	2	c. 1590–1600

at all is indicative of the professional nature of the volume. Holmes likely recorded the lute pieces as soon as he came upon them. Some of the titles provided in Holmes's anthology provide names of people with whom Dowland associated, such as "Dr. Case's pavan," "Mrs. White's nothing," "K. Darcy's spirit," "K. Darcy's galliard," and "Lady Russell's pavan," which sometimes helps with chronological dating of the works.

Dr. Case refers to John Case, the Oxford lecturer and physician who mentioned Dowland in a 1588 treatise, praising *"Birdum, Mundanum, Bullum, Morleum, Doulandum, Ionsonum, aliosque hodie permultos instrumentorum peritissimos iustis suis laudibus non persequamur"* (Byrd, Munday, Bull, Morley, Dowland, Johnson, and many others who are very skilled in the instruments of our day), a sure indication that Dowland was one of the best-known musicians of his time.[27] The listed composers represent a diverse range of musical styles. The presence of Dowland and Johnson toward the end indicates a move toward greater appreciation of lutenists alongside keyboardists. Case's tract was printed the same year Dowland received his Bachelor of Music degree from Oxford. Intriguingly, Holmes's first manuscript volume opens with a Latin epigram sometimes attributed to Case. When that epigram is considered alongside the inclusion of Dowland's "Dr. Case's pavan," it seems that the Oxford man was not only a Dowland patron, but also supported Holmes.[28] Case did not become a medical doctor until 1589, so the piece was composed, or at least copied, after that time.

Katherine Darcy was the daughter of Sir Henry Darcy. Her name, as listed in the titles of the lute solos in Holmes's collection, suggests that "K. Darcy's spirit" and "K. Darcy's galliard" were composed prior to her 1591 marriage to Gervase Clifton, a Knight of the Shire. A later version of the galliard appears in Robert Dowland's 1610 *Varietie of Lute-Lessons*, with Darcy-Clifton acknowledged in the dance title "The right honorable, the Lady Clifton's spirit," using her new title after her husband was raised to baron.[29] That Darcy received multiple tributes may indicate an especially close connection to the composer.

Lady Russell refers to Elizabeth Russell, daughter of Sir Anthony Cooke, who married second husband John, Lord Russell, heir to the Duke of Bedford. She never officially became a duchess because her husband's death preceded that of her father-in-law, although she still styled herself as a dowager duchess. Russell was already very wealthy and quite powerful even before she wed Lord Russell, bringing to her marriage property, including Bisham Abbey in Berkshire, inherited from her first husband, Sir Thomas

Hoby.[30] Russell and her associates would have been lucrative connections for Dowland, if the opportunity arose, as Lady Russell had many useful connections. Her sister Mildred was married to William Cecil, first Baron Burghley, and was mother of Dowland's sponsor Robert Cecil. Russell's son Sir Edward Hoby married Margaret Carey, sister of George Carey, who became Baron Hunsdon and was dedicatee of Dowland's *First Booke*. Members of this arts-supporting circle were especially desirable patrons for musicians of the 1580s and 1590s.

In addition to pieces with titles naming public figures, Dowland's "Lachrimae" appears in three versions in Holmes's first manuscript volume, all in fairly close proximity, confirming the work was already a core part of Dowland's repertoire. With so many Dowland pieces in Holmes's first lutebook, the composer must have established a prominent presence in the copyist's environment. Dowland made direct contact with Holmes's manuscripts at least once. He signed his "Farewell" fantasia in Holmes's second volume at some point after 1595.[31] The sprightly "Mrs. White's nothing" in Holmes's volume is even attributed to "Jo. Dowlande, Bachelor of Music," drawing a strong connection between Dowland's and Holmes's activities in Oxford.[32] That the designation reads so closely to Dowland's own practice in his printed anthologies suggests the composer requested his work be recorded that way.

While Holmes's volumes are especially valuable for Dowland aficionados, more typical of the time were the personal manuscripts kept by those learning to play the lute or collecting music to play in their own household, such as the *Folger-Dowland Lute Book*, which dates to the 1590s.[33] Lute students, both male and female, often came from upper-class households, as learning to play a musical instrument was respected for its role in a well-rounded education. Pupils typically purchased blank manuscript paper or books to build their collection of lute music and for study between lessons. These manuscripts reflect a pedagogical convention of the time, in which lute teachers left music sheets for students to copy onto their own folios. This process helped students learn the intricacies of tablature notation, theory, and rhythm, as well as aiding memorization.[34] Sometimes, however, instructors copied music into a student's book themselves. When separate sources include enough similarities, evidence often suggests they may have been copied from a common source, like that of a teacher with many students. This method of music transmission, however, also accounts for the many musical variants found across manuscripts due to time, space, error, and perhaps more importantly, musical taste and adaptation for the owner's skill level.

Dowland's professional activity as a lute instructor is confirmed within the *Folger-Dowland Lute Book*. The manuscript pages, possibly owned at various times by a Yorkshire gentlewoman named Anne Baylon and someone by the name of William Browne, include a dozen lute pieces by Dowland—once again the composer with the most pieces represented—as well as many by others, including five by royal lutenist John Johnson. It seems the volume's first scribe copied much of the initial music and a second, perhaps the first's teacher, made corrections and added new pieces. At least seven, and perhaps as many as ten, other hands follow. One of the later scribal hands may be that of Dowland's son Robert.[35] If so, the manuscript stretches over many years. Johnson signed some of his pieces, perhaps at the behest of the owner's teacher. At some point, John Dowland added his own signature to a number of his compositions that had been copied previously. While some scholars suggest he signed to confirm he had viewed and approved the copy, the script may simply indicate that the student valued and collected autographs from respected musicians.[36]

Parts of at least three pieces in the manuscript are copied in Dowland's own hand: "My Lady Hunsdon's allmande," "What if a day," and an untitled version of "Lady Clifton's almain." The first of these is also signed by the composer. Dowland again declares his credentials, clearly indicating "Jo: Doulande, Bachelor of Music." Patrons and acquaintances named in composition titles in the Folger collection include [Mrs.] Winter, Mr. Smith, and Lady Laiton. Winter and Smith are quite common names and thus more difficult to link with specific individuals, but Lady Laiton is likely Elizabeth Knollys, wife of Sir Thomas Laiton of Shropshire, Captain of Guernsey, who was knighted in 1579, or possibly the wife of Lady Elizabeth's son Thomas, née Elizabeth Gerrard.[37] Most significantly, the piece "My Lady Hunsdon's Allmande" again links Dowland to the Carey family and to Baron Hunsdon, dedicatee of the *First Booke*. Whether Dowland provided regular instruction or simply a few lessons to the owner of the Folger book is difficult to discern. Scholar Matthew Spring describes the pieces in the Folger volume as "suitable for beginners—short, simple, and attractive," a contrast to the Holmes collection, which presents more complex musical examples.[38] The two collections stand as tangible reminders of the connectedness created by music during the era, in which professional performers, amateurs, teachers, students, and patrons all converged.

Moreover, the Holmes manuscript reflects the sort of music Dowland was composing from the beginning of his career. It was through performances of such lute solos that the musician achieved his initial fame and respect. As Dowland traveled and as time progressed, his music began appearing in more remote locations, both in print and in manuscript, arranged for a wider variety of mediums, and with increasing variants. And even as he later produced printed music for a larger market enamored with singing, he remained an advocate for his own instrument, the lute an integral part of "becoming Dowland."

NAVIGATING THE CONTINENT

5
"A man to serve any prince in the world"
(German Lands, 1594–1595)

When John Johnson, lutenist in Queen Elizabeth's service, died in the summer of 1594, Dowland was the most accomplished and recognized lutenist in England. With his past diplomatic service, degree from Oxford, and flattery of important courtiers, Dowland expected consideration for Johnson's appointment, placing himself atop any list of persons who might be named as "musician for the three lutes."[1] His petitions for the post, however, met with no success. Although Elizabeth declined to appoint anyone right away, Dowland did not wait long before moving on, and away, from England. In response to an invitation to visit the court of Heinrich Julius, Duke of Brunswick, Dowland sought travel permission to the German lands from Privy Councillors Robert Devereux, second Earl of Essex, and Secretary of State Robert Cecil. Cecil and Essex, both extremely powerful, had engaged in a political struggle since at least 1590, each hoping to become Elizabeth's right-hand man. Cecil ultimately prevailed, obtaining an official appointment as Secretary of State in 1596. Often those seeking favors found themselves in the position of choosing sides, but Dowland astutely tied himself to both important courtiers. That he approached these men is a testament to his connections and standing within courtly circles. He later recalled to Cecil:

> And according as I desired there came a letter to me out of Germany from the Duke of Brunswick, whereupon I spake to your honor and to my Lord of Essex, who willingly gave me both your hands (for which I would be glad if there were any service in me that your honors could command).[2]

Permission for foreign travel, especially when granted by someone like Cecil, typically recognized an expectation that the recipient would convey appropriate intelligence in aid of country, whenever and wherever gleaned.

Dowland's offer to provide "service" then takes on new meaning. Musicians often found themselves in a unique position, as they were permitted into spaces in which important meetings took place, often unobtrusively placed and unnoticed. Information overheard became intelligence to be passed on. Thus, the lutenist's request held potential benefits both to himself and to a senior statesman like Cecil. Dowland's earlier experiences in Cobham's embassy in Paris had prepared him for such pursuits. The north German lands were solidly Protestant and therefore allied with England, but many important political and religious figures traveled through Duke Heinrich Julius's court. Valuable information exchange was a distinct possibility.

Dowland arrived again on the Continent in the late summer or early autumn of 1594. He later wrote nostalgically of his time in the German lands:

> I bent my course toward the famous provinces of Germany, where I found both excellent masters, and most honorable patrons of music: Namely, those two miracles of this age for virtue and magnificence, *Henry Julio*, Duke of *Brunswick*, and learned *Maritius Landgrave* of *Hessen*, of whose princely virtues and favors towards me I can never speak sufficiently. Neither can I forget the kindness of *Alexandro Horologio*, a right learned master of music, servant to the royal prince the *Landgrave* of *Hessen*, and *Gregorio Howet*, lutenist to the magnificent Duke of *Brunswick*, both whom I name as well for their love to me, as also for their excellency in their faculties.[3]

Heinrich Julius von Braunschweig-Lüneburg was surely pleased with the Englishman's arrival in Wolfenbüttel. Dowland recalled a generous show of welcome:

> When I came to the Duke of Brunswick he used me kindly, and gave me a rich chain of gold, £23 in money with velvet and satin and gold lace to make me apparel, with promise that if I would serve him he would give me as much as any prince in the world.[4]

A December 1594 German register confirms these details, indicating monetary payment to "an English lutenist."[5] The listing also notes compensation to a merchant who regularly supplied fine fabrics to the court, referencing the same types of goods recalled in Dowland's description. The ruler was obviously hoping for a long-term relationship with the lutenist and thus presented him with valuable, enticing gifts that would allow him to fashion himself in a manner expected within a court of such esteem.

Heinrich Julius, who was about the same age as Dowland, became Duke of Brunswick-Lüneburg and ruling Prince of Brunswick-Wolfenbüttel in 1589, following the death of his father. Highly educated, at age twelve he was named founding rector of the University of Helmstedt, which, when established in 1576, was the first north German Protestant university. During the duke's official reign, he reformed legal and educational systems, enlarged his father's official library to over 4,300 volumes and, although Protestant, at times maintained a moderate stance toward Catholics, allowing priests in his domain to retain their titles.[6] An educated artist like Dowland would have found such attributes attractive. Yet the duke also took pleasure in persecuting Jews and witches, while maintaining his own interest in alchemy, and was also known for alcoholic overconsumption. Perhaps because of his propensity for extravagant overspending, Heinrich Julius's court was an artistically vibrant one. In 1592, an English acting troupe arrived in Wolfenbüttel. A number of the players remained in the duke's employment for two decades. During this time, the company staged some of the ten dramatic works the ruler authored and published himself in 1593 and 1594, the most popular ones including *Susanna* and *Von Einem Buler und Bulerin*.[7] The duke-prince's second wife, Elisabeth, was the sister of Christian IV, future King of Denmark and Dowland's eventual employer. Two of Heinrich Julius and Elisabeth's children were born during Dowland's time in Germany, although after the lutenist had already left Wolfenbüttel. Heinrich Julius may have first enjoyed entertainment by English actors and resolved to establish his own troupe when he traveled to Denmark for his wedding to Elisabeth in 1590. It may also have been through these actors, many of whom were previously sponsored by the Earl of Leicester, that Heinrich Julius first heard of Dowland's prowess on the lute.

In addition to his actors, the duke employed a number of dedicated musicians and maintained an active musical household, both in Wolfenbüttel and in Gröningen.[8] He built up the musical company put in place during the reign of his father, who in 1573 instructed, "So we would also like to have all sorts of other musical instruments such as trumpets, cornetts, viols, flutes, crumhorns, bombards, and others."[9] In the early 1590s, the duke hired a young Michael Praetorius as organist. Dowland surely heard this talented musician (who remained with the duke for most of his career, eventually being named *kapellmeister*) perform while at the Brunswick court.

Conversely, the organist became familiar with Dowland's music at some time, for two consort versions of Dowland's "Mrs. Winter's jump," arranged for four instruments, are found in Praetorius's only printed collection of instrumental works, *Terpsichore* (1612). In this musical volume, the pieces are labeled "Incerti."[10] It seems Dowland's musical influence remained long after he left Germany, in manuscript form and in courtly practice, but authorship of his music was not recognized by Praetorius so long after the lutenist left.

Heinrich Julius already employed a personal lutenist when he invited Dowland to Germany. Belgian musician Gregory Howet officially began working for the duke in 1591 and served the court his entire career.[11] Originating from Antwerp, Howet was a highly regarded performer throughout the German lands and one of the best-paid musicians in the duke's court. In 1594, the duke built a new residence in Wolfenbüttel, renovated others, and erected a new building at the university in Helmstadt. Enlarging his musical presence as well would enhance his image as leader of one of the most vital and cultured courts in all of Europe and he may have felt the time was right to add another highly accomplished lutenist to his entourage, hence Dowland's invitation.[12]

It seems Dowland and Howet hit it off well enough, for they traveled together soon afterward. Dowland later referenced the kindness of his new friend, who was just old enough to have served as sort of a mentor to him. A manuscript of the late 1630s belonging to Johann Stobaeus indicates Howet may have introduced Dowland to modern Continental lute techniques related to right-hand thumb use.[13] Few of Howet's lute compositions survive, but those that do often appear in the same German sources in which Dowland's music is featured, indicating a common sphere of influence. Most of these musical volumes date to the second decade of the seventeenth century, after Dowland had returned to England. One might surmise that John and Gregory remained in contact with each other and that Howet was in part responsible for Dowland's continued musical presence in the German lands. Dowland's son Robert featured one of Howet's fantasias in his *Varietie of Lute-Lessons* (1610), placing the composition just before one of his father's.[14] This fantasia is the only Howet composition preserved in English sources. The same Howet piece, with minor variants, appeared earlier in a 1594 Adrian Denss anthology printed in Cologne, which Dowland may have acquired while in Germany, referencing the print later for his son's collection.[15] Lute scholar Godelieve Spiessens noted that at least four of Howet's compositions exhibit material or themes borrowed from Dowland.[16]

In late 1594, not too long after Dowland first arrived, Heinrich Julius sent Howet and Dowland, along with other musicians and actors, to the Kassel court of his friend Mortiz, the Landgrave of Hesse. Howet was given 27 guilders on 29 October 1594, perhaps for travel, although no details beyond amount are provided in the financial register.[17] The two lutenists reached Kassel, some eighty-five miles from Wolfenbüttel, in early winter. Ludwig Brockmann of Kassel requested payment for fifteen weeks of lodging for two English lutenists in December 1594. The invoice does not specify whether the fifteen weeks are partially in arrears or if the request is for full prepayment.[18] Alessandro Orologio, a visiting Prague-based Italian composer, reported that Wolfenbüttel musicians arrived in Kassel on 1 November 1595.[19] The information in Orologio's letter fits the Dowland-Howet trip well, so some scholars contend the date was copied incorrectly on the original document. Others argue that the musicians could not be Dowland and Howet. Complicating matters further, Wolfenbüttel registers dated 22 December 1594 show gifts to Dowland from Duke Heinrich Julius, indicating the lutenists either did not leave for Kassel until after that date, or that the receipts were recorded at a later time. Regardless, Dowland and Howet both remained in Kassel at least until 25 March 1595, enjoying the landgrave's hospitality.[20] Dowland seems to have cemented a close friendship with the nobleman, who later offered him employment.

> From thence I went to the Landgrave of Hessen (who gave me the greatest welcome that might be for one of my quality), who sent a ring into England to my wife valued at £20 sterling, and gave me a great standing cup with a cover gilt, full of dollars with many great offers for my service.[21]

Moritz inherited his titles just two years prior to Dowland's arrival and soon was acclaimed for his virtuous nature. Like Heinrich Julius, he was especially well educated. The landgrave spoke multiple languages and employed scientists and lawyers. His support of the arts is well established, both through his own group of English actors and the many musicians he sponsored and employed. Yet he also maintained a strict rule over his districts, acting both as authoritarian and enlightened leader. Many years later, Dowland's friend and neighbor Henry Peacham noted:

> But above others, who carrieth away the palm for excellency, not only in music, but in whatsoever is to be wished in a brave prince, is the yet living

Maurice Landgrave of *Hessen*, of whose own composition I have seen eight or ten several sets of motets, and solemn music, set purposely for his own chapel; where for the greater honor of some festival, and many times for his recreation only, he is his own organist. Besides, he readily speaketh ten or twelve several languages: he is so universal a scholar, that coming (as he doth often) to his University of *Marburg*, what questions soever he meeteth with set up (as the manner is in the *German* and our universities), he will *ex tempore*, dispute an hour or two (even in boots and spurs) upon them, with their best professors. I pass over his rare skill in chirurgerie, he being generally accounted the best bonesetter in the country. Who have seen his estate, his hospitality, his rich furnished armory, his brave stable of great horses, his courtesy to all strangers, being men of quality and good parts, let them speak the rest.[22]

With so much in common, it is not difficult to understand both the closeness and competitiveness evidenced between Prince Moritz and Duke Heinrich Julius (Fig. 5.1). The two often found themselves attending the same ceremonial festivities in various courts. Further, they formed an alliance of sorts, along with Christian IV of Denmark, that advocated for common political, religious, intellectual, and artistic interests. They traveled to each other's courts and received dedications and solicitations for patronage from many of the same individuals.[23] Moritz stood as godfather to the duke and duchess's first son in 1591.[24]

The landgrave hired permanent musicians into his court from not only the German lands, but also from England, Austria, France, and Italy, in a sort of race to see if he might prevail in establishing the most artistic court in Europe.[25] An inventory of Prince Moritz's library from 1613 lists music collected from across the Continent, both original prints and copied in manuscripts.[26] Such a library would hold great appeal to an English musician interested in current musical trends. The prince himself composed over one hundred musical works, including a pavan printed in *Varietie of Lute-Lessons* (1610), as well as five courantes surviving in the landgrave's daughter's lutebook, a manuscript that also features versions of eight Dowland lute solos, copied around the same time.[27]

Moritz's first child and heir apparent, Otto, was born in December 1594. Christian of Denmark (then only seventeen years old and not yet crowned Christian IV) traveled to Kassel in January 1595 to assume his place as godfather in celebratory activities, which brought together important

Fig. 5.1 Heinrich Julius, print by Heinrich Ulrich; Moritz, print by Crispijn de Passe © The Trustees of the British Museum. All rights reserved.

representatives from several nearby courts.[28] German nobility had long established a precedent of hosting lavish festivities marking celebratory occasions such as weddings, baptisms, and coronations, all of which also served diplomatic ends. Throughout his 1595 tour of the north German lands, Christian—known for active participation in tournaments—was treated to displays of pomp and grandeur.[29] How much exposure Christian had to Dowland during this short trip remains uncertain, but it seems quite likely that, if the landgrave was hosting two impressive lutenists, Howet and Dowland were at some time called upon to perform for visiting dignitaries. In fact, in a letter to Heinrich Julius the following March, Moritz asserted that Dowland took advantage of any opportunity to perform.[30] Thus, in January 1595, Dowland first crossed paths with the man who would employ him above all others just a few years later. Before the end of the month, Christian left for a stay in Wolfenbüttel and the subsequent baptism of his niece, daughter of his sister Elisabeth and Heinrich Julius.[31]

Dowland and Howet were probably first sent by Heinrich Julius to Kassel to participate in Otto's baptismal festivities, as a goodwill gesture to Moritz. The two musicians were then expected to return to Wolfenbüttel before celebrations began for Heinrich Julius's own child around the same time that

Christian went on to Wolfenbüttel. If this was the plan, Heinrich Julius was justifiably upset that one of the lutenists did not return until March and that the other did not return at all. Although his initial reaction is not available, a response, written by the landgrave to the duke in March 1595, issues an apology for keeping the musicians longer than expected:

> Venerable and high-born prince, dear affectionate uncle and cousin, brother-in-law, brother and godfather, we have received your Grace's letter and read it, hearing what happened to your Grace and the lutenists GH and JD. On the contrary, Johan Dulandt is not in our employment, but only stays here, performing as the occasion arises. It was to our great satisfaction that your Grace sent the lutenists and musicians to us. And if we held them up beyond their allotted time, we kindly ask that they be excused on our behalf. As far as their art is concerned, we heard them both play, each in comparison to the other, and although we do not fully understand the lute, we think they are both good, agreeing with your Grace that the lutenist Gregorius Hawitten is an experienced, practiced performer, and his madrigals cannot be surpassed. On the other hand, we find the other, Dulandt, is a good composer. If, as your Grace has reported, [Dowland] disparaged your lutenists and offended them in some way, he regrets and apologizes most vehemently.
>
> So as not to abuse your Grace's cordiality, and sent from Kassel, 21 March 1595. Moritz Landgrave Hessen.[32]

If Dowland did not return to the duke's court after Heinrich Julius treated him so generously upon his arrival, thereby severing any implied or hoped-for service commitment, Moritz needed to tread lightly in his response. To extend goodwill, Heinrich Julius's own lutenist is rated "experienced and practiced," while Dowland's talent is recognized somewhat offhandedly, one of two good performers. More importantly, the landgrave goes out of his way to assure his noble friend that Dowland is not in his own employ, whether or not a position had been extended to him at this time. Yet in his *First Booke* (1597), Dowland states that the prince granted "favors towards me I can never speak sufficiently" and in a later letter, Moritz refers to Dowland as "my loving friend."[33] Perhaps their relationship grew upon Dowland's subsequent return to Kassel. More likely, the prince simply did not want to upset the duke, for when Moritz later offered Dowland a permanent placement, he makes clear his esteem for "a man of your worth."[34] Howet may have profited most from the sequence of events. He returned to an offer from his Wolfenbüttel employer to purchase him a house, apparently an attempt by the duke to solidify a long-lasting commitment from his star lutenist after Dowland's snub.[35]

The Dowland apology conveyed in the landgrave's letter is worth consideration. Did Dowland, with a chip on his shoulder after being passed over by his own monarch, do or say something to antagonize the musicians in Heinrich Julius's court during his Kassel stay? Did they relay something negative to the duke in an attempt to distance themselves from one who chose not to accept their patron's graciousness? It is not unreasonable to think that Dowland was still nursing his disappointment of the previous summer. After all, it had been less than a year since he applied for Johnson's job without success. An unattributed letter copied into an English manuscript to an unnamed recipient dated 20 January 1595 reads:

> Most honorable, and my only singular good lord:
>
> About twelve years past, through little regard to myself I fell into some misgovernment, for the which (as others) I might allege youth for my excuse (if not for warranties). But trusting especially that my sundry willing and ready endeavors in the service of her majesty and my country had cancelled those former error, I gave little heed unto them. The while (now of late) malice making large blots of those heedless stains, hath urged them (by false and injurious evidence) against me, and caused them to be censured against my reputation and fame. In my distresses heretofore (most honorable) having found your Lordship the only helpful star that hath availed me, may it now please the same to shine upon me favorably, before I perish utterly. A most happy (unhappy) man should I be (your honor abling me thereunto), if I might in foreign travel employed (I wreck not the danger whatsoever), either by industrious service and daring adventure, wipe out this my homebred blemish, or with my blood shedding testify the duty I owe to your honor, and get beyond fortunes and the world's spite. Unto this my humble petition thrice noble Lord listen, by the excellency of those virtues that renowns you forever. And my perpetual prayers to God shall be, that your honor's pity in this case may be accepted of him as great piety, and to reward it with present and ever—following unfailing happiness.[36]

The letterbook in which the document was copied contains transcriptions of two other pieces of Dowland primary source material, letters received by the musician the following year, one from English patron Henry Noel and the other from Prince Moritz. While not attributed to Dowland, or any author for that matter, the 1595 letter is of the sort Dowland might have penned to Robert Cecil after having sought permission to travel in order to distance himself from rumors of disloyalty to his homeland because of religion. Once in Germany, if the musician still felt the sting of his rejection at home and also feared disappointing the patron who first invited him abroad, perhaps he was already looking toward moving on. Such a letter hints that the writer, whoever he was, sees his best way to prove loyalty to the English court is through an offer to aid the Crown, by methods available only to one traveling in the queen's service. The letter expresses the same sort of angst appearing in Dowland's Cecil letter, written less than a year later. In 1595 Dowland decided to travel beyond the Kassel court. Knowingly or not, the musician would soon place himself in locations ripe with opportunities to provide intelligence, a potential gesture of loyalty to his monarch at home. The added allure of exploring new musical vistas in the Italian lands must have seemed like a fine adventure at the time.

6

"I founde the Cities furnisht with all good Artes"

(Italy, 1595)

In the spring of 1595, Dowland left Germany to travel to the Italian lands. He later claimed a single goal for the trip: to meet famed Italian madrigal composer and lutenist Luca Marenzio, who was residing in Rome. During his journey, he covered at least 1,800 miles in eight months or less. At the time, Italian city-states served as centers of innovation, promoting emerging musical genres, styles, and philosophies that would spread throughout all of Europe, influencing Western musical culture for decades—even centuries—to come. Visiting these cities allowed Dowland to evaluate and assimilate the newest trends into his own compositions. Questions abound related to Dowland's Italian travels. When exactly did he leave the German lands? Did he depart directly from Kassel? What was his route, and what forms of transportation did he utilize? Did he have traveling companions? Was the trip self-funded, or was he patronized by English or German supporters? What was his itinerary? Even as these questions remain unanswered, Dowland's tour can reasonably be reconstructed, based on the experiences of others who traveled similar routes at approximately the same time. In his *First Booke of Songes or Ayres* (1597), the musician wrote:

> I passed over the Alps into *Italy*, where I found the cities furnished with all good arts, but especially music. What favor and estimation I had in *Venice, Padua, Genoa, Ferrara, Florence*, and diverse other places I willingly suppress, least I should any way seem partial in mine own endeavors.

Dowland did not leave Kassel until at least the spring of 1595 and he returned to Germany by early November. He could not have remained for too long in any one city. Just over a decade later, Englishman Thomas Coryat described a personal journey completed in five months, in which he

Fig. 6.1 Dowland's Italian travels

visited cities in France, Italy, Switzerland, Germany, and the Netherlands, including a six-week stay in Venice.[1] Much of the time he moved by foot. By the end of the sixteenth century, travel had become quite common for royalty, diplomats, wealthy merchants, and the sons of aristocrats, and standard routes were well established. While it was not unusual for artists and servants to travel, they most often were included in the entourage of an employer, as Dowland had been when in France with Cobham, or they journeyed for a particular purpose, such as study, purchase of goods, or oversight of print publications, often sponsored by a patron. Curtis Price notes that English aristocrats traveled by many means, "on horseback, by public coach, mail packet, post-chaise and canal boat or on foot—often on the same day."[2]

A direct route from Kassel to Venice comprises over 500 miles, including mountainous travel. With constant progress and no weather delays or unforeseen circumstances, it would take someone weeks to reach the city on foot. Coach or horseback would be a much more efficient method but would also increase expenses considerably. Poulton suggested that Dowland likely carried with him at least two lutes, each with wooden or leather cases, as well as regular clothes and attire suitable for royal performance, therefore probably requiring a pack horse and servant to transport all of his belongings over the mountains.[3]

The relationship Dowland established with Moritz, Landgrave of Hesse, may have been especially important to his Italian travels. The landgrave, known later for his support of international study for musicians, may have served as Dowland's sponsor for the first portion of his trip to Venice, as he did later for Heinrich Schütz in 1609. Dowland's itinerary suggests that acquisition of instruments, either for himself or the landgrave, may have been a primary goal. The first four cities listed in his *First Booke* description, Venice, Padua, Genoa, and Ferrara, all were home to German-descended luthiers.[4] Many years after Dowland's trip, his friend Henry Peacham created an epigram in honor of Dowland that reads, "Your word, *Hine ille lachrimae,* beneath a Venice lute within a laurel wreath."[5] Dowland may have purchased a favorite instrument while in Venice, or at the very least, Peacham understood the importance of Venice as an especially thriving lute-making center.

No documents survive pertaining to the permission Dowland first received from Cecil and Essex to leave England, and he may have been granted travel only to Wolfenbüttel. According to the 1595 Cecil letter, Dowland "desired to get beyond the seas, which I durst not attempt without license from some of the Privy Council, for fear of being taken and so may have extreme punishment." If Duke Heinrich Julius's invitation was presented as the sole purpose for going abroad, Dowland may not have revealed that he was hoping to extend his trip farther, if that was the case. In the final decades of the sixteenth century, the Privy Council granted permission to visit internal portions of Italy only to select individuals, because of inquisition dangers that might affect English subjects.[6] If Dowland was perceived by the Privy Council as holding any remaining loyalties to Catholicism, his original request most certainly would have been denied. Still, in order to proceed to Venice and beyond, Dowland needed some sort of paperwork explaining who he was and the purpose of his journey. His new friend Moritz was in just such a position as to grant this. Might the prince have encouraged Dowland in his further quest toward Rome to meet Marenzio? Did fellow musician Alessandro Orologio's kindness in Kassel extend to advising Dowland on how best to travel and what to do once in Venice? The musician's German acquaintances could have been quite useful for an Italian sojourn.

Venice functioned as a republic rather than a ducal court or papal entity like so many of the other Italian city-states. The highly cosmopolitan commercial center, famous for its unique canal system, was situated at the crossroads of inter-European trade. As an important port city, she welcomed merchants and dignitaries from all over the world. Venice's population fluctuated in the 1580s and 1590s due to plague and other factors but averaged about 150,000 residents, making it one of the largest cities in Europe.[7] After his time in London and Paris, Dowland should have felt comfortable in a city of that size, perhaps more so than he did in the German towns from which he arrived. In a 1578 Italian-English language tutor, John Florio described the destination for his readers: "You shall see a fair city, rich, sumptuous, strong, well furnished, adorned with fair women, populated of many people, abundant, and plentiful of all good things."[8] When his imagined reader questions an implied exaggeration, he replies: "Nay, rather I am not able to praise it enough as it deserves." Coryat referred to the port as "the most glorious, peerless, and maiden city of Venice: I call it maiden, because it was never conquered."[9] Sonically, Dowland may first have noticed Venice's bells, which tolled regularly from the city's hundreds of churches.[10]

Venice established a reputation for producing fine musicians, as well as instruments. In England, the practice of importing Venetian instrumentalists dated back to the court of Henry VIII. The children and grandchildren of some of these performers still served during Elizabeth's reign.[11] Venice's most heralded musicians were employed at St. Mark's Basilica, around which the state's musical activity flourished. If Dowland made it to the maritime republic by late April, he was present on the occasion of the coronation of a new Doge, Marino Grimani, held at St. Mark's. The church's *maestro di cappella*, Baldassare Donato, oversaw the music for the festivities. Anyone fortunate enough to attend heard famed cathedral organist Giovanni Gabrieli.

Dowland singled out just one Venetian musician in his 1597 *First Booke* introduction: "Not to stand too long upon my travels, I will only name that worthy master Giovanni Crochio, Vicemaster of the Chapel of St. Mark's in Venice, with whom I had familiar conference." Although prominent in Venetian church music, Croce was also known for his secular music, producing nine anthologies of madrigals, canzonettes, and masquerades. His works were also included in many mixed anthologies.[12] In 1622, perhaps inspired by Dowland's recollection, Peacham similarly described Croce as

> that great master, and master not long since of St. *Mark's* Chapel in *Venice*; second to none, for a full, lofty, and sprightly vein, following none save his own humor, who while he lived, was one of the most free and brave companions of the world.[13]

After religious activities sponsored by St. Mark's, the second most important and elaborate Venetian musical events were sponsored by six city confraternities, the *scuole grandi*, companies of laypersons and city church parishes.[14] Singers and instrumentalists associated with these occasions were often acquired from the official rosters of St. Mark's.[15] Croce was assigned oversight of three *scuole* at various times, including the Scuola di San Rocco, which sponsored several feast days each year with especially elaborate celebrations related to the church namesake's Feast of San Rocco. In 1608, Coryat described one small part of the scene utilizing theorbos, instruments of the lute family:

> This feast consisted principally of music, which was both vocal and instrumental, so good, so delectable, so rare, so admirable, so super excellent, that it did even ravish and stupify all those strangers that never heard the like ... Those that played upon the treble viols, sung and played together, and sometimes two singular fellows played together upon theorboes, to which they sung also, who yielded admirable sweet music, but so still that they could scarce be heard but by those that were very near them. These two theorbists concluded that night's music, which continued three whole hours at the least. For they began about five of the clock, and ended not before eight.[16]

The feast took place each year in mid-August, after Dowland had moved on to Florence, but he may have heard about preparations for this especially large and elaborate celebration from Croce, or perhaps he had even returned by then.

Venice was also a major center for music publishing. Unlike London and Paris, where individuals held music printing patents granted by authoritarian monarchs, Venice's capitalistic system encouraged multiple printers and publishers.[17] In the 1580s, Venetian printers produced upward of eighty distinct volumes of music each year. When Dowland arrived in 1595, he was surely already familiar with Italian music of the time. Moritz collected numerous Continental volumes in his library, including the "Englished" madrigals introduced in England in 1588 and 1590, as well as the authentic Italian ones that preceded. He also owned at least six musical anthologies printed and released in Paris during the years Dowland resided in France that consisted partially or completely of Italian settings.[18]

If the lutenist was looking to secure newly produced musical anthologies for himself or the landgrave, he had plenty from which to choose. Among others, 1595 saw Venetian releases of ecclesiastical works by Aichinger, Banchieri, and Belli, all for eight voices; five- and six-voice madrigal settings by Cirullo, Zanchi, del Mel, and de Monte; psalm, mass, and motet settings for up to twelve voices by Cortellini, Massaino, del Mel, Flandrus, and Patarini; a posthumous print of Andrea Gabrieli's second book of ricercari; and Molinaro's first book of canzonettas. Of special note, in that same year, Dowland's friend Croce released his second book of eight-voice motets in Venice, as well as his *Triaca musicale*, a set of four- to seven-voice madrigals; Marenzio, whom Dowland hoped to meet, produced his sixth and seventh books of madrigals; and Orologio, Dowland's associate from Kassel, worked with the Gardano press to produce his second book of madrigals, dedicated to the landgrave in 1595, and his canzonettes for three voices in 1596. Both were recorded in Venice in the autumn of 1595, raising the possibility that Dowland accompanied Orologio to or from Venice at the beginning or end of his trip.[19]

Padua and Ferrara, cities Dowland lists in his Italian itinerary, are located close to Venice. Both housed established lute makers. Dowland may have traveled to these cities on his way to Florence, or visited while based in Venice. Padua, a protectorate of Venice just one long day's walk away, would have offered quite a contrast for Dowland. At the time, the famous university there was much better known for its medical innovations than its musical ones. The city featured several intriguing attractions associated with the university, including the city's medical theatres, the first permanent spaces specifically built for viewing dissections and surgeries. One of these venues was built in 1594 and completed in 1595, the year of Dowland's journey.

The new lecture hall-type facility provided a set space for these productions. A strange pedagogical juxtaposition of medical procedures with processions and music, begun around the time that Dowland visited, was instituted by university Lecturer in Surgery and Professor of Anatomy Hieronymous Fabricius of Aquapendente.[20] Dowland might have been interested in the inclusion of musicians, specifically lutenists, who featured prominently in a description of one 1597 dissection:

> On the 12th of December, in order to please the anatomy spectators and to raise them from their sad look, lute players led by the anatomy students had been brought into the theatre ... those musicians were present as well for many days, following, and the expenses were hardly to be regretted by those on whom they were imposed, since when they watch and listen as spectators to them, they normally sit above away from the tumult and stomping; thanks to this tranquility the anatomical theatre will be able to persist for quite a long time, unharmed for some years.[21]

Quite a few English students attended the university in the fifteenth and sixteen centuries and the city seems to have been exempt from Italian travel bans, likely because of its distance from the papal states. Dowland may have met with some of his fellow countrymen while there.

In 1595, Ferrara, twice as far from Venice as Padua, was the home of Carlo Gesualdo, Prince of Venosa, an accomplished composer and lutenist in his own right. The prince became notorious in 1590 when he murdered his wife and her lover in Naples.[22] Publicity following the grotesque tragedy only increased public interest in both the prince and his music. In 1594, Gesualdo married again, this time to Eleonora d'Este, first cousin once removed to Duke Alfonso II of Ferrara. Gesualdo arrived in the city prior to his February 1594 wedding ceremonies and remained through most of 1596, engrossed in his own musical activities. The nobleman journeyed to his castle in Gesualdo with lutenist Fabrizio Filomarino in the late summer of 1595, not returning until December. Thus, Dowland probably had no chance to meet the prince, unless he visited Ferrara in the late spring or early summer.[23] Still, the Este court in Ferrara was famous for highly skilled and virtuosic musicians, and Dowland may have heard some of them perform.

A logical itinerary would send Dowland from the areas surrounding Venice directly to Florence, traveling through Bologna, and thus leaving only Genoa remaining on his list of cities visited (see Fig. 6.1). The tone of the musician's November letter to Cecil, however, sounds as if his decision to leave Italy was made in haste from Florence. A side trip to Genoa in the opposite direction at that point seems unlikely. Perhaps he instead traveled to Bologna from Ferrara, cut across to Genoa, and then looped southward toward Tuscany. Bologna was an especially important Italian musical center, both for printing and instrument making.[24] Although a papal state, Bologna maintained its own city senate, made up of nine senators from the aristocratic class and a cardinal legate and vice-legate. Artists and musicians were sponsored both by the Roman church and by independent patrons. Wealthy families sought to secure the finest musicians for their households, and the city's academies, confraternaties, and a multitude of churches regularly hosted dramatic musical events and festivities. Music printing, especially that of madrigals, was established in 1584. In the late 1590s, Bologna developed the madrigal comedy, a predecessor of opera. Dowland named several men he met while there, but mentioned no musical connections: "At Bologna I met with two men, the one named Pierce an Irishman, the other named Dracot. They are gone both to Rome."[25]

If Dowland was seeking out musicians when he arrived in Genoa, lutenist-composer Simone Molinaro seems a likely candidate. Molinaro's late uncle, Dalla Gostena, was famous for his lute fantasias, a genre that Dowland fully embraced. Four years after Dowland visited, Molinaro produced a lute anthology that included not only his own works for six-course lute, but also twenty-five fantasias composed by his uncle.[26] Molinaro himself favored *pass' e mezzi* (equivalent to the pavan), each paired with a galliard, mirroring Dowland's own preferred dances. Giulio Caccini, one of the most famous Florentine composers of the time, visited Genoa in 1595. Although Dowland never mentioned meeting the esteemed musician, two of Caccini's songs for lute, voice, and bass appear in Robert Dowland's 1610 *Musicall Banquet*.[27]

Although Dowland was headed to Rome to meet Marenzio, his Italian travels peaked in Florence, where he arrived at least by early June.[28] The walled-in city had a population of about 60,000, half that of Venice, but was still larger than the other Italian locations the composer visited.[29] Historically, Florence was a very wealthy republic-in-name, guided by the banking Medici family, a city-state that experienced periods of both prosperity and decline. Dowland's visit was during a time of financial and political recovery. By 1595 the city had become a ducal state and, like much of Tuscany, had submitted to Spanish rule. This is especially noteworthy, as Dowland later warned Cecil of Spanish influence and plots against England, as conveyed by Italian contacts. Dowland no doubt absorbed the flourishing

Florentine musical style. The city was home to the famous "camerata," started in the 1570s, the academy so often credited with the modernization of music through an elevation of monody. This intellectual think tank, much like the Académie du Palais operating in Paris during the Dowland's time there, was made up of scientists, poets, musicians (including Caccini), and men of multivarious talents who influenced the artistic output and resulting musical soundscape of the city in 1595.[30]

The formation of academies was not a new idea, and the city, like others in Italy, held long traditions of musical events sponsored both publicly and privately, including street pageants, *carri* (parades of floats, each depicting a scene with accompanying madrigals), and *intermedi* (musical scenes between play acts). Often the subject matter of these dramas served as propaganda heralding both the state and the Medici family. By the 1590s, Jacopo Corsi led the camerata, whose members were already at work creating the early opera *Dafne*, even though it was not premiered until 1598. Dowland might or might not have known of the camerata's activities, although in the seventeenth century, poet Carol Roberto Dati wrote that "the house of Jacopo Corsi, Florentine nobleman, was always open, like a public academy, to everyone who had intelligence or talent in the liberal arts."[31] One of the main musical ideas espoused by this group was the monodic concept of aria, with an emphasis on the perfect combination of singer and a single accompanying instrument, reminiscent of Dowland's lute songs. Variations on repeated lines as a means for virtuosic elaboration were standard, a convention also used in many of Dowland's lute solos.

A highlight of Dowland's travels must have been his performance in Florence for Grand Duke Ferdinando I de' Medici.[32] The duke often received guest musicians at his Palazzo Pitti residence, a short walk across the river from the famous Piazza del Duomo.[33] An acquaintance such as Caccini, who had long been sponsored by the duke and whom Dowland may have met in Genoa, was the sort of person who could gain an interested performer entrance to the court. The grand duke was in Florence from May through November 1595, with a few weeks spent just outside Florence in September and October at the Villa di Pratolino.[34] Dowland stated he received "great favors" for his ducal performance.

Dowland may even have approached the court looking for Luca Marenzio, the madrigalist who inspired his trip. Marenzio was one of the most famous Florentine-sponsored musicians of his day. At the time, the Italian musician was in Rome, from whence he eventually wrote to Dowland, offering up a meeting. In his *First Booke,* Dowland transcribed:

> Most Magnificent, my most observant Lord,
> From a letter from Signor Alberìgo Maluezi, I understand you have expressed with kind affection your desire to join me in friendship, and I, infinitely thanking you for your good spirit, offering to meet you if I can help in any way, as I am grateful for your infinite virtues and qualities that deserve the admiration of all who observe them, and for the sake of this, I bask in your hands. From Rome the 13th of July, 1595.[35]

Marenzio, who had been in the service of Ferdinando I for three years, left Rome some time in the fall of 1595, under command of the Pope, to become *maestro di cappella* for Zygunt III Wasa of Poland. Grand Duke Ferdinando provided reference letters for him on 10 September to pick up on his way.[36] He and Dowland, however, were not destined to meet.

About the time Marenzio wrote his letter to Dowland, the Englishman's situation began to change dramatically. It seems Dowland made it known in Florence that he was seeking introductions to grant him safe travel to Rome. It would have been quite convenient to bring up his Catholic associations of the past to aid this quest. Dowland later reported to Cecil that one day while he was walking on the plaza, a man approached him, claiming he had seen the English priest "Skidmore" in town. Dowland then met with this priest. Described by Dowland's acquaintance as "son and heir to Sir John Skidmore of the Court," the man was undoubtedly the similarly named second son of Sir John Scudamore of Holme Lacy, Herefordshire. Scudamore the son, not much younger than Dowland, had previously served Francis Walsingham, but arrived on the Continent in 1591 to attend the English College in Rome, where he was ordained a Catholic priest in 1592.[37]

This contact might not have been arranged by new Italian acquaintances, but through established English ones, for the man who became Dowland's primary connection to Rome, Scudamore, was the son of a good friend of George Carey, dedicatee of Dowland's *First Booke* just two years later. The senior Scudamore, Sir John, was also a fellow Gentleman Pensioner of Henry Noel, who corresponded with Dowland after the musician returned to Germany.[38] Further, Scudamore's response to Dowland, "telling him my name, he was very glad to see me," indicates that he was previously known to the priest, at least by name. Dowland's supposed reputation as a Catholic raises a question here, for when he claims his troubles at home were due to the queen's perception of him as "an obstinate papist," Scudamore replied, "Mr. Dowland, if it be not so, make her words true."

Dowland's meeting with Scudamore must have taken place in early June or sooner. Scudamore had arrived just recently in Florence with a group of other priests for the purpose of meditation and study at the convent Sancta Maria Novella.[39] As reported to Cecil, the two spoke of politics and religion, Dowland professing that he did not believe that any priests would plot to kill the English queen. Scudamore then revealed to him that there were many clergymen in Rome who wished her overthrow, although he clarified these were Spanish-influenced Jesuits. The priest claimed that, while he would like the queen to be Catholic, he would still defend his monarch and country if necessary.[40] Both men assuredly chose their words carefully, not knowing who would ultimately be privy to the conversation. Before they parted, Scudamore promised to deliver papers to Dowland that would secure his travel to Rome.

The next day Dowland dined with a group of gentlemen, including one "Lord Gray." If this was Thomas Grey, fifteenth Baron Grey of Wilton, the lutenist surely was courting both sides—playing the Catholic card to secure a travel recommendation from his priestly associates and then reporting his conversations back to Grey, a staunch Protestant with Puritanical tendencies and connections to the English court.[41] Dowland contended that by revealing Scudamore's words, he gave warning, presumably to the threat of Spanish animosity. Lord Grey seems to have approved of Dowland's duplicitous actions, especially after the musician renewed his vow of loyalty to the queen, for "he liked well, and bade me keep that secret." Lord Grey and his associates moved on.

Dowland did not hear from Scudamore again for more than a month, but finally received the promised travel documents, which were delivered to him by an English priest from Yorkshire named Bailey. The lutenist opened the letter in the company of Josias Bodley, who had a long record of international service to the crown.[42] He also showed the document to others, keeping it in his possession to send back to Cecil later. Scudamore's recommendation read:

> Right worshipful Mr. Fitzherbert,
> I know the fame of Mr. Douland our countryman for his exquisiteness upon the lute and his cunning in music hath come to your ears long ago and now

shortly you are like to see him in person and be judge yourself of his music, wherein he will I assure give you content. My request to you ... according to your loving nature would give all kind and courteous entertainment to him which that you may the safer do, though his coming from England might be some occasion of hindrance. I do assure in *verbo sacerdotis* that he is no meddler but rather inclined to the good and only for the fame of Lucca Emarentiana [Marenzio] and love of music hath undertaken this voyage so that I hope there will be no occasion to hinder you from doing him what favors you can, which I pray you again and again to show him for my sake and I shall be always bound to you for this, as for many other your exceeding courtesies to me showed—so praying god to bless you and us all do take leave.

Florence, 7 July 1595
Yours always at command,
John Scudamore, priest

In content, Scudamore's letter is unremarkable, affirming nothing more than that which Dowland requested—an endorsement for a musician seeking the famous Marenzio, as well as a plea for hospitality. Bailey's spoken words to Dowland were more heavy laden. The friar told the musician that his reputation had preceded him to Rome and that he was welcome there—as a Catholic exile serving the Pope. He was promised employment and the support of papal officials in the form of "a large pension of the pope, and that his holiness and all the cardinals would make wonderful much of me." Bailey went on to tell him that if he chose such a path, arrangements could be made for Dowland's wife and children to escape to Italy, for if they remained in England "they would lose their lives." In the end, it seems that Dowland's use of his perceived religion, in order to gain protection traveling to Rome, had spiraled into a much larger opportunity, one that if taken would require him to abandon his nation entirely.

There are certain pivotal moments in which a future-altering choice resounds with earthshaking profundity. Dowland had happened upon such a moment. He had set in motion events that transformed a professed desire to meet an exalted musical figure into a situation that jeopardized his safety and that of his family, which threatened to unravel all the connections he had built in his homeland. He was playing a dangerous game by associating with two powerful opposing forces and was suddenly forced into an awareness that his current situation had become untenable. Dowland's angst in addressing Cecil is clear:

> I called to mind our conference and got me by myself and wept heartily, to see my fortune so hard that I should become servant to the greatest enemy of my prince, country, wife, children, and friends, for want, and to make me like themselves. God knoweth I never loved treason nor treachery nor never knew any, nor never heard any mass in England, which I find is great abuse of the people, for on my soul I understand it not, wherefore I have reformed myself to live according to her majesty's laws, as I was born under Her Highness, and that most humbly I do crave pardon, protesting if there were any ability in me, I would be most ready to make amends.

It was time to make things right again. Dowland departed Florence and headed back toward Germany, never to return to the Italian lands again.

7

"You shall not neede to doubt of satisfaction here"

(German Lands, 1595–1597)

Dowland's Psalmes

Dowland made his way back to the German lands through Venice. He met with acquaintances along the way and noted in his letter to Cecil that speculation about Spanish aggression toward England in the upcoming year was circulating both in Italy and Germany.[1] Whether Dowland traveled from Venice into Germany alone or with others remains uncertain. Orologio was preparing his musical prints in Venice in the fall, before traveling back to Kassel by November. Did Dowland reconnect with his colleague for his return trip? Whatever the case, by 10 November, Dowland arrived in Nuremberg. He penned his heartfelt tome to Robert Cecil, detailing his adventures across Italy, overtly professing his loyalty to England at every instance, and revealing as much intelligence as he could muster.

The piece of correspondence brings up many issues related to religion, loyalty, connections, and intelligence. The challenge today is to read this letter as an artifact reflecting one particularly illuminating moment rather than an indictment of a man's entire life and career. Dowland needed to defend his honor and put to rest any rumors insinuating he had papal connections that might get back to London. It was vital that he reassure his most important English ally that he was trustworthy, valuable even, by reporting what he had seen and heard. He had narrowly escaped a precarious situation and was shaken to the core. Yet once back in safe territory, Dowland still had a future to consider. His greatest accomplishments—diplomatic, musical, and entrepreneurial—were still to come.

From Nuremberg, Dowland eventually returned to Kassel, leaving behind his Italian intrigues and deepening his relationship with Landgrave Moritz. An influential Protestant German leader, Prince Moritz was an ardent artistic supporter. The landgrave, known as "der Gelehrte," spoke multiple languages, started a school, sponsored actors and musicians, and wrote plays and poetry himself.[2] After visiting the Kassel court in 1596, Englishman Edward Monings reported,

> His education prince-like, generally known in all things, and excellent in many, seasoning his grave and more important studies for ability in judgment, with studies of pastime for retiring, as in poetry, music, and the *mathematics*, and for ornament in discourse in the languages, *French*, *Italian*, and *English*, wherein he is expert reading much, conferring and writing much he is a full man, a ready man, an exact man, and so excellent a Prince that a man may say of him without flattery as *Tully* did of *Pompei, unus in quo summa sunt omnia,* and for my private opinion I think there are but few such men in the world.[3]

Dowland's and Moritz's circles overlapped in terms of individual acquaintances, although not always at the same time. Lutenist Charles Tessier, whom Dowland likely met in Paris a decade earlier and who was in England in 1597 just after Dowland returned to London from Germany, probably met Moritz in Portiers in 1602 or 1603.[4] The following year, Tessier dedicated his second music book, *Aires et villanelles*, to the landgrave. While there are other avenues through which the two may have met, one wonders if Dowland spoke of Tessier to the landgrave while he was in the German lands or if instead he viewed his fellow lutenist-composer as competition. As for courtly contacts, Robert Devereux, second Earl of Essex, to whom Dowland appealed for permission to travel to Germany in the first place, personally knew and corresponded with Moritz, at times through one of the landgrave's English theatrical players. Robert Browne delivered at least one letter from Essex to Kassel in January 1595 when Dowland was present.[5] The lutenist may have communicated with his patrons and family back home in England through this same system of envoys.

The court of Hessen maintained a relationship with England even before Moritz assumed his office in 1592. Recommendations back and forth between Elizabeth I and Moritz's father show sustained communication.[6]

This comradery extended into the Moritz era. Continuing the Kassel court's tradition of diplomacy, Moritz formally appointed ambassadors to visit the English court, hoping to foster closer ties. When anticipating the birth of his first daughter, the prince solicited Queen Elizabeth to serve as godmother.[7] This was not an unusual request for the queen, as she took on the role for more than one hundred children during her reign.[8] She did not, however, have the time nor the inclination to be present for all her honorifics so, as was often the case, she sent a delegation to participate in the baptismal ceremonies dedicating her new German namesake. Elizabeth appointed Henry Clinton, second Earl of Lincoln, to serve as a special ambassador and proxy. In July, the earl led a group of English diplomats to Germany, returning in early October. The entourage first went to the court of Heinrich Julius, where Moritz sent an ambassador to meet them, after which they traveled on to Kassel. If Dowland remained in the city through the late summer and early autumn of 1596, he was present for baptismal festivities celebrating the birth of Moritz's daughter Elisabeth. The impressive events in which the delegation participated were recorded in detail by Monings. The Englishman, unfortunately, seemed more interested in those attending the festivities and the architecture of the landgrave's estate than musical details.[9] Dowland is not mentioned in this eyewitness account, but Monings gives few particulars related to entertainments that took place.[10]

Music was certainly part of Elisabeth's life. French lutenist Victor de Montbuysson later compiled a manuscript book of lute music for the landgrave's daughter around the year 1610. The collection includes a dozen arrangements of Dowland compositions, including several intabulations of "Come again," a lute song that appeared in Dowland's *First Booke*, and five courantes composed by Moritz.[11] Montbuysson was appointed lutenist to Moritz's court sometime between 1596 and 1598, perhaps after Dowland turned down the landgrave's offer of employment, and was one of the prince's most well-paid musicians.[12] It might reason that Dowland's music was copied somewhere into court collections while he was staying at the Kassel court and then later found its way into Elisabeth's book so many years later. However, the arrangements are quite different from Dowland's official versions. A more likely explanation suggests that Hessen scribes copied Dowland's music from other printed Continental anthologies.[13]

A December 1596 letter from Sir Henry Noel proves that Dowland kept up regular correspondence with his English patrons during his time at the Kassel court. More importantly, the communication demonstrates that

Dowland retained supporters back in England. Noel was a Gentleman Pensioner, serving in the ceremonial guard for the queen and thus ranking highly within Elizabeth's circle of respected gentleman courtiers. Part of the circle surrounding Sir Walter Raleigh, Noel was awarded a set of lands from Elizabeth in 1589 for a period of fifty years.[14] It was from this and other grants, such as a monopoly on pottery and stoneware arranged by Robert Cecil, that Noel managed his lavish courtier's lifestyle, although some reports characterize him as perpetually in debt.[15] Listed among "Memorable Persons" of Leicestershire, Thomas Fuller later described him thus:

> Henry Noel Esq; I will incur the reader's deserved displeasure, if he appear not most *memorable* in his generation. He was younger son to Sir *Andrew Noel* of *Dalby* in this county, who for person, parentage, grace, gesture, valor, and many other excellent parts, (amongst which, skill in music) was of the first rank in the court. And though his lands and livelihood were small, having nothing known certain, but his *annuity* and *pension*, as gentleman to Queen *Elizabeth*, yet in *state, pomp, magnificence*, and *expenses*, did ever equalize the barons of great worth. If any demand whence this proceeded, the *Spanish proverb* answers him, *That which cometh from above let no man question*.[16]

When Noel wrote to Dowland, the coveted court lutenist position left vacant by John Johnson's death a year and a half earlier was yet to be filled. Noel reassured his friend that he was still remembered and valued within the English court's musical circles.

> To Sir John Dowland at the Landgrave's Court ... I take well your several remembrances to me by letters which ere this time I would have answered, but for the uncertainty of your abiding.

> Now I understand that you remain in the landgrave's court: A Prince whom I honor for his high renowned virtues, being thereby desirous to see him, and have determined (God willing) as I pass those parts, with his favors to kiss his hand, if it be not presumption. I wish he knew my desire to do him service, and whereso ere I become, I will with honor and reverence speak and think of him. It is reported here of his purpose to see the queen. I wish it for that good of either, hers, to see a prince without peer, his to see a queen without comparison.

You shall not need to doubt of satisfaction here, for her majesty hath wished diverse times your return: Ferdinando hath told me her pleasure twice, which being now certified you, you may therewith answer all objections. Therefore forbear not longer than other occasions (than your doubts here) do detain you. I have heard of your estimation everywhere, whereof I am glad, and take that with other parts of your service once to me, for which I will do you all the pleasures I can. I wish you health and soon return and commit you to God.

Your old master and friend: H. Noel[17]

That Queen Elizabeth looked upon Dowland with favor would be welcome news to the lutenist, counteracting any lingering doubts he still harbored as to the monarch's esteem. Now a decision was at hand. Should Dowland return, as his friend and patron Noel suggested, or would he remain in the court headed by Moritz, a man who addressed him as "my loving friend" and who offered him continued service? Dowland heeded Noel's call, for Moritz later references "the letter impending little less which called you home."[18] John Dowland, England's musical treasure, would soon be back on native soil.

The lutenist, perhaps keeping his options open, remained in contact with Moritz even after his return to London. Many years later, the first pavan in Robert Dowland's *Varietie of Lute-Lessons* is attributed to Moritz, declaring, "Here beginneth the pavans: of which the first was made by the most magnificent and famous Prince Mauritius, Landgrave of Hessen, and from him sent to my father."[19] This pavan might have arrived after Dowland first returned to England, saved all the many years until the lute volume was produced in 1610, or might have been acquired any time in the interim. In 1612, Henry Peacham included an emblem and poem in his *Minerva Britanna* honoring Moritz, noting his "admirable knowledge in all learning, and the languages, hath excellent skill in music. Mr. Dowland hath many times showed me 10 or 12 several sets of songs for his chapel of his own composing."[20] Moritz also remained knowledgeable about Dowland's situation and offered him support. A 1598 letter written by the prince illuminates:

Honorable, my loving friend Mr. John Dowland, Bachelor in Music: London

Mr. Dowland, I imagined your departure from me had been either to serve her majesty or at the least for some other preferment fit for a man of your worth: the letter impending little less which called you home, the which I understand since hath took no place, either for want of good friends to prefer you, or by some particular ill hap that many times follows men of virtue, but to the purpose. If you do think it the acceptance of my service may any way better your estate, I will assure you that entertainment, that every way, you shall hold yourself content. Thus referring you to your best consideration, together with the council of your Friends, I rest, expecting your answer.[21]

Unfortunately for Dowland, Noel died in February 1597. Without his dedicated support, the implied English court position was not to be.[22]

In honor of his friend, Dowland composed a collection of spiritual pieces titled *Mr. Henry Noell, his funerall Psalmes*. This was not the first time Dowland experimented with setting sacred texts. No Englander of the time could escape the importance of psalms in both church and domestic settings. The Old Testament poetic scriptures were utilized by Protestants of all sorts, as well as the recusant Catholic community. In fact, the most successful musical volumes printed in the Elizabethan era were those devoted to psalm singing. About the same time that Dowland was born, the first edition of *The Whole Booke of Psalmes* (1562) was printed by John Day. Day held the printing monopoly for select sacred works from 1559 until his death in 1584, at which time the privilege remained in the control of his son Richard, who then assigned the right to various other printers. The *Whole Booke* featured all 150 psalms, Englished in metrical translation, with added melodic musical notation.

Many of the English rhyming texts had been known for more than a decade, the work of two translators, Thomas Sternhold and John Hopkins. The music in the *Whole Booke of Psalmes* was presented as a single melody line and could be sung alone or corporately in domestic settings or by a congregation or clergy in church services. Because of the metrical nature of the poetry, specific melody lines could be fit to multiple psalms. Therefore, many fewer melodies were presented than texts, and rather than wasting ink on repeated musical notation, the phrase "Sing this as the $[x]^{th}$ psalm" appears regularly. The book was so popular that it was published every year thereafter through the 1630s, with few exceptions, and often in multiple yearly editions, demonstrating the importance of psalm singing during the era.[23]

In 1592, thirty years after Day's initial *Whole Booke* run, printer Thomas East compiled his own collection of psalms under a similar title.[24] For his version, he solicited contemporaneous composers, including Dowland, to provide four-part harmonizations. In the resulting volume, all four voice parts were printed in a sort of choirbook format, in which the cantus voice sits atop the tenor on the left of two facing pages, and altus and bassus are arranged similarly on the right. Primary melodies are found in the tenor voice. Someone who purchased the volume could sing alone or in harmony with others, or simply read the texts for meditative reflection. A number of the psalms in East's volume provide more than one metrical translation for specific psalms, marked "Another of the same." Musically, some settings are matched to only one text, while others are used for multiple psalms or prayers. Unlike the earlier *Whole Booke* monophonic settings, notated music is provided for every individual psalm. Thus, repeated music is reprinted with new words in each additional use. Composer credits are consistent throughout.

John Dowland contributed six harmonizations to East's collection.[25] The most oft-used Dowland composition appears initially with Psalm 38, "Put me not to rebuke, O Lord," and features a tune in the tenor that was first seen in a 1564 Scottish Psalter with a different scripture (Ex. 7.1).[26] East used the Dowland harmonization alongside twenty-two different psalm texts in the 1592 tome. Later 1594, 1604, and 1611 editions increase the setting's use to more than thirty entries.[27] The harmonization's straightforward homorhythmic texture, narrow voice ranges, and simple voicings are representative of typical hymn settings of the time, which made them especially

Ex. 7.1 Psalm harmonization first used with Psalm 38 (East, 1592)

well suited for use in domestic situations. The entries also speak to Dowland's familiarity with psalms intended for Protestant worship.

Psalm 100, "All people that on earth do dwell," features Dowland's harmonization of an especially famous tune.[28] The setting is also repeated twice toward the end of the volume in a section of prayers, attached to "A psalm before morning prayer" and "A psalm before evening prayer." The tenor melody, originally composed by Louis Bourgeois and used in the 1551 Genevan Psalter, became known as "the Old Hundreth." Day did not use this text or tune in his 1562 volume for Psalm 100, but the melody is found in a Continental English psalter issued in 1560 and reprinted in London in 1561.[29] The tune then appeared in the 1563 edition of the *Whole Booke*, but with a different textual translation. The "All people that on earth do dwell" text was not used in Day's *Whole Booke* until the mid-1560s, but became the standard text Dowland knew for most of his life. Dowland's Psalm 100 setting later appears in lute intabulation in a manuscript of the early seventeenth century, an arrangement that, given his life's passion, surely would have pleased the composer-lutenist.[30]

In the final years of his life, Dowland reset Psalm 100 for a new version of the *Whole Booke of Psalmes*, this time compiled by Thomas Ravenscroft in 1621. Ravenscroft's anthology, like East's, featured four-part settings most probably intended for domestic use.[31] In his introduction, Ravenscroft states:

> The singing of psalms (as say the doctors) comforteth the sorrowful, pacifieth the angry, strengtheneth the weak, humbleth the proud, gladdeth the humble, stirs up the flow, reconcileth enemies, lifteth up the heart to heavenly things, and uniteth the creature to his creator, for whatsoever is in the psalms, conduceth to the edification, benefit, and consolation of mankind.[32]

Ravenscroft crafted many of his collection's harmonizations himself, but he also included some by contemporaries such as Martin Peerson and Thomas Tomkins, as well as a few older ones by Thomas Morley and John Farmer, who had died decades earlier. Dowland by this time was more closely associated with an older generation of musicians, and his inclusion may have been a sign of respect offered up by the St. Paul's chorister. Unlike East's psalm book, Dowland no longer dominates the volume with his musical entries. He is represented with just this one psalm harmonization. His

Ex. 7.2 Psalm 100, *Whole Booke of Psalmes* (East, 1592) and (Ravenscroft, 1621)

tenor voice again sings the same Bourgeois "French tune" for Psalm 100, and the "All people that on Earth do dwell" translation is also present. Yet rhythmic alterations at phrase endings extend the lengths of several notes and more closely match the Genevan original. The other voices are markedly different, exhibiting more rhythmic independence and interwoven lines that create a beautiful rendition (Ex. 7.2).

In a place of honor at the end of East's 1592 volume is a "Prayer for the Queen's most excellent Majesty," with music composed by Dowland. Both the prayer and its music are original to East's collection. The extended text clearly reaches out to Elizabeth and provides a bit of nationalistic pride.

> O God of power omnipotent,
>   and goodness infinite,
> Whose name is more than excellent,
>   and works all exquisite,
> Enlarge our hearts, our mouth, our tongue
>   that thou in greater store,
> Mayst have thy worthy praises sung,
>   then erst thou hadst before.
> For showing like the drops of rain
>   from out thy bounteous hands,
> Thou pow'rest thy gifts on us amain,
>   the sea hath fewer sands.
> A special token of thy love,
>   we have (which passeth all),
> A prince whose nobleness doth prove
>   herself heroical.
> Thou blessest England for her sake,
>   with peace and gospels truth.
> Her foreign enemies all do quake,
>   to leave what England doth.
> Do thou her battles ever fight,
>   and strengthen up her hand,
> That all the world may say by right,
>   God dwelleth in her land.
> And bless her with a length of days,
>   make all her study be,
> To serve thy majesty always,
>   in pure sincerity.
> And keep us that our sins do not,
>   her happy days make less,
> For then full soon will be forgot,
>   our former happiness.
> Direct her in thy righteousness,
>   and shield her with thy grace,
> And grant her subjects faithfulness,
>   fail not in any case.[33]

One wonders if Dowland seized the opportunity to flatter the queen in a new way, with hopes of a future appointment.

When Henry Noel died in 1597, Dowland again turned to creating psalm arrangements. In honor of his friend and patron, the musician composed a set of funeral psalms, opening with one labeled *Lamentatio Henrici Noel*.[34] These psalm settings are quite different from those provided to East and Ravenscroft. First, Dowland's earlier psalm settings harmonize completely different texts from those he set for Noel, with the exception of one. His settings for East, like others in that volume, are simple and conjunct, with limited voice ranges. The melody is placed in the tenor. The Noel collection features melodies in the upper voice and utilizes larger ranges, with more complex voice parts and more florid lines. Because of this, scholar Diana Poulton suggested the songs were written to be sung by the Westminster Abbey choir for Noel's interment at St. Andrew's Chapel. The choice of text then might be seen as curious, for if Dowland was composing specifically for Noel's service, he could have instead focused upon texts of the Anglican funeral sentences, found in the *Book of Common Prayer* with the instruction to be spoken or sung.[35] Instead, he produced a set of psalms and other spiritual texts in honor of his Protestant friend.

The collection consists of seven funeral songs featuring verses from four of the seven penitential psalms, interspersed with three psalm-like prayers, all harmonized in a four-part texture with each voice copied in a separate partbook. The pieces stand as the only other scriptural settings the composer attempted beyond his *Whole Booke* contributions.[36] Ravenscroft, in his 1621 psalm collection, stressed the consoling properties of the penitential psalms' dark texts by asking:

> Wouldst thou make a confession, and repent thee of thy sins? Then sing with remorse and humility the seven penitential psalms of *David*, and thou shalt feel the sweet mercy of God and thy mind refreshed with spiritual joy.[37]

As a complete set for a specific occasion, the spiritual songs for Noel take on special meaning.

Several Dowland contemporaries composed penitential psalm sets that may have served as models for his tribute. The first seven selections in William Byrd's *Songs of Sundrie Natures* (1589) are three-voice imitative part songs with English metrical text translations of the seven psalms, the lyrics penned by an anonymous author.[38] Continental composers, such as Orlando Lassus and Andrea Gabrieli, also set versions of the penitential psalms.[39]

Dowland's Venetian friend Croce created a unique collection, using Italian textual paraphrases by Francesco Bembo, titled *Li sette sonetti penitentiali*. This anthology was first printed in Venice in 1596, reissued in Germany with Latin texts in 1599, and translated into English and printed by Thomas East in 1608.[40] None of Croce's settings bear musical similarities to Dowland's compositions, but may have provided the lutenist inspiration in the collection's aesthetic as a set of *madrigali spirituali*—pieces with vernacular texts intended for a domestic audience. Dowland's friend Henry Peacham later wrote, perhaps based on the recollections and assessments of his friend, "[Croce's] penitential psalms are excellently composed, and for piety are his best."[41]

As an Italian, Croce approached the scriptures from a Catholic viewpoint, even though the pieces were not specifically liturgical. Noel, however, was Protestant, and buried in a church at the heart of the Church of England. It is curious, then, that the copyist of Dowland's songs for Noel ascribes each partbook to "Gio. Dolandi infælice Inglese. Baccalario in Musica" and labels the four psalm settings with their Latin reference titles: *Domine ne in furore* (Psalm 6), *Miserere mei deus* (Psalm 51), *De profundis* (Psalm 130), and *Domine exaudi* (Psalm 143). Perhaps these titles indicate Dowland began his psalm set during or soon after his Italian sojourn, inspired by Croce, and then found use for them upon Noel's death. Still, the English lyrics and obvious connections to the Protestant *Whole Booke of Psalmes* tie Dowland's settings back to a solid foundation in the Church of England, which developed its burial service directly from the Sarum rite, even though it did not officially retain any of the penitential psalms in the service prescribed in the *Book of Common Prayer*.[42]

The lyrics Dowland set in his seven Noel pieces include English translations of Psalms 6, 51, 130, and 140 and their Latin titles, as well as *Lamentatio* (with words from the traditional *Whole Booke* "Lamentation of a sinner"), "The humble suit of a sinner," and "The humble complaint of a sinner." These texts first appeared together in John Day's 1562 print of the Sternhold and Hopkins *Whole Booke*. Dowland's words match the first verses of the *Whole Booke*, and associated melodies are similar in four of Dowland's seven pieces.[43] Yet when he was composing his Noel settings, the primary musical source from which Dowland gathered those four melodies, as well as all of his texts, was East's 1592 volume, the same one to which the lutenist had contributed. Dowland no doubt owned a copy.

Not only do the words from the Noel set correlate more closely to the 1592 volume than earlier renditions of all seven songs, but (in the four movements

Ex. 7.3 Comparison of Lamentation melodies in *Whole Booke of Psalmes* (1562), *Whole Booke* (East, 1592), and psalms for Henry Noel (1597)

with matching melodies) rhythms, spellings, and phrasal barlines mirror almost exactly. (Ex. 7.3). These songs include "O Lord turn not away" (Lamentation), "O Lord consider my distress" (Psalm 51), "O Lord of whom I do depend," (Humble suit of a sinner), and "Where righteousness doth say" ([Humble] complaint of a sinner). Unlike the 1592 *Whole Booke* settings, Dowland places the hymn tune in the soprano voice in his new harmonizations, rather than in the tenor. The three psalms that do not replicate melodies from the *Whole Booke* set the texts "Lord in thy wrath reprove me not" (Psalm 6), "Lord on thee I make my moan" (Psalm 130), and "Lord hear my prayer" (Psalm 143). The hymn tunes are not present in any other identified English source of the time, so Dowland may have composed them himself. The most curious choice to provide a new melody is for Psalm 130, for it was Dowland who harmonized the 1592 East version. Thus, he was especially familiar with the original *Whole Booke* tune.

The single set of Dowland-Noel partbook manuscripts was listed in a 1636 inventory of William Cavendish, first Duke of Newcastle, who resided much of the time at his Welbeck estate in Nottinghamshire.[44] No direct connection between Dowland and Newcastle is known, although Robert Dowland was employed by Newcastle's uncle, also named William Cavendish, in the early

Ex. 7.3 (*cont.*) Comparison of Lamentation melodies in *Whole Booke of Psalmes* (1562), *Whole Booke* (East, 1592), and psalms for Henry Noel (1597)

seventeenth century. Noel knew of and supported the political and personal interests of Newcastle's father, Sir Charles Cavendish.

Dowland's manuscript psalm collection may have made its way into the library of another of the duke's uncles, Edward Talbot, eighth Earl of Shrewsbury, and his wife Jane. On the front inside cover and first folio page of the manuscript, a Francis Farthing signed his name, inscribing the volume "books for the lord." Farthing was employed by Lady Shrewsbury. When she died in 1626, Lady Shrewsbury bequeathed her possessions to her sister, Newcastle's mother, Katherine. The books likely then ended up in the Newcastle collection at Welbeck. There the Italian inscriptions found good company, for the duke's father, Charles Cavendish, was quite interested in Italian music, and the Newcastle collection included at least four print anthologies of Italian secular songs.[45] Thus, this seemingly straightforward set of psalms for a dead English Protestant gentleman takes on a sort of international significance.

In hindsight, Dowland's psalms for Noel portray add an aura of disappointment and unfulfilled dreams to the musician's story. If Dowland anticipated that Noel and his support would gain him the court lutenist position he longed for before traveling to Germany—and that was still vacant—his composed laments may have signaled not only his loss of a friend and true supporter, but also his once more dashed hopes of officially joining Elizabeth's entourage.

8

The First Booke of Songes or Ayres

(1597)

John Dowland's return to England may have been disappointing in terms of his employment goals, but the year that followed was nonetheless fruitful. In 1597, Dowland's *First Booke of Songes or Ayres* was printed in London, eventually becoming the most successful secular musical anthology of its time. As such, the volume served as an exemplar of Dowland's talents and his ability to adapt to any musical circumstance, thus advertising his artistic abilities to potential patrons in an innovative and well-produced songbook.

From 1575 through 1596, only a few men controlled all music rolling off London presses. In 1575, Queen Elizabeth granted a twenty-one-year monopoly on the printing of music paper and all musical editions, excepting metrical psalms, to William Byrd and his fellow composer and mentor Thomas Tallis. That same year, the two Chapel Royal musicians together created *Cantiones quae ab argumento sacrae vocantur*, a collection of thirty-four Latin motets dedicated to the queen. It was another thirteen years before the next English volume of songs became available, when Byrd's *Psalmes, Sonets, & songes* (1588) broke the publishing drought three years after Tallis died. From that time forward, Thomas East was Byrd's chosen printer.

Over the next nine years, several especially important musical anthologies stand out among the two dozen authorized for print. In addition to a second songbook and a number of fully sacred volumes by Byrd, the first editions of Italian madrigals in English translation were introduced by Nicholas Yonge and by Thomas Watson. East spearheaded a four-voice volume of the *Whole Booke of Psalmes*, to which Dowland contributed.[1] And while neither Yonge, Watson, nor East was a composer, Thomas Morley, Byrd's print culture heir apparent, produced his first five self-composed, multi-voice Italianate songbooks in the madrigal style. With the exception of two didactic volumes published by William Barley and printed by John Danter, all music books issued from 1588 through 1596 were printed by East.[2]

The English music printing world entered a new era in 1597. Byrd's patent had expired and was not reissued to another musician until late in 1598. Perhaps capitalizing on the ability to put forth music without permission and, equally important, without associated fees, nine new secular music books were printed in the year following the monopoly's expiration, more than double that of any previous year. East's press was responsible for four: *Le Premier Livre de Chansons & Airs* by Charles Tessier, *The first set of English Madrigalls* by George Kirbye, Thomas Weelkes's *Madrigals to 3. 4. 5. & 6. voyces*, and a sequel to Yonge's Englished Italian madrigals, *Musical Transalpina*. All these partbook volumes align closely with types of music previously printed by East. The other music books of 1597 were produced on the presses of printer Peter Short.[3] Two of these collections, sets of canzonets by Morley (one original and one collected from Italian composers), were similar in content to those issued by East and likewise produced as partbooks, with separate volumes for each voice. The other three presented new alternatives for music prints in England. These included Morley's theoretical treatise *A Plaine and Easie Introduction to Practicall Musicke*, Anthony Holborne's *The Cittharn Schoole*, and, most significantly, John Dowland's *First Booke of Songes or Ayres*.

Other basic music theory treatises had previously appeared in England, but Morley's *Plaine and Easie Introduction* remains the most famous and important English singing and composition manual of the era. Likewise, Holborne's *Cittharn Schoole* raised the standard for instrumental prints beyond William Barley's rather clumsy 1596 lute tutorial and anthology. In both cases, Short set a new level of production expectations. *Cittharn Schoole* is an anthology of music for a plucked string instrument similar to the lute. The book includes not only cittern solos, but also duos with bass, as well as texted songs composed by Holborne's brother William.[4] It seems that Short used both *Cittharn Schoole* and *Plaine and Easie Introduction*, as well as Morley's five- and six-voice *Canzonets*, to practice the logistics he would need for Dowland's lute song collection. Holborne's volume features cittern tablature, utilizing a grill-type print not previously seen in England. For ensemble pieces, both instrumental and vocal, all parts are printed on facing pages, in "choirbook format," thus rendering the need to purchase separate partbooks unnecessary.[5] This setup is replicated in the cantus partbook of Morley's *Canzonets*, with lute tablature on the page facing the highest voice. Owners, however, still needed to purchase additional partbooks for Morley's other voices.

A Plaine and Easie Introduction uses this same choirbook format in singing examples, but the placement of parts is altered further in the third portion of the volume, where at least one voice on each facing page is rotated so that singers sitting around a table could view their parts straight on.[6] This "tablebook format" is then used fully throughout Dowland's *First Booke*, with one page featuring a primary voice atop printed lute tablature and additional voices appearing on the facing page right side up, upside down, and to the side (Fig. 8.1). The format became the new standard for music with instruments. Twenty-nine lute songbooks that followed in England over the next twenty-five years used this same template.[7] The physical dimensions of the volume were twice the height and width of other recent music prints, with folio rather than quarto-sized pages, ensuring visibility for multiple performers sitting around different sides of the table. Once the pages were cut and bound into books, the sheer size of the music would have been striking in comparison to previous music volumes familiar to the public.

The *First Booke* is often credited with initiating tablebook format. However, as early as 1538, French printer Jacques Moderne issued his first

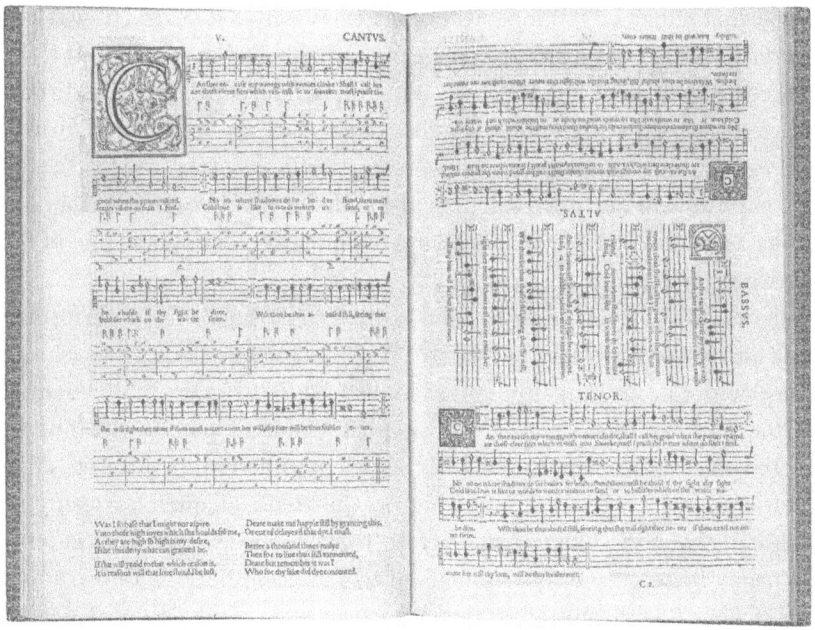

Fig. 8.1 Tablebook format, *First Booke of Songes or Ayres*, C1v–C2r. STC 7091. Used by permission of the Folger Shakespeare Library.

volume of *Le Parangon des Chansons*, a collection of polyphonic French songs by multiple composers that was laid out with one of two voices on each page printed upside for viewing across a table.[8] While seemingly successful— Moderne followed with ten similar collections in a series over five years— the format was not embraced by other printers. In England, at least one sixteenth-century manuscript of textless music from the Tallis-Byrd generation was beautifully copied as a tablebook.[9] Who proposed this same format for the English 1597 prints? Perhaps Short was introduced to the concept when acquiring his tablature print from a French source. It is possible that while in Paris, Dowland came across Moderne's volumes. Dowland may also have been privy to Morley's proofs for the *Introduction* treatise and realized its usefulness for his own purposes. Morley's *Introduction* and Dowland's *First Booke* also share the same title page artwork. Further, Short registered Dowland's *First Booke* with the Stationers' Company on the same day as Morley's *Canzonets*.[10] Thus, Short's 1597 prints collectively suggest some sort of collaboration among Morley, Short, and/or Dowland.

Although Dowland's *First Booke* cannot be credited as the first English print utilizing this innovative format, it was the first full collection of lute songs for voice with lute accompaniment printed in England, a category of music that remained fashionable for the next twenty-five years. His was also the first volume to include the singer's part with both notation and lyrics placed directly above lute tablature. With this design, Dowland created a paradigm for what an English lute song should be, not only in logistical format, but also in musical aesthetic. Truly, if the *First Booke* was Dowland's only accomplishment during his lifetime, the anthology would surely garner ongoing accolades on its own, rendering the lutenist-composer as one of the most outstanding musicians of his day.

Dowland's business sense led him to offer songs that could be performed in a variety of ways for the widest possible commercial appeal: as solo songs with lute accompaniment, as multi-part vocal songs in the manner of the popular English madrigal, as mixed-consort pieces with one or more voices and/or instruments, or some combination thereof. Yet while Dowland was certainly capitalizing on the trend of multi-part singing that had swept the nation since before Yonge's 1588 *Musica Transalpina*, he firmly believed that instruments played an essential role in the music of his *First Booke*, indicating that his works were to be accompanied by "lute, orpharion, or viol de gamba." In fact, the voices beyond the cantus are those he suggests as expendable, "so made that all the parts together, or either of them severally may be sung." All of this is in keeping with Dowland's affirmation of the lute as his own "first labor," claiming it to be "the most musical instrument."[11]

In his *First Booke* note "To the courteous reader," Dowland accuses:

> There have been diverse lute lessons of mine lately printed without my knowledge, false and unperfect, but I propose shortly myself to set forth the choicest of all my lessons in print, and also an introduction for fingering, with other books of songs, whereof this is the first.

Most scholars point to Barley's 1596 publication as the source to which Dowland was referring when he claimed his works were being offered incorrectly and without permission. Barley's anthology, which used a clumsy sort of woodblock tablature printing, is divided into sections featuring individual instructions and music for each of three plucked string instruments: the lute, the orpharion, and the bandora. After lutenist Francis Cutting's music, Dowland's is the most represented in Barley's anthology, with three pieces in the section for lute, including "Lachrimae," "Piper's pavan," and "Fortune," and four in the section for bandora: "Solus cum sola," "A galliard made by J. D." (more well known as the Essex galliard), "Go from my window," and "Mrs. Winter's jump."[12] To his credit, Barley did acknowledge Dowland in his introduction as one of "some of the best authors professing this excellent science of music."

Dowland's music fit Barley's professed prefatory philosophy well, as music intended for "a melancholy and troubled mind," and similarities to Dowland's work quickly become apparent. The opening non-musical poem in Barley's volume follows the same six-line iambic pentameter as many verses in the *First Booke*, including Dowland's initial song, "Unquiet thoughts." With an eerie resemblance in topical tone, Dowland's text stands almost as an answer.

(Barley)

Thoughts make men sigh, sighs make men sick at heart,
Sickness consumes, consumption kills at last:
Death is the end of every deadly smart,
And sweet the joy where every pain is past:
But oh, the time of death too long delayed,
Where tried patience is too ill apayed.

(Dowland)

> Unquiet thoughts your civil slaughter stint,
> And wrap your wrongs within a pensive heart:
> And you my tongue that makes my mouth a mint,
> And stamps my thoughts to coin them words by art:
> Be still, for if you ever do the like,
> I'll cut the string that makes the hammer strike.

Even more remarkable, one of Barley's prefatory verses opens with the words "Flow forth abundant tears," drawing a direct parallel to the words "Flow my tears" that were added to Dowland's "Lachrimae" tune in his 1600 *Second Booke of Songs*. Dowland's music, as well as pieces by Cutting, Jones, Rosseter, and others, were not the only "borrowed" portions of Barley's book. Most of the lute instructions proceeding the musical selections are taken directly from Adrian Le Roy's earlier lute tutorial, the one available in England during Dowland's formative years.

Barley himself was not a musician, but a skilled, if at times unethical, publisher and bookseller who worked with a number of different printers in London.[13] He likely collected music for his volume from circulating manuscripts, perhaps with the help of a musical acquaintance, for he states that he paid dearly for the works included. His compensation was certainly not passed on to Dowland, as the modern concept of copyright did not yet exist. In any case, Dowland's complaints were justified, as musical errors abound in the Barley collection, and whoever gathered the music was not especially discerning in terms of quality of material. The difference in care taken by Dowland and Short just one year later is striking.

The *First Booke* introduces Dowland's earliest datable vocal songs. Most previous manuscript sources include only lute tablature, in accord with the musician's reputation as one of the premier instrumental performers of his day. Yet several of his *First Booke* song texts are linked to previous entertainments, and he informs his readers that some of the compositions are ripe with age. The choice to produce a songbook was an astute one, for it allowed Dowland to fashion an anthology around texts exuding courtly ideals, bringing the composer closer to those of influence and power who might aid him in finally securing an official English post. Dowland exuded a certain confidence that this would not be his only songbook publication, for by titling the work his first book of songs, he implied that another would follow, a promise fulfilled in 1600. What Dowland might not have foreseen was the popularity of the *First Booke* as a singular entity. The volume received reissues in 1600, 1603, 1606, and 1613—more than any other secular music book of the era. Although subsequent editions are marked as "newly corrected and amended," changes are minor and do not much affect the music or text.[14]

As Dowland's first public print offering, the *First Booke* presented an opportunity to establish his credentials and reputation and to form a carefully crafted artistic persona. From the very first page, the lutenist presents a clear vision of who he is and what the volume includes: *The First Booke of Songes or Ayres of fowre partes with Tableture for the Lute: So made that all the partes together, or either of them seuerally may be song to the Lute, Orpherian or Viol De gambo*. A beautiful woodblock illustration featuring astronomical symbols and practitioners—the same featured on Morley's *A Plaine and Easie Introduction*—graces the title page. The term "title page border" does not really suffice for this dominating image. Used at least twenty times since 1559 in books of various disciplines, most especially those related to the sciences, the image suggests a depth of knowledge, intellect, and care by its creators (Fig. 8.2).[15] The title page also touts Dowland's educational status, listing him as "Lutenist and Bachelor of Music in both the Universities," which implies Oxford and Cambridge. No extant record verifies a second degree, but perhaps this is not surprising, as Thomas Fuller's history of Cambridge University noted that University Registrar Thomas Smith was extremely negligent in his duties from 1588 to 1601, leaving much information unrecorded.[16] Dowland's second degree was possibly bestowed via incorporation, in which one university recognizes a degree granted previously by another.

Placed underneath the title, the Latin phrase *Nec prosuit domino, quae prosunt omnibus, artes* hints at the dissatisfaction Dowland may have felt in his standing with the English government. Translated roughly as "while the arts are meant for all, they do not benefit the master," the motto's scholarly Latin tone is at once academic and personal. The book's "To the courteous reader" provides a glimpse of Dowland's vulnerability, opening with testimony about how difficult it is to offer up one's work to public scrutiny, not knowing how it will be received.[17] Whether this is a heartfelt expression or simply a hopeful gesture for creating a closer connection with the book's readers is irrelevant, for it allows Dowland to present his résumé, complete with names and places that establish him as an internationally respected

Fig. 8.2 Title page, *First Booke of Songes or Ayres*. RB59102. The Huntington Library, San Marino, California.

artist. He reveals his intended audience as an elite one, stating, "the courtly judgement I hope will not be severe against [my songs]," calling upon the communities in which his music first appeared. Yet Dowland also implies that some works were performed at the universities.

Dowland then reveals more biographical information than in any other source outside his 1595 Cecil letter, cataloging his travels to France, Germany, and Italy. A reference to the "sundry letters" he received from Italian composer Luca Marenzio is accompanied by his transcription of one of them, placing himself in league with one of the most popular and internationally recognized madrigalists of his time.[18] Dowland then honors Marenzio in the sixteenth song of the book, "Would my conceit," with a parody of the opening few bars of Marenzio's madrigal "Ahi, dispietata morte," using similar pitches with manipulated rhythms at the beginning (Ex. 8.1).[19] One of Dowland's more intriguing prefatory allusions is to Giovanni Croce, whom he met in Venice in 1595. Croce's madrigals first appeared translated into English in Yonge's second *Musica Transalpina* of 1597, the same year the *First Booke* appeared. Also in 1597, Morley's four-voice *Canzonets* includes five songs with music attributed to Croce. Dowland's passing mention of the Italian composer serves to elevate his own status. Those paying close attention might realize that Morley, who earned his degree at the same time as Dowland and who now was a Gentleman of the Chapel Royal, might have known Croce's works well enough to present them to the English public, but Dowland personally knew the Italian musician.

Dowland's dedication cements the *First Booke* within the courtly atmosphere he hoped to convey. George Carey, Baron Hunsdon, receives a traditional obsequious dedicatory text. Hunsdon was also the dedicatee for Morley's 1597 five- and six-voice *Canzonets*, the volume recorded with the Stationers' Company the same day as Dowland's. This additional connection between Dowland's and Morley's books again suggests either close collaboration or competition—or perhaps both. A full-page crest placed opposite Dowland's dedication, one not included in Morley's volume, heralds the statesman's importance. Carey's honorifics are then listed in Dowland's dedication as "the most honorable Order of the Garter Knight: Baron of Hunsdon, Captain of her Majesty's Gentlemen Pensioners, Governor of the Isle of Wight, Lieutenant of the County of Southampton, Lord Chamberlain of her Majesty's most royal house, and of her Highness['s] most honorable Privy Council." Most significant for Dowland were the final two.

Ex. 8.1 Marenzio, "Ahi, dispietata morte" / Dowland, "Would my conceit," openings

As Elizabeth's Lord Chamberlain and a member of the Privy Council—roles Hunsdon had recently assumed after his father's death—the baron was especially well positioned to influence courtly appointments for musicians. Dowland references "honorable favors" he received from Carey in his dedication and hopes for continued kindnesses, suggesting a previous relationship. Dowland goes on to name Carey's wife, for whom the composer elsewhere named a lute solo, as "my honorable mistress, whose singular graces towards me have added spirit to my unfortunate labors."[20] The single instrumental work in the volume, "Galliard for two to play upon one lute," is placed after all the songs. Its titular instruction brings forth images of a teacher and student, parent and child, or pair of lovers intertwined in a playful feat of musicking.

Hunsdon was noted as a lutenist in Morley's five- and six-voice *Canzonets*. Perhaps Dowland envisioned the Baron making music with one of his own children or his wife. Considering his dedication, Dowland may have worked in the Carey household, perhaps after returning to England to find his intended supporter Henry Noel—a man closely connected with Hunsdon—already dead.[21]

The *First Booke*'s prefatory material also includes a Latin tribute from lute enthusiast Thomas Campion. In it, the gentleman poet attests to Dowland's skills, which are portrayed as descending from Orpheus. This was not the first time Campion heralded Dowland's talents. In the Latin *Poemata* (1595), Dowland is afforded an epigram among more than one hundred presented, the only poem in Campion's book addressed to a named professional musician. The verse is notably longer than most of the epigrams surrounding it.

To John Dowland

O, whose lute makes the high heavens sound
And those who dwell in dark Styx's shadows,
How soft is the murmur, like a wave eclipsing Lygia,
Wet with dew as she dries her hair.
How softly the murmur strikes the drooping ear,
While sleep intrudes on tender eyes?
Like a scythe, a rose dissected from its purple head
Drops her scattering leaves to the ground,
Here I slip, so weak in sleep,
And my limbs fall heavily to the ground.
You steal my miserable mind from me
My breathless heart plucked of your gut.
Which deity brought his power
To direct your trembling fingers among the gods?
Let the great performer keep his rightful place.
You alone bring credence to ancient things,
So I not surprised that Orpheus stood atop Rhodope
Commanding rocks and wild beasts.
But, oh, blessed, stay thy divine hands,
For now, for a little while stay these divine hands.
My soul melts, how carefully you steal it from me.[22]

Campion's later Latin commendation in Dowland's *First Book* is shorter, but echoes the poignancy of his original *Poemata* sentiment, again associating the lutenist's talents with those of Orpheus:

Fame, which posterity granted Orpheus,
Musica gives to him, and even better,
Suppressing the fleeting sounds that came before.
What delights he has presented to the ears,
He now also makes visible to eyes in the light.[23]

Campion was an apt choice for solicitation of a laudatory commendation. A well-educated London-born gentleman, he was also a poet and musician. While not a full-time professional musician like Dowland, his songs appeared in five collections of ayres from 1601 through 1617, by which time he had received his physician's degree. Campion also actively participated in royal entertainments during the reigns of both Elizabeth and James. He was featured in Gray's Inn masques in the 1580s, performing in front of courtiers and possibly even the queen herself. His poems began appearing in printed English verse anthologies soon afterwards. In the 1590s, he served in at least one military campaign led by the Earl of Essex. As a well-respected gentleman with courtly connections, Campion was someone who bridged the gap between those at the highest levels of nobility and professional artisans such as Dowland.

Dowland's *First Booke* includes twenty-one strophic lute song–airs, set for cantus voice and lute plus alto, tenor, and bass voices or instruments (Table 8.1). The previously mentioned lute duo is placed at volume's end. While prefatory material indicates that many of the compositions in the anthology were not new, there is no indication whether these older works were first created as songs or in another format. In some cases, they were certainly composed as lute solos to which Dowland later added words, aligning the melody and creating additional voice parts to cater to a clientele used to multi-voice singing. At least six of the *First Booke* songs are found as lute solos or in instrumental consort versions in manuscripts, five of them in collections predating the *First Booke*.[24]

The quality of the poetry that Dowland set to music and the scenarios the texts evoke also support the notion that the *First Booke* was intended for a courtly audience.[25] As with most songbooks of the age, authors of featured

Table 8.1 Contents of *The First Booke of Songes or Ayres* (1597)

(songs to four voices and lute)

I. Unquiet thoughts
II. Whoever thinks or hopes of love
III. My thoughts are winged with hopes
IV. If my complaints could passions move
V. Can she excuse my wrongs
VI. Now, O now I needs must part
VII. Dear if you change, I'll never choose again
VIII. Burst forth my tears
IX. Go crystal tears
X. Think'st thou then by thy feigning
XI. Come away, come sweet love
XII. Rest awhile you cruel cares
XIII. Sleep wayward thoughts
XIV. All ye whom love or fortune hath betrayed
XV. Wilt thou unkind, thus reave me of my heart
XVI. Would my conceit that first enforced my woe
XVII. Come again, sweet love doth now invite
XVIII. His golden locks Time hath to silver turned
XIX. Awake sweet love, thou art returned
XX. Come heavy sleep
XXI. Away with these self-loving lads

(lute duo)

A Galliard for two to play upon one Lute

verses receive no attribution but were likely Elizabethan courtier-poets. This practice adhered to a "stigma of print" philosophy, in which publicly acknowledging the writings of courtiers was deemed unseemly.[26] Because of this stigma, only a few of Dowland's verses have been concretely linked with specific poets, including two ("Whoever thinks or hopes" and "Away with these self-loving lads") excerpted from Fulke Greville's *Caelica*.[27] Greville's Petrarchan-inspired poetic cycle takes as one of its mistresses the figure Cynthia, a character regularly used to symbolize Queen Elizabeth in dramatic allegory. Scholar Gavin Alexander suggests the *Caelica* poems were likely given to Dowland by Greville himself.[28] "My thoughts are winged with hopes," another song featuring the character Cynthia, sets lyrics likely penned by George Clifford, third Earl of Cumberland.[29]

> My thoughts are winged with hopes, my hopes with love,
> Mount love unto the moon in clearest night,
> And say as she doth in the heavens move
> In earth so wanes and waxeth my delight:
> And whisper this but softly in her ears,
>   Hope oft doth hang the head, and trust shed tears.
>
> And you my thoughts that some mistrust do carry,
> If for mistrust my mistress do you blame,
> Say though you alter, yet you do not vary,
> As she doth change, and yet remain the same:
> Distrust doth enter hearts, but not infect,
>   And love is sweetest seasoned with suspect.
>
> If she for this with clouds do mask her eyes,
> And make the heavens dark with her disdain,
> With windy sighs disperse them in the skies,
> Or with thy tears dissolve them into rain;
> Thoughts, hopes, and love return to me no more,
>   'Til Cynthia shine as she hath done before.

Words in the first verse correspond to the title border image perfectly, with evocative wordplay describing the moon, heavens, and earth, all images also found in other songs in the book. More evocatively, the second-verse imagery portraying Cynthia "as she doth change, and yet remain the same" uses language associated with Elizabeth's motto *Semper eadam*, solidifying the impression of a never-aging queen who "shine[s] as she hath done before."[30] The music to "My thoughts are winged" shows up later in consort arrangement in Dowland's *Lachrimae* (1604) with the title "Sir John Souch, his galliard," referring to the gentleman to whom Dowland's *Third Booke* was dedicated and who married the daughter of Henry Berkeley, a close friend of collection dedicatee Carey. Other *First Booke* lyrics hold associations with individual courtier poets via their subject matter or through eponymous connections of later renditions of the music. In one instance, "His golden locks" presents a poem sung at the 1590 tiltyard retirement of Sir Henry Lee, with words likely written by Lee himself.[31]

One of Dowland's most popular *First Booke* songs, "Can she excuse my wrongs," has been framed by many scholars as a plea to the queen by royal favorite Robert Devereux, second Earl of Essex. The courtier maintained a volatile relationship with his monarch, falling into and out of grace as his hotheaded ego often led him to action before considering possible consequences. This pattern eventually led to his downfall and execution in 1601. The earl rose to power quickly after 1587. A decade later, he stood as the leader of one side of an ongoing power struggle at court between his followers and those of Robert Cecil. Elizabeth used this rivalry to her advantage as a way to keep her advisors in line as they simultaneously were required to work together for ongoing national concerns. For Essex, that meant significant rewards for his accomplishments, but swift rebukes when he moved beyond the bounds of his authority, an occurrence that became more frequent as the decade progressed.[32]

In 1596, Essex was ascending the heights of public popularity after leading a successful military mission to capture the Spanish city of Cadiz, one of England's most decisive victories in its conflict with Spain. The following year, the same in which the *First Booke* was printed, Essex led an expedition to the Azores, actively defying specific orders while there. This back and forth of circumstance required constant apologies to his queen. Those purchasing the *First Booke* likely knew of these events, and some might have sought out the volume as a means to decipher gossip of the court, especially that related to the queen's inner circle. "Can she excuse" does not "name names" outright. It might be read simply as a song with poignant lyrics. Still, its textual mood mirrors those of Essex's many letters to the queen, written when he was sent away to cool off.

> Can she excuse my wrongs with virtue's cloak?
> Shall I call her good when she proves unkind?
> Are those clear fires which vanish into smoke?
> Must I praise the leaves where no fruit I find?
>
> No, no, where shadows do for bodies stand,
> Thou mayst be abused if thy sight be dim.
> Cold love is like to words written on sand,
> Or to bubbles which on the water swim.

Wilt thou be thus abused still,
Seeing that she will right thee never.
If thou canst not o'ercome her will,
Thy love will be thus fruitless ever.

Was I so base that I might not aspire
Unto those high joys which she holds from me?
As they are high, so high is my desire.
If she this deny, what can granted be?

If she will yield to that which reason is,
It is reason's will that love should be just.
Dear, make me happy still by granting this,
Or cut off delays if that die I must.

Better a thousand times to die
Than for to live thus still tormented.
Dear, but remember it was I
Who for thy sake did die contented.

Elizabethan courtiers such as Essex and others in the Sidney-Essex circle were often the same individuals who made lasting impressions as poets. Many wrote a type of apologetic poetry aimed at reinforcing the portrayal of a supreme female royal mistress who held in her palm the futures of her subjects.[33] This style is found in much of Essex's poetry. While the words of "Can she excuse" have not been found in any Essex holographs, a *Lachrimae* (1604) instrumental consort version by Dowland is titled "Earl of Essex galliard." Son Robert labels the music similarly in a lute solo found in *Varietie of Lute-Lessons* (1610), strengthening the connection between courtier and music. Proven attribution of text, however, is not as important as the impression listeners of the time held. If they heard the song and thought of Essex and his circumstances, then meaning afforded in the lute song was achieved.

Other pieces in the volume can similarly be interpreted as reflections of publicly recognized events in the Elizabethan court. "Now, O now I needs must part," for example, is reminiscent of the end of a long-discussed courtship between the queen and the French Duke of Anjou and Alençon.[34] Francis, youngest son of French King Henri II and Catherine de' Medici, was first suggested as a match for Elizabeth in 1579, with hopes of negotiating an English alliance with France against Scotland. The duke was twenty-two years younger than the queen but the two seemed to develop a certain affection for each other, as evidenced in a rich trove of correspondence. Elizabeth even nicknamed Francis "her frog." Many English people were not in favor of the match, largely because of the duke's Catholic background. The Privy Council was split on the matter. While Dowland was in France in 1581, Walsingham undertook a diplomatic mission to Paris, during which the French king wanted confirmation of a marriage contract. Walsingham, however, left for home without resolving the matter. Housed at the English embassy at the time, Dowland surely was knowledgeable of the affair.

Francis visited England twice in an effort to woo the queen. She seemed to waffle in her intention to wed and used negotiations over the years to her advantage. Regardless, during the French duke's 1581 London stay, it became apparent that a marriage would not take place. The duke was afforded a grand send-off by many important members of court, including George Carey, Henry Noel, Fulke Greville, and even Elizabeth herself. English officials accompanied the duke and his entourage across the country toward port, some continuing on to France. Elizabeth and Anjou said goodbye just a few days before he boarded *The Discovery*, attended by the Earl of Leicester:

> [E]ither part took their leave of other, not without great grief and show of very great amity, especially between her majesty and the monsieur. Which thing was perceived also in the lords and gentlemen of both nations, and likewise in the ladies, to all whom it was like grief to depart after they had been conversant and had lived friendly and brotherly together by the space of three months, without any change or alteration of good wills. But the honor which enforced his highness, assuaged his grief, and made him proceed on his journey with the said prince and lords of both nations.[35]

Elizabeth wrote a poem inspired by the occasion.

> I grieve and dare not show my discontent.
> I love, and yet am forced to seem to hate.
> I do, yet dare not say I ever meant.
> I seem stark mute, but inwardly do prate.
> I am and not; I freeze and yet am burned,
> Since from myself, my other self I turned.

My care is like my shadow in the sun,
Follows me flying, flies when I pursue it,
Stands, and lies by me, doth what I have done.
His too familiar care doth make me rue it.
No means I find to rid him from my breast,
'Til by the end of things it be suppressed.

Some gentler passions slide into my mind,
For I am soft and made of melting snow.
Or be more cruel, love, and so be kind,
Let me, or float, or sink, be high or low.
Or let me live with some more sweet content,
Or die, and so forget what love ere meant.
      Eliza Regina, upon Monsieur's departure.[36]

Dowland's lyrics for "Now, O now I needs must part" evoke the same feeling of loss emanating from the queen's poem, expressed as an answer from her intended. The verses even conclude with a similar living-dying sentiment.

Now, O now I needs must part,
Parting though I absent mourn.
Absence can no joy impart,
Joy once fled cannot return.
While I live I needs must love.
Love lives not when hope is gone.
Now at last despair doth prove,
Love divided loveth none.

Sad despair doth drive me hence.
This despair unkindness sends.
If that parting be offense,
It is she which then offends.

Dear when I from thee am gone,
Gone are all my joys at once.
I loved thee and thee alone
In whose love I joyed once.

And although your sight I leave,
Sight wherein my joys do lie.
'Til that death do sense bereave,
Never shall affection die.

Dear if I do not return,
Love and I shall die together.
For my absence never mourn
Whom you might have joyed ever.
Part we must though now I die,
Die I do to part with you,
Him despair doth cause to lie,
Who both lived and dieth true.

Like "Can she excuse," the music to which "Now, O now" is set finds concordance in other Dowland manuscripts and prints as a solo lute galliard, including the Holmes manuscript, the same one that features the "Earl of Essex galliard" without title.[37] The manuscript contains two versions of the music heard in "Now, O now." The first, a simpler one, is copied untitled. The second is labeled "The frog galliard," providing a direct reference to Elizabeth's term of endearment for Anjou. The tune became popular and shows up in several dozen manuscript and print collections of both lute and consort music over the next fifty years, often retaining its "frog" title. One of these appeared not long after Dowland's *First Booke*, the last of six arrangements of Dowland works for mixed consort found in Thomas Morley's 1599 *First Booke of Consort Lessons*.[38]

"Can she excuse" and "Now, O now" are clear examples of the ways in which songs in the *First Booke* provided imagery related to Elizabeth's court. They exhibit the standard practice of using in-text coded language understood within the context of contemporaneous political and social events. Surely such messages weave their way throughout the entire volume, in ways that are difficult to decipher more than four hundred years later. From another vantage, in some ways the sentiments of the "complaint poetry" featured in the *First Booke* songs also might be applied directly to Dowland himself, a musician whose professional hopes rested on Queen Elizabeth and members of her court.

Yet Dowland was not simply providing courtly inspired balladry for his consumers. The composer also fashioned a public artistic persona within his *First Booke*. Already well known for his famous "Lachrimae," the lute pavan that musically depicts his own tears, Dowland builds on a fashionable trend surrounding a so-called cult of melancholy, while maintaining a pleasant exterior. The dedication to Carey carries no pessimistic tone, but the Latin motto on the title page expresses a sort of dissatisfaction from the outset. Similarly, the note to the reader presents only one negative thought, of imperfect presentation of Dowland's music by other publishers, but the overarching impression is one of a successful, well-traveled practitioner who found contentment in his art. Thus, the transition to a group of songs tinged with sadness creates a performative aesthetic. Dowland's tears find literal realization in lyrics of the songs "Burst forth my tears" and "Go crystal tears," as well as in the interior text of "Come again, sweet love," in which the narrator sits, sighs, weeps, faints, and dies. In "Come heavy sleep," the singer's "weary weeping eyes . . . spring of tears doth stop my vital breath and tears my heart with sorrows sight swollen cries." Likewise, "All ye whom love" expresses "tears, sighs, and ceaseless cries alone I spend." Themes of sleep, sorrow, and darkness permeate Dowland's lyrics. To be fair, not all of the songs in the collection are somber. In fact, some such as "Awake sweet love" and "Away with these self-loving lads" sound quite uplifting or spirited. Still, enough contain lyrics of despair and resignation to color the whole. Darker themes are then balanced by expressions of redeeming love and a clear celebration of a worshiped queen in the form of Cynthia, enhancing a perception of their creator as a brilliant but tortured soul.

Musically, Dowland turns his four-note descending "Lachrimae" motive into a sort of emblem outlined throughout the *First Booke*. No fewer than four of the songs open or end with the melodic outline of the "Lachrimae" motive, while two begin with the theme in inversion. Another four open or close with the second subphrase of "Lachrimae," in which the first note of the descending tetrachord is lowered (Ex. 8.2). Such short melodic segments certainly might be viewed as the natural side effect of a composer who wrote predominantly stepwise melodies, especially with rhythmic alteration, but their placement creates an overarching aesthetic, coincidental or not. Harmonically, the composer was not thinking in terms of major-minor tonality as modern musicians do, but the songs tend toward a minor mode, often accentuated by carefully placed chromatic-second movement in a sort of weeping trope. And yet, if a foreboding aura encompasses the larger volume, the mood is still just a shadow. Unbeknownst to anyone at the time, Dowland's darkest works were yet to come.

Ex. 8.2 "Lachrimae" theme outline examples in openings and endings of *First Booke* songs

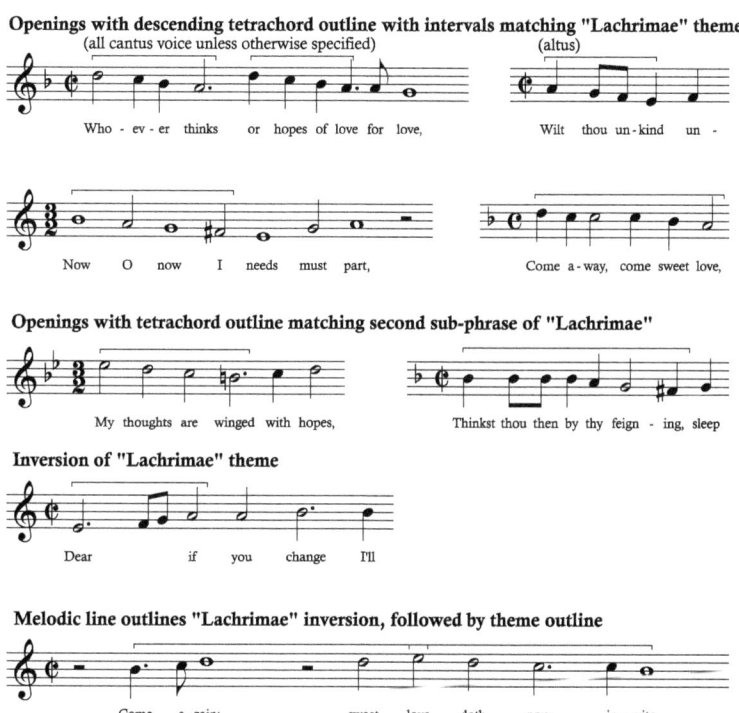

If Dowland created his *First Booke* as an appeal for recognition in the English court, building upon the reputation he had been formulating in the decade since his 1588 degree from Oxford and creating a powerful artistic image for himself, he did not wait long to see if the venture would yield positive results. About the same time the lute songbook was printed, his old patron Moritz extended an invitation for Dowland to return to Kassel. The offer would have been valued by many, and perhaps was by Dowland. With the success of his *First Booke* propelling him forward, and no court position tying him to English soil, Dowland was free to pursue his passions wherever he pleased. He might also have decided to remain patient, applying himself to his goal of a national court position. But the enterprising musician was offered a more profitable path. Denmark awaited.

SERVING TWO NATIONS

9

"Personal Lutenist to the King"

(Denmark, 1598–1602)

By all accounts, 1598 marked a high point in John Dowland's career. His musical anthology of the previous year was a success, his reputation was at an all-time high both on the Continent and at home in England, and he was offered employment in two of the most enlightened courts in all of Europe—those of Moritz, the Landgrave of Hesse, and Christian IV, King of Denmark. He chose the latter. Dowland was not a typical member of Christian's entourage. Any musician would be envious of his position, a prestigious one in which he could remain for life should he desire, secure in his exorbitant salary and his unique title, "Personal Lutenist to the King." For a while Dowland was content, serving his new employer, exploiting his worth as an agent for procuring new musicians and instruments for the court, and benefiting from Christian's generous travel allowances. And yet, for Dowland, working for Christian IV was not ultimately the perfect placement, for it was not in England.

When Dowland arrived home from the German lands in 1597, John Johnson's position as court lutenist still had not been filled.[1] Did the queen envision Dowland in the role, but waited for him to exhibit a more appropriate courtly disposition as he matured? Is it possible that, because of Christian's especially favorable terms, Dowland would have chosen Denmark even had Elizabeth offered him employment? Beyond the English court position, Dowland had other choices, as evidenced by Moritz's invitation. Yet the opportunity to travel to Denmark held appeal on several levels. Foremost was the substantial compensation Christian offered. Dowland's salary was set at 500 daler per year, a sizable income for a court musician. The Danish financial register notes:

> His Royal Majesty has graciously appointed and accepts Johann Doulande to be a lutenist in the service of his majesty, wherefore his said Royal Majesty intends yearly to let him have for his sustenance 500 daler out of

his majesty's public treasury, in accordance with the contents of his letters of appointment, a copy of which has been deposited here. Dated Frederiksborg on the 18th November in the year 1598.[2]

This salary was unprecedented for a musician in the Danish court.[3] The same day that Dowland began, another English musician named Robert Bosan was hired for 60 daler per year plus 7 daler per month for board, and free livery, or a total of 144 daler per year.[4] Even this amount was three times the rate received by ordinary workers in other areas of the royal household. The higher pay scale for musicians was likely due to enhanced literacy, allowing for use of such employees beyond musical activities.[5] When Dowland began his service, even especially valued musicians such as court organist and eventual *kapellmeister* Melchior Borchgrevinck earned only around 200 daler per year.[6] William Brade, the English gambist who worked on and off again for Christian from 1594 through 1622, may have helped paved the way, for he was compensated at 320 daler.[7]

Dowland's salary did not include the usual stipend for board and livery, indicating that he was either responsible for those expenses himself, or that Christian provided lodging within the royal residences, at least initially. The absence of livery may indicate that Dowland was not expected to don an official court uniform but was free to dress in any manner he chose, providing it was appropriate for a given occasion. In later years, Christian offered the same provisions for several other highly paid musicians, including organist Vincentius Bertholusius, who in 1609 received a salary of 1000 daler, and lutenist/violist Jacobus Merlis, who received 600 daler.[8] Englishman Thomas Cutting was also hired under similar terms when he was summoned to Denmark as lutenist in 1608 after Dowland had left, although he received a lower compensation rate of 300 daler per annum.[9] Dowland's generous Danish offer not only benefited him financially, but also demonstrated to Queen Elizabeth his value to other distinguished monarchs, thus increasing his perceived worth at home.

In some ways, the Denmark appointment finally put to rest old questions related to Dowland's religion. After his unfortunate associations with Catholics in Italy, Dowland returned to the staunchly German Protestant court of Moritz, who was in league with other similarly leaning figures such as Heinrich Julius in Wolfenbüttel, as well as Christian IV in Denmark. Christian's 1597 marriage to Anna Katrine of Brandenburg was specifically engineered to bring together two of the strongest Lutheran state strongholds and, as Duke of Schleswig-Holstein, Christian was in a natural position to help fortify the Protestant cause in the north German lands. Dowland's previous associations with Church of England advocates such as Cecil, Sidney, and Noel, and his experience as a contributor to the *Whole Booke of Psalmes* surely prepared him for the theological atmosphere cultivated by the Danish monarch, in which he was not simply observing, but fully immersed.

Secretary of State Robert Cecil may have encouraged Dowland to take the position in Christian's court.[10] Dowland was well acquainted with the expectations of international diplomacy from his time in Cobham's English embassy in Paris and had already proven himself useful in providing foreign-source information in his 1595 letter sent to the statesman from Nuremberg. In October 1598, Cecil noted that subjects were in place to provide information "in such states as are friends to us, as Scotland, Holland, Zeeland, Italy, Germany, Denmark, and Swedland."[11] Mrs. Dowland and the Dowland children may even have been denied permission to travel to Denmark, specifically to maintain Dowland's ties to England and assure his ongoing allegiance.[12] Regardless of his reasons for accepting the job, Dowland packed his bags and arrived in Denmark, presumably in November 1598.

If it is useful to consider Dowland's reasons for choosing Denmark, it is equally valuable to examine Christian IV's motives for seeking out the services of the English lutenist. In 1596, Christian had only recently officially taken the throne, for when his father Frederik II died eight years previously, the crown prince was not yet eleven years old. As a result, the kingdom was governed by a state council until Christian was deemed adult enough to rule on his own in 1596.[13] Growing up, the Danish monarch was provided an excellent education in academics, languages, arts, and physical pursuits, and he also participated in many social functions, exposing him to the inner workings of court hierarchy, behind-the-scenes politics, and social graces. By the time he began his approved rule, Christian was determined to make his realm the greatest and most admired kingdom in all of Europe. Part of his vision included enhancing the reputation of the court musical establishment by enlarging its numbers, securing international musicians, and preparing Danish musicians for high levels of artistry, either by apprenticing them to court instrumentalists or sending them elsewhere for training.

Christian IV fit the image of a well-rounded renaissance courtier (Fig. 9.1). After attending the king's 1596 coronation, one German nobleman noted the monarch's athletic, artistic, and musical acumen.[14] Earlier, at the wedding of his sister to Heinrich Julius, the princely heir demonstrated his prowess on

Fig. 9.1 Christian IV, detail, print by Robert Dunkerton. NPG D34884 © National Portrait Gallery, London.

trumpet, lute, cornet, violin, and trombone.[15] As a musician and statesman, the monarch held high standards for those whom he employed. With tightly controlled oversight in all areas of his kingdom, Christian insisted upon only the best musicians. These artists were not simply entertainers, but also served a propagandous role, creating a well-publicized cultural image of the Danish court.

A lutenist position opened up in Denmark with the 1596 death of Johann Spaltholtz.[16] No candidates may have been available in the convening two years and Christian was surely picky when choosing someone to fill the role, perhaps even deciding on a slow recruitment campaign. Dowland's reputation and talent certainly would have been alluring as the young monarch built up his chamber. Christian may have heard Dowland play when he visited Kassel and Wolfenbüttel in 1596. The king spent time in conversation with Alessandro Orologio on his German tour and likely met other musicians as well.[17] Perhaps Christian waited, hoping to entice the English lutenist to his court after hearing Dowland play in Germany. At the very least, the king had access to reports of Dowland from the leaders of those cities, his brother-in-law Duke Heinrich Julius and friend Moritz, Landgrave of Hesse.

Christian fully accomplished his goal to build a world-famous musical establishment. During the course of his almost sixty-year reign, the monarch employed over 300 different musicians, many of whom came from other countries, including France, England, Germany, Poland, Netherlands, and Italy. When his father Frederik II died, forty-seven musicians were on the payroll. By the time of Christian's coronation, that number had expanded to at least sixty-one, including twenty-three singers and thirty-eight instrumentalists, twenty-three of whom were trumpeters.[18] Christian's travels to the German lands no doubt influenced his desire to increase his retinue, especially after he experienced the ways in which musicians enhanced celebratory court activities. Upon entering Christian's service, Dowland joined a solid contingent of professional musicians. The group was small enough that all were well known to one another, but large enough to be impressive in its breadth of talent. German Prince Christian of Anhalt-Bernburg noted that smaller subgroups of this large company often performed when visitors were present. In this way a different ensemble entertained each day, providing constant variety and showing off the wide range of skills available to the Danish king.[19]

From 1595 on, Christian IV was in contact with Orologio, Dowland's old musical acquaintance from Germany. The musician dedicated works to Christian, and in 1599, the monarch requested assistance from Orologio in finding Italian musicians for employment in the Danish court.[20] Christian also sent agents to England to secure instrumentalists and singers. Looking to Dowland's homeland for artists was not a new practice for the Danish court. Christian's father had, upon recommendation of the Earl of Leicester, engaged a troupe of English comedians in the 1580s.[21] By 1598, Dowland had already spent time in England, France, the German duchies, and Italy. He likely had a command of several languages and was reputed to be one of the finest lutenists anywhere. Such a figure would stand as a jewel in the crown of the prince's entourage, an aid to the young king as he formed his own international reputation. Dowland's wide range of talents allowed him to function not only in a musical capacity, but also as a diplomatic advisor and as cultural ambassador to the many visitors to the Danish court in Elsinore and Copenhagen.

Christian sent musician Melchior Borchgrevinck to England in 1597 as part of a delegation to return the Order of the Garter that had been presented to Christian's father. While there, Borchgrevinck was charged with purchasing new instruments for the Danish court.[22] Perhaps he was also tasked with filling the court lutenist position. Did he meet Dowland? Did Dowland aid him in other duties? During his time in London, Borchgrevinck heard lutenists play on at least two different occasions, each time providing them compensation.[23] The names of these musicians were not recorded in reports of either event, but Dowland may have been one of them. The Dane may also have presented Dowland with an offer from his king. If so, it is possible that Dowland then traveled with Borchgrevinck on the organist's return trip across the North Sea.

A 1598 letter written from Denmark by William Leighton, possibly the same gentleman who compiled *The Teares or Lamentacions of a Sorrowfull Soule* (1614), which includes two songs by Dowland, brings up the possibility that Dowland's arrival in Elsinore may have overlapped with Leighton's stay.[24] Leighton may even have recommended Dowland for employment to someone in the Danish court. One curious document found in the Berkeley Castle archive, however, records a payment of 40 shillings "given in reward to Dowland and his consort."[25] The receipt is dated January 1599. If Dowland received this payment himself on that date, he was not yet in Denmark at the beginning of his service term. Perhaps he was held on retainer while fulfilling previously accepted obligations, although, based on 1599 Danish payment records, it was more likely that the payment record was postdated or reflected compensation made afterwards to a representative.

Dowland's arrival in Denmark may have produced a bit of culture shock for the English musician. While he certainly knew of Christian IV's reputation, the land was an unknown. Geographically, the Danish Empire was one of the largest in Europe. In addition to the area encompassing modern-day Denmark, Christian also ruled over Iceland, Norway, parts of present-day

Sweden, and some German lands (Fig. 9.2). While Christian eventually built up one of the most modern kingdoms in Europe, featuring bustling trade, impressive architecture, educational opportunities, and self-sufficient supply chains, the monarch needed time to accomplish his goals. Copenhagen in 1596 boasted only about 15,000 residents.[26] A sustained royal presence was not re-established in the city until the 1590s. Before that time, the main center of court and all things political was Elsinore, which, although just as well known as Copenhagen, had far fewer residents. Most other Danish and Norse towns figured in populations below 1,000.

Compared to the large cities in which Dowland had spent time—Paris, London, Venice, and Florence—his new Danish abode was downright provincial. Although Kassel was similar in size to Elsinore, the German city was much closer in proximity to other large populations, and Moritz's principality of Hesse surpassed 100,000 residents.[27] King Christian's ingenuity in modern architecture may have offset the small-town feel of his two largest cities. In several of his residences, the king requested that special rooms be built below dining areas, from which acoustically placed pipes delivered

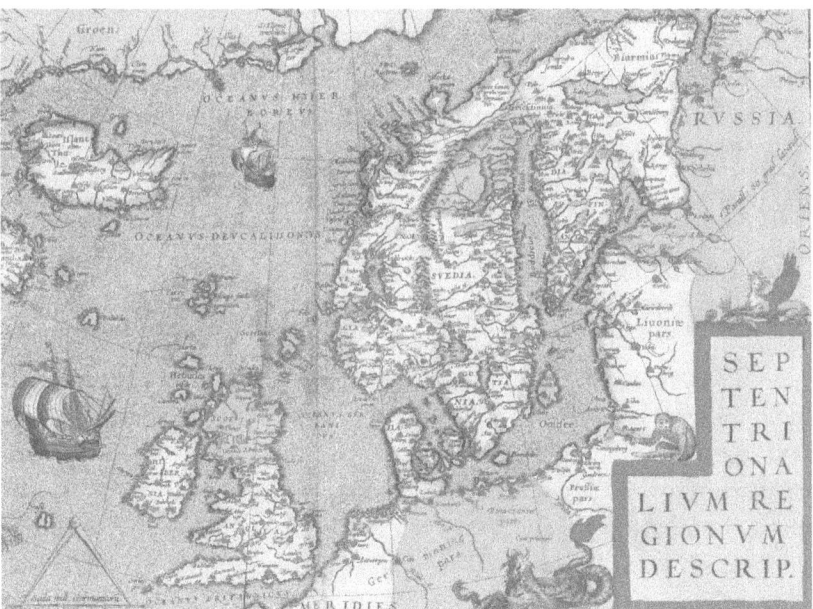

Fig. 9.2 Northern Europe, map by Abraham Ortelius, *Theatrum orbis terrarium* (1570), plate 102, detail. STC 18855. Used by permission of the Folger Shakespeare Library.

"unseen" performances into entertaining spaces.[28] Not only did this provide a novel experience for important visitors, but the layout may also have negated issues of close placement of musicians who might listen in on privileged conversations.

Christian traveled frequently, both within his own kingdom and beyond. As was often the case with rulers, his musicians regularly escorted him. In this way, they could provide entertainment and handle other miscellaneous tasks that might arise.[29] John Case, in his *Praise of Musicke* (1586), noted the importance of musicians on such journeys, stating "that wayfaring men, solace themselves with songs, and ease the wearisomeness of their journey, considering that music as a pleasant companion, is unto them instead of a wagon on the way."[30] Dowland likely joined Christian on some of his tours.

In April 1599, Christian embarked by sea to the North Cape of Norway to address and oversee shipping channel issues. Reports indicate it was a dangerous, and at times unpleasant, journey. The weather was bad. The ship, the *Victor*, ran up upon rocks and was damaged, but continued onward. The vessel required repair before journeying home. The king was accompanied by musicians, for his secretary Jonas Charisius noted that Christian preferred to spend his time in his cabin with music.[31] There is no evidence that Dowland was one of the musicians who took part in this particular progress. Yet he did not receive his first salary payment until August 1599. If he were with Christian, who returned 13 July, the gap in payments, which were normally provided quarterly in February and May in other years, makes more sense.

In 1599, Christian sent a group of musicians, including Borchgrevinck, Hans Nielsen, and Mogen Pedersøn, to study for a year with Giovanni Gabrieli in Venice.[32] Dowland was not included in the sojourn. Of course, he had not been in Christian's employ for long at the time. He himself had visited Venice in the recent past and was already renowned for his compositions. He may also have been traveling with Christian or been placed in charge of musical activities in Elsinore. The king seemed especially interested in improving the quality of homegrown musicians. Starting in 1600, he sponsored four students each year to study abroad with individual stipends of 400 daler per year.[33] To keep his best at home to oversee those who remained, while sending off other top Danish musicians for outside training, seems like a prudent move.

One certainty is Christian's trust in Dowland during the musician's initial years of service. In addition to his generous employment terms, the

Englishman was titled "Royal Lutenist to the King." Only one other musician at the time ranked so highly—court organist Borchgrevinck. By 1603, Borchgrevinck was titled "the King's Chief Instrumentalist." Other musicians in the household were listed in court records simply as "instrumentalist" or "singer." On 28 July 1600, Dowland received 600 daler beyond his normal salary, acknowledged by written receipt.

> I, Master Johannes Dowlannd, His Royal Majesty's lutenist, acknowledge that by the instruction and command of the honorable and noble Christopher Walckendorff of Glorup, Lord High Steward of the Kingdom of Denmark, I have received from the honorable and noble men, Eenvold Krussse of Hiermitslevgaard and Sivert Beck of Førslev, His Royal Majesty's treasurers, six hundred old dollars which His said Royal Majesty has upon this time graciously given and presented to me. In acknowledgement of this I have signed the present receipt with my own hand.[34]

Given Christian's faith in Dowland, it seems the two grew close during the lutenist's first months in Denmark. And yet the musician surely knew his place. Dowland could never truly hope to advance beyond the status of glorified servant, for the Danish king placed himself in a sphere completely separate from all others. In one instance, noted court astronomer Tyge Brahe positioned himself on a plane equal with the king. He was swiftly berated for thinking too highly of himself and ordered to render his service submissively, offering it humbly before his monarch.[35] Singer John Meinert and gambist Daniel Norcome, who were hired the year following Dowland, stayed in Denmark only two years and then left the court without seeking permission. Christian, livid at the situation, unsuccessfully sent agents to retrieve the two.[36] Dowland was some fourteen years older than the young king, who wielded his newly gained power with a brash stroke. The musician may have recognized some of his own youthful tendencies in his new employer and even supported them, but as a well seasoned professional, he surely took better care to watch, listen, and avoid offense than he might have earlier in his career.

Dowland's Denmark years were especially creative ones. During his time in residence in King Christian's court, the composer produced two songbooks (1600 and 1603) and his consort music collection *Lachrimae* (1604). Sales of his *First Booke* continued to thrive, with reprints in London in 1600, 1603, and 1606. These volumes speak to his ongoing connections in England, for he had other options for printing and publication. After Christian sent Borchgrevinck, Nielsen, and Pedersøn to study in Venice in 1599, both Nielsen and Pedersøn returned to the Italian lands in the first decade of the seventeenth century to publish madrigal volumes in the city known for its musical printing presses.[37] Unlike his colleagues in the Danish court who took their fruits to Venice or to printers in closer proximity to Copenhagen in cities such as Antwerp, Amsterdam, or the many German printing centers, Dowland looked to England. Perhaps he was capitalizing on the success of his *First Booke*. Certainly he was astute enough to realize that the place for his English-texted songs was London, but he also may have held onto hope for the possibility of that elusive English court position. Maintaining his presence and his reputation in his homeland could only serve him well. In fact, Dowland's printed output flourished, more so than it ever did during the years he actually lived among his countrymen.

The Second Booke of Songs or Ayres was prepared and completed in "Elsinore in Denmark, the first of June 1600."[38] Dowland sent the manuscript to his wife, who remained in England. She in turn agreed that George Eastland would serve as publisher. In August 1600, after Mrs. Dowland received agreed-upon compensation for the *Second Booke*, she met with John Baxter, a musician of Christian's court who had arrived in London to secure trumpeters for Christian's service. Mrs. Dowland either loaned Baxter money to cover his expenses or gave him the *Second Booke* publication fee to take back to her husband. The trumpeter then spent the funds for his own tasks, as Danish records indicate Baxter requested further compensation once he returned.

> Johann Bagster, His Royal Majesty's ship trumpeter, who, on his said Royal Majesty's behalf, again shall perform and give to Johan Stockis and Master Lamb of London in England, also to master John Dowland (His Royal Majesty's lutenist) his wife the mentioned money he had borrowed and lent of them in England. And which money then was given in the hands of the five English trumpeters, whom he according to His Royal Majesty's gracious command in the present year 1600 in England has appointed and accepted in the service of His Royal Majesty.[39]

Dowland finished the *Second Booke* before Baxter left for England, so it is quite possible the trumpeter was entrusted with the manuscript to deliver to Mrs. Dowland. This might explain why Baxter then approached her later.[40]

The scenario is one more example of Christian using his valued musicians to solicit new employees and carry out international business. Baxter's access to monetary resources, of which he was provided 30 daler up front, pales when compared with the finances provided to Dowland for his own impending journey to England the following year.

During Dowland's first year in Denmark, he received no pay for almost nine months and borrowed 200 daler from grocer Herman Rose, presumably to cover living expenses.[41] Once he was established in his post, by 1600 Dowland received regular quarterly payments every November, February, May, and August. This continued into 1601.[42] In June 1601, however, Dowland was advanced six months' salary, representing the time since his last May payment through the next November.[43] This was just the first of several prepayments that would follow in succeeding years. The king seemed happy to front him the money. On that same June date, Dowland and several others received a portrait of the king, made of crown gold, presumably as a gesture of esteem.[44] Dowland's first advance anticipated the king's progress, on which he journeyed without his favored musician.[45] The lutenist himself would soon be traveling on business for Christian. Three months later, in September 1601, Dowland was given 300 daler to "purchase instruments in England," including string instruments, an Irish harp, and instrumental accessories.[46] He was also to acquire a harpist and a dancing master, as well as gifts for the queen and king. The 300 daler Dowland received for expenses is impressive, totaling more than most court musicians made in a year. To have trusted a servant with such a large sum reasserts Christian's confidence in Dowland's business acumen. This trust is especially revealing when considering Christian's reputation as an authoritarian ruler who had difficulty delegating even trivial matters.[47]

Dowland did not return until May 1602. He found a suitable dancing master in Henry Sandon, who was hired for 330 daler in October 1601. Charles O'Reilly was promised 200 daler and secured as harpist. A suitable Irish harp was acquired at the same time. Christian then stood as the only Continental ruler with an Irish harp and dedicated harpist in his retinue.[48] Several foreign diplomats and rulers heard O'Reilly play, each commenting on the sound of the harp. This particular instrument remained in Christian's collection even after the harpist left Denmark.[49] Both Sandon and O'Reilly were promised an additional 10 daler per month pension, although it is not clear if this was authorized by the king or if Dowland took it upon himself to negotiate additional funds.[50] Both men were hired for one year only, suggesting they were brought to Denmark for a specific occasion, perhaps for festivities related to the departure of Christian's younger brother Prince Hans before he left for Russia in August 1602 to marry the daughter of Tsar Boris Godunov.[51] Dowland, Sandon, and O'Reilly arrived in Denmark in May. On the basis of Dowland's salary advance through November 1601, it seems he was expected to return much sooner but stayed almost a year. In fact, by the time the musicians arrived, only three months remained in Sandon and O'Reilly's employment contract. Dowland attributed the tardiness to weather-related, travel-inhibiting conditions.

It was another year before Dowland was reimbursed for expenses beyond what was originally advanced to him. The record shows:

> According to His Majesty's own most gracious command, returned and satisfied John Dowland, His Royal Majesty's lutenist, who on behalf of his said Royal Highness out of his own purse most humbly had taken with him and spent in London in England: first, 140 daler which he has given to a harp-player and a dance-master whom at that place he has according His Royal Majesty's most gracious command appointed and employed in the services of his majesty on account of their future salary and board which also has been given them and settled here in His Royal Majesty's public treasury a short while ago; also given for some English gloves, which he has purchased for His Royal Majesty and for His Royal Majesty's beloved wife, the high-born princess Queen Anna Catharina: 72 daler; for racket strings: 15 daler; for a case of viols: 102 daler; and 20 daler for expenses which arose from transferring the mentioned case from England to this kingdom to His Royal Majesty; furthermore, for an Irish harp and extra strings: 104 daler; then for the board of the mentioned John Dowland and the aforementioned harp-player and dance-master which they have spent on the travel from England to this kingdom: 100 daler; also for lute strings and a golden cord around His Royal Majesty's lute: 3 daler; thus his expenses amount to in total as written above: 506 daler, in accordance with the handed in statement and list which is signed by His most gracious Royal Majesty himself. Against his above-mentioned expenses which he on His Royal Majesty's behalf has raised on a bill of exchange in London in England (from some English merchants which are called the "Mellsingsche Company"): 289 daler; thus on this occasion he has now according to this settlement of accounts received what he by His Royal Majesty's public treasury has been disbursed and paid as above mentioned: 217 daler.[52]

The amount Dowland spent in England was considerable for what was ordered. He obviously felt very confident in the king's trust. With so much time between expenditures and repayment, Dowland must have been especially well off from his own entrepreneurial pursuits, or else he was quite creative in making ends meet.[53] In 1602 and the first half of 1603, Dowland adjusted back to his regular schedule of quarterly salary payments, before once again visiting home to pursue his own artistic and political opportunities.

10

The Second Booke of Songs or Ayres (1600) and *The Third and Last Booke of Songs or Aires* (1603)

Dowland's *The Second Booke of Songs or Ayres, of 2. 4. and 5. parts: With Tableture for the Lute or Orpherian, with the Violl de Gamba* features twenty-two songs plus a lute and bass viol duo, closely resembling the organization of his *First Booke*. The songbook reproduces the same tablebook format from the *First Booke*, but exhibits greater variety in number of voices, construction of lyrics, and contrast of musical settings. As indicated in the title, the number of voices increases throughout the volume, moving from two to four, both with lute, and then concludes with two vocal works that, when the lute is counted, are composed in six parts. The second of these songs is a dialogue for two solo singers, lute, viols, and three additional voices that answer in chorus, a model for the dramatic musical dialogue that became increasingly popular through the end of the century.[1]

Dowland provides clues within the *Second Booke* as to his professional circle by offering mini-dedications attached to two of the songs. The first entry in the collection, "I saw my lady weep," is dedicated to Anthony Holborne, who served Robert Cecil in the 1590s and whose cittern anthology Peter Short printed the same year as the *First Booke*. "O sweet woods" names Hugh Holland, a poet of certain contemporaneous renown. This was not the first time the three men appeared together in a single volume. Holborne, Holland, and Dowland each contributed one of four commendatory poems found at the start of Giles Farnaby's *Canzonets* of 1598, also printed by Short.[2]

The logistics of the *Second Booke*'s creation were understandably complicated by Dowland's employment in Denmark. Manuscript copies of his music were sent by messenger to Mrs. Dowland, who remained behind in England. She sold publication rights for the songbook to George Eastland, who positioned himself as Dowland's friend in the print's prefatory remarks.

The whole volume is dedicated to Lucy Harington Russell, Countess of Bedford, seemingly chosen by Dowland, who addresses her in his dedication.[3] Just nineteen years old at the time of the *Second Booke*'s printing, Russell had already established herself as one of England's leading patrons of the arts. Lucy's father negotiated an advantageous marriage to Edward Russell, third Earl of Bedford, for his well-educated and reportedly beautiful daughter when she was only thirteen years old. Bedford inherited the title of earl eight years previously when his father died but had just assumed control of his estate upon turning twenty-one. Over the years, Lucy lent her support to poets and playwrights such as Michael Drayton and Ben Jonson. She corresponded with John Donne and even penned her own poetry, including one lyric that begins with the words, "Death be not proud," answering Donne's holy sonnet.[4]

Like the *First Booke*'s cover art, the *Second Booke*'s title page border was used previously in other prints, with alterations to title and printer information. One unique feature inserts two staves of music into an oval at the top of the page (Fig 10.1). This short bit of notation provides the melody for a three-voice canon, underlaid with the opening words of Psalm 150, "Praise God upon the lute and viol." Such a choice brings attention to the instruments used in the volume and perhaps also acknowledges the Countess's strong religious beliefs. As a Calvinist, she knew the importance of psalm study for corporate worship and domestic devotions. A duo for lute and bass viol titled "Dowland's adieu for Master Oliver Cromwell" at volume end brings about a secular balance. Cromwell was an English gentleman who served as both Member of Parliament and as a judge within the court system during James I's reign.[5] He married the daughter of Thomas Bromley, whom volume dedicatee Lucy Russell may have known, for her grandfather Robert Kelway was an overseer of Bromley's will.[6]

Dowland's dedication to Lady Bedford stresses his absence from London and then continues on to praise his patroness's knowledge of and dedication to the arts, all while elevating the status of women as protectors of music:

> I send unto your Lady from the court of a foreign prince, this volume of my second labors. As to the worthiest patroness of Music, which is the noblest of all sciences, for the whole frame of Nature, is nothing but Harmony, as well in souls, as bodies. And because I am now removed from your sight, I will speak boldly, that your Lady shall be unthankful to Nature herself, if

Fig. 10.1 Title page, *Second Booke of Songs or Ayres*. RB59101. The Huntington Library, San Marino, California.

you do not love, and defend that Art, by which, she hath given you so well-tuned a mind.

Your Ladyship hath in yourself an excellent agreement of many virtues, of which, though I admire all, yet I am bound by my profession to give especial honor to your knowledge of Music, which in the judgement of ancient times was so proper an excellency to women, that the Muses took their name from it, and yet so rare, that the world durst imagine but nine of them.

I most humbly beseech your Lady to receive this work into your favor. And the rather, because it cometh far to beg it of you. From Elsinore in Denmark the first of June, 1600.

The remainder of the book's prefatory material was provided by publisher Eastland, the only time in any of Dowland's six printed volumes that the composer did not write a personal note to the reader. Eastland took on this role easily, asking for continued favor for himself and his absent friend. Inserted before the note is an acrostic poem in honor of Lady Bedford.

G. Eastland. To J. Dowland's Lute.

L ute arise and charm the air,
U ntil a thousand forms she bear,
C onjure them all that they repair,
I nto the circles of her care,
E ver to dwell in concord there.

B y this thy tunes may have access,
E ven to her spirit whose flow'ring treasure,
D oth sweetest Harmony express,
F illing all ears and hearts with pleasure.
O n earth, observing heavenly measure,
R ight well can she judge and defend them.
D oubt not of that for she can mend them.

The creation of an acrostic, in which the first letters of each line spell out an important word or name, is an impressive novelty, but generally would not restrict the writer from following poetic structural norms. Yet Eastland's poem reads a bit clumsily, with lines of irregular syllable lengths and stresses.

The instruction above the verse, however, intimates that the acrostic is not all that it seems.

"To J. Dowland's Lute" is the type of directive placed at the top of ballad sheets of the time, on which new words were printed with instructions to sing them to a well-known song. While no tune survives with an identification of "J. Dowland's Lute," the composer's lute solo "Lachrimae" had already entered the public consciousness. A texted song version of "Lachrimae," now titled "Flow my tears," even appears as the *Second Booke*'s second song. With only a few rhythmic adjustments to later strains of the piece, Eastland's poem easily replaces Dowland's unattributed lyrics when sung without repeats, explaining the uneven nature of Eastland's poetic contribution (Ex. 10.1). As such, the panegyric offers praise for the Countess while reminding her of Dowland's most famous song—two classics ahead of their time. The inclusion of Dowland's lachrimae-inspired "Flow my tears" alone might have enticed buyers to purchase the entire volume, and the piece certainly would have been mentioned in any publicity. To reference the composition as musico-poetic contrafactum before the song appears was a stroke of genius.

Lucy Russell, or Lady Bedford as she was addressed, was closely connected to the Sidney-Essex courtly circle, the same group that produced so much esteemed poetry of the era. Her husband's uncle William was knighted by Robert Dudley, Earl of Leicester (stepfather to Essex) in Holland in 1586 alongside Henry Noel, Henry Unton, Robert Devereux, and Robert Sidney, all of whom are named in assorted Dowland musical titles.[7] Lucy, in her own right, was connected even more closely to Philip and Robert Sidney as a first cousin, once removed, on her mother's side. She also knew of and mixed with many of the same courtly individuals associated with Dowland's *First Booke* texts. The *Second Booke*, then, reads almost as a sequel to the *First*.

Yet if the earlier volume stood as a larger commentary on courtiers of the Elizabethan court, the *Second Booke* more decidedly evokes images directly related to Robert Devereux, second Earl of Essex. The nobleman was introduced at court in the 1580s, probably by his stepfather, the queen's first favorite, the Earl of Leicester. Essex rose rapidly in Elizabeth's esteem in the late 1580s and 1590s and was named a member of the Privy Council in 1593. As Essex's power and position grew, so did his altercations with the queen. In 1599, the year before the *Second Booke* was released, Elizabeth appointed the earl Lord Lieutenant of Ireland. After ineffectively leading an offensive in the contested land, the earl entered an unauthorized truce with Irish forces before returning to London, explicitly ignoring orders from the

Ex. 10.1 Eastland-Dowland, "Lute arise" contrafactum

queen to remain. Essex was subsequently tried, confined to his quarters, and removed from his positions of power.[8] The overall aesthetic of the *Second Booke* mirrors those dark days.

Dowland's gloomy, affective style is evident from the outset and remains so throughout the first five songs (Table 10.1). The first words of each confirm a realized pathos: "I saw my lady weep," "Flow my tears," "Sorrow, sorrow stay," "Die not before they day," and "Mourn, mourn, day with darkness fled."[9]

Table 10.1 Contents of *The Second Booke of Songs or Ayres* (1600)

(songs to two voices and lute)
I. I saw my lady weep
II. Flow my tears
III. Sorrow stay, lend true repentant tears
IV. Die not before thy day
V. Mourn, mourn, day is with darkness fled
VI.–VIII. Time's eldest son, old age the heir of ease

(songs to four voices and lute)
IX. Praise blindness eyes, for seeing is deceit
X. O sweet woods, the delight of solitariness
XI. If floods of tears could cleanse my follies past
XII. Fine knacks for ladies
XIII. Now cease, my wand'ring eyes
XIV. Come ye heavy states of night
XV. White as lilies was her face
XVI. Woeful heart with grief oppressed
XVII. A shepherd in a shade
XVIII. Faction that ever dwells in court
XIX. Shall I sue, shall I seek for grace
XX. Toss not my soul

(five voices, lute, and treble viols)
XXI. Clear or cloudy, sweet as April show'ring

(canto-bass dialogue, lute, four viols, five-part chorus)
XXII. Humor, say what mak'st thou here

(lute and bass viol)
Dowland's adieu for Master Oliver Cromwell

Dowland sets these five works, and the three that follow, for only two voices with lute. This more transparent texture not only provides greater clarity for the texts, but also aurally simulates the sort of loneliness marked by removal from society. The bass voice can either be sung or played on viol, or the two might reinforce each other. The foundational emphasis on the bass line accentuates the mournful tone of the music even further. For instance, in "Sorrow stay," opening chromatic movement in the bass, which moves to the leading tone and back, affords an appropriate sighing effect. Later in the song, an especially moving duet between the canto and bass accentuates the words "down, down, down I go," as each voice literally moves downward on alternate beats, mirroring a rhythmic collaboration from the song's opening phrase before "arising" as appropriate (Ex. 10.2). Notably, of the opening five

Ex. 10.2 "Sorrow, sorrow stay," opening and text painting

pieces, the most musically ambiguous is the last. Even as its lyrics ask the listener to mourn, a hopeful musical aesthetic returns. Still, in the middle of "Mourn, mourn, day with darkness fled," the words "in darkness learn to dwell" revisit the line "Hark you shadows that in darkness dwell" sung prophetically in "Flow my tears," and foreshadow the title of Dowland's bleakest of songs, "In darkness let me dwell," printed later in *A Musicall Banquet* (1610).

The entries that follow, "Time's eldest son," "Then sit thee down," and "When others sing *venite*," continue the Henry Lee saga in a setting of three parts (see Chapter 3). The pieces provide a breath between the opening set's gloom and the four-voice songs that follow. Together the three-part composition nostalgically reminds the reader of a less contentious time within the court and recalls the older generation of favorites imbued in the *First Booke*.[10] Considering Essex's military activities of the previous year, one line stands out, a reference to "gallant youth in martial prowess please." While this allusion might apply generally to any of the men involved in the ceremonial tilting activities at Lee's 1590 retirement, it was Robert Devereux who dominated attention in the annual tournaments from that time onward, using the public platform to further his courtly ambition and public popularity.

The next twelve songs of four voices noticeably shift the tone of the volume, not only in terms of texture, but also by interspersing songs with an uplifting musical spirit amongst those of despair. Topically, they imagine a feminine authority, plead for forgiveness, and wallow in self-pity. The three that open the section stand central to the volume. The harmonic movement and triple meter of "Praise blindness eyes" aurally recalls Dowland's "Can she excuse" from the *First Booke*, which features lyrics some scholars have suggested were penned by Essex. The lyrics of the *Second Booke* song fall within the same courtly trope, matching style both poetically and musically. "O sweet woods," which follows "Praise blindness eyes," poignantly returns to an exile theme. The song also features two lines of text from Philip Sidney's *Old Arcadia*.[11] Together, these songs recall themes from the *First Booke* that were becoming even more relevant in 1600.

After the Earl of Essex's censure and confinement, many of his family members were not allowed to visit him. Some remained at Wansted, the estate where Philip Sidney entertained the queen, where Leicester secretly married Essex's mother without royal permission, where Essex exiled himself in earlier years upon receiving the queen's disfavor, and where the earl's followers and family often gathered.[12] The final stanza of "O sweet woods" mentions Wansted by name, directly tying the song to the situation in which the nobleman found himself in those dark days of 1600.

> You woods, in you the fairest Nymphs have walked,
> Nymphs at whose sight all hearts did yield to Love.
> You woods, in whom dear lovers oft have talked,
> How do you now a place of mourning prove?
> Wansted, my Mistress, saith this is the doom.
> Thou art loves Childbed, Nursery, and Tomb.

The distraught woman mentioned in "I saw may lady weep," the song placed at the beginning of the anthology, might easily be associated with one of those mourning the earl's exile and concerned for his future. "O sweet woods" is also the piece labeled, "To Master Hugh Holland." While Holland's association with the work is uncertain, in 1599 he preached a sermon in defense of the theatrics surrounding the queen's annual Accession Day festivities—the same events that so enhanced Essex's fame.[13]

As if in answer, the song that follows sounds much like the apologetic poetry sent to Elizabeth by Essex in those early days when he was banned from court, neatly concluding with a reference back to the blind eyes that began the first song of four voices.

> If floods of tears could cleanse my follies past,
> And smokes of sighs might sacrifice for sin,
> If groaning cries might salve my fault at last,
> Or endless moan, for error pardon win,
> Then would I cry, weep, sigh, and ever moan,
> Mine errors, fault, sins, follies past and gone.
>
> I see my hopes must wither in their bud.
> I see my favors are no lasting flowers.
> I see that words will breed no better good,
> Than loss of time and lightening but at hours.
> Thus when I see, then thus I say therefore,
> *That favors, hopes, and words, can blind no more.* (emphasis added)

The text first appeared as the last of a set of poems appended to the unauthorized 1591 first printing of Philip Sidney's *Astrophel and Stella*, following a number of verses by Samuel Daniel, another Lady Russell beneficiary.[14] In the context of 1600, the poem takes on new meaning, moving from Sidney, who in 1591 was still being mourned after his 1587 battlefield death, to Essex, Sidney's assumed heir as Protestant defender of the faith. Essex's initial promise, which helped him secure his exalted status in the Elizabethan regime, was coming into question. Modern scholars have justifiably read the *Second Booke* songs as commentary on Essex and his situation.[15] The texts Dowland uses, however, never explicitly name the earl, thus avoiding accusations of direct support or disapproval. In this way, Dowland shielded himself from criticism while appealing directly to his hoped-for patroness, whose familial ties and close friendships brought her close to Essex's activities.

In 1601, the year after the *Second Booke* appeared, Essex met his final disgrace. Frustrated by unsuccessful attempts to obtain an audience with the queen, the earl gathered his supporters in an effort to force his way into her presence chamber, either to plead his case or in hopes of instigating a coup d'état. Lucy Russell, a close friend of Essex's sister Penelope Devereux Rich and others in the earl's circle, came dangerously close to the events that precipitated Essex's execution. Lucy's husband, Edward, joined Essex's followers at Essex House on the day of the earl's march toward London. Although implicated in subsequent depositions, Edward claimed under examination that he went to Essex House upon invitation from Penelope, not knowing the earl's intentions, and that he slipped away from the crowd once he fully understood the situation.[16] For his participation, Edward was punished with an astronomical £20,000 fine and exiled from court, still a much better outcome than that of some of his fellow nobles who were present that day. The Essex conflict was already percolating in 1600, and rumors of tensions between the earl and the queen were a favorite topic of public gossip. Dowland and the purchasers of his book could not have fully foreseen the drama that was about to unfold, and consequences were weighty. Even those in Essex's circle who were cleared of complicity in his alleged uprising experienced setbacks in their courtly status. And yet, two years later upon James I's accession to the throne, those who endured saw great relief. Lucy, Lady Bedford, was even named to the new queen's bedchamber.

While Dowland's lyrics alluded to the escalating tensions surrounding Essex, another sort of drama was taking place related to the production of the *Second Booke*.[17] George Eastland agreed to pay Mrs. Dowland, who was representing her husband while he was in Denmark, £20 and half any amount received from the book's dedication for the right to publish the songbook. Eastland then secured Thomas East to print a run of 1,000 songbooks. A draft agreement outlining the transaction was scripted, but final details were agreed upon verbally. Eastland was to pay East 40s. to cover the advance patent fee due to Thomas Morley, who now held the music printing monopoly, and £10 for East's printing services.[18] A patent fee of £7. 10s. was also to be paid before print completion. In return, East would print the songbooks for delivery to Eastland, who could then sell them for his own profit. As printer, East registered the book into the Stationers' register on 15 July 1600.[19] This meant that once Eastland had sold his 1,000 copies, East would retain the right to print and sell future editions. East completed the print run on 2 August. Eastland had not yet paid the patent fee and East granted him an extension. As part of their verbal agreement, and according to standard practice, East was allowed to print extra copies of the book in its first offering from paper left over from the print run. These extra copies became the source of a legal squabble preserved in court records.

Eastland hoped to delay public circulation until after he could present Lady Bedford with her copy of the songbook but became aware that some copies had already been sold by East's employees. Even though he could not prove this happened with East's knowledge, and although the copies should have belonged to East anyway, Eastland sued the printer. East countersued, as he had not received the remainder of the patent fee for which he was liable to Morley. The court sided with East. Eastland persisted and the case worked its way through the courts. Eastland claimed his output for the venture exceeded £100 and that he should be compensated by East for printing and selling numerous unauthorized copies that harmed his ability to sell his stock. East responded with an itemized cost for what Eastland's fees truly were, totaling only £47. 12s. And so it continued. Finally, in the autumn of 1601, the Court of Requests decided that evidence from both sides was contradictory and that fault could not be determined. No damages were ordered, nor court fees covered for either side. The final ruling: "it is ordered that the same matter shall be from henceforth clearly dismissed out of this court forever."[20] Yet Eastland was still not satisfied. He took the issue to the Privy Council, as well as the Court of Chancery, but to no avail. Eastland's dealings with both East and with Dowland seem to have ended there.

For his third songbook in 1603, Dowland turned to Stationer Thomas Adams as publisher, who recontracted the *First Booke*'s Peter Short for printing services. The song collection was registered in February, less than two months before Queen Elizabeth died. In the same words found on the eventual title page, Dowland is listed with his credentials: "Bachelor in Music, and Lutenist to the most high and mighty Christian the Fourth, by the grace of God, King of Denmark and Norway."[21] In many ways, Dowland's *The Third and Last Booke of Songs or Aires* functions as a continuation of, or perhaps an apology for, his *Second Booke*. Twenty-one songs in groups of two voices with lute, moving to four voices and concluding with a dialogue for five voices plus instruments, follows the organizational structure of the previous collection (Table 10.2). Some of the poetry set is associated with courtly figures, including Essex, and themes of weeping return. Yet there are many more pieces of a sprightly nature than in the *Second Booke* and, in spite of structural and musical similarities, this volume puts forth its own individual identity. While the first group of songs is written for voice, lute, and bass, as in the *Second Booke,* the bass line here remains untexted, unambiguously emphasizing an intention that the compositions be realized as solo songs. Of course, for Dowland, the harmonic accompaniment could only be accomplished on lute.

Dowland deliberately solicits attention from outside courtly circles in *The Third Booke*, while reserving his loyal praise for the queen alone. A Latin motto on Dowland's title page, *Bona quò communiora eò maeliora*, translates to "The more common the goods, the better." Then in his note to the reader he states, "My labors for my part I freely offer to every man's judgment," marking his music as for all. For the first time, Dowland grants his volume dedication to a member of the gentry: "To my honorable good friend, John Souch, esquire," acknowledging a gentleman four generations removed from the nobility, although one who maintained connections within the elite hierarchy. Zouch (as his name was more commonly spelled) was associated with the circles to which Dowland had previously appealed, participating in one of the Essex-Raleigh expeditions in 1591. Before this, Zouch married Mary Berkeley, daughter of Henry, seventh Lord Berkeley.[22]

A late 1590s Berkeley Castle payment record shows that Lord Berkeley hired "Dowland and his consort" to play for some occasion.[23] Berkeley, and thus presumably Zouch, were closely connected to George Carey, Baron Hunsdon, dedicatee of Dowland's *First Booke*. Carey's daughter Elizabeth married Berkeley's son Thomas, meaning Zouch and Thomas Berkeley were in-laws. The song "My thoughts are winged with hope," from that same *First Booke*, is first found as a lute solo in Mathew Holmes's Oxford lute book and then retitled "Sir John Souch's galliard" in Dowland's 1604 *Lachrimae* consort version. It is enticing to think that this last adaptation was the one performed at the 1598 Berkeley affair by "Dowland and his consort," although the Zouch-Berkeley union was not a happy one and Zouch abandoned his marriage fairly quickly.[24] Shortly after Dowland's *Third Booke* was recorded in the Stationers' record, Zouch was knighted as one of fifty Knights Bachelor who gathered at Belvoir Castle in April 1603 to welcome the new king, James I. A generational accomplishment, his father, also Sir John Zouch, had received his knighthood upon the 1559 coronation of Elizabeth.[25]

Dowland's *Third Booke* features lyrics that suggest pastoral scenes and characters, comment on love and beauty, and portray Cupid throughout. In this way, Dowland's volume moves closer thematically to the esteemed sonnet sequences of Elizabethan writers such as Edmund Spenser and Thomas Watson than any other he produced. Collectively, however, the poetry in the volume reads less consistently in terms of quality and form than his first two books but still creates a more cohesive narrative. Each individual song would serve well as appropriate fare in the entertainments regularly presented to Queen Elizabeth. In fact, at least two of the songs in the *Third Booke* were included in or inspired by entertainments placed before the queen.

The ghost of the Earl of Essex, protagonist of Dowland's previous volume, hovers conspicuously close. Lyrics for "Behold a wonder here," in which Love has his sight restored by an Elizabethan Cynthia, were likely written by Essex as part of the 1595 Accession Day festivities. In it, a blind Indian prince has his sight renewed by the queen before revealing himself as Cupid.[26] The text of Dowland's song fits the scenario perfectly.

> Behold a wonder here!
> Love hath received his sight,
> Which many hundred years,
> Hath not beheld the light.
>
> Such beams infused be,
> By *Cynthia* in his eyes,
> As first have made him see,
> And then have made him wise.

Table 10.2 Contents of *The Third and Last Booke of Songs or Aires* (1603)

(voice, lute, and bass viol)
I. Farewell, too fair
II. Time stands still
III. Behold a wonder here
IV. Daphne was not so chaste as she was changing

(songs to four voices and lute)
V. Me, me, and none but me
VI. When Phoebus first did Daphne love
VII. Say Love, if ever thou didst find
VIII. Flow not so fast, ye fountains
IX. What if I never speed
X. Love stood amaz'd at sweet Beauty's pain
XI. Lend your ears to my sorrow good people
XII. By a fountain where I lay
XIII. O what hath overwrought my all amazed thought
XIV. Farewell unkind, farewell
XV. Weep you no more sad fountains
XVI. Fie on this feigning, is love without desire
XVII. I must complain, yet do enjoy my love
XVIII. It was a time when silly bees could speak
XIX. The lowest trees have tops
XX. What poor astronomers are they

(canto-bass dialogue, two lutes, three viols, five-part chorus)
XXI. Come when I call, or tarry till I come

Love now no more will weep
For them that laugh the while,
Nor wake for them that sleep,
Nor sigh for them that smile.

So powerful is the beauty
That Love doth now behold,
As love is turned to duty,
That's neither blind nor bold.

This beauty shows her might,
To be of double kind,
In giving love his sight
And striking folly blind.

The 1595 entertainment was created at a time when Essex was pressing his case to be named Elizabeth's principal secretary, competing for the position with Robert Cecil. More notably, it was on this occasion that Essex held up the ceremonial tilts for some twenty minutes, seeking the queen's attention. She was not moved.

The song following "Behold a wonder" shifts sentiment. "Daphne was not so chaste" references "the false light of thy traitorous fires." Certainly, the most explosive traitorous events of recent years were those connected to the fall of Essex. Later, the same Daphne is featured in "When Phoebus first did Daphne love." In its lyrics, Phoebus cannot persuade Daphne to his will, ultimately raging against the cause—her oath of virginity. He goes on to declare that "none but one should live a maid."[27] In Elizabethan England, that "one" could refer only to a particular person—the Virgin Queen. As for Phoebus, the character was at various times associated allegorically with several persons, including both Philip Sidney and James VI of Scotland, the future king of England.[28] But Thomas Watson, in dedicating his *Italian Madrigalls Englished* (1590) to the Earl of Essex states, "*Phoebus eris*" (Phoebus you shall be).[29] Placed between these two songs, "Me, me, and none but me" references death and speaks of flying to heaven to join "my beloved turtle dove." Although the ascription is highly debated, some scholars have proposed Essex as the turtle dove to Elizabeth's phoenix in the Shakespearean "The Phoenix and the Turtle," first published in Robert Chester's *Loves Martyr* in 1601.[30] The turtle and phoenix also reappear in later songs in the *Third Booke*. In the context of Dowland's full anthology, the allusions again nod toward Essex and Elizabeth.

One might question the wisdom of evoking the spirit of Essex before Elizabeth so soon after the dramatic events of 1601. The lyrics of "When Phoebus first did Daphne love," however, herald Elizabeth's alter ego Cynthia as the one who holds power over Cupid, "giving love his sight and striking folly blind." "Behold a wonder" sanctions the steadfastness of the queen. Further, with the hindsight of 1601, Elizabeth's choice to officially confirm Cecil rather than Essex as Secretary of State in 1596 showed a long-range wisdom ultimately rewarded. In this light, Dowland's volume apologizes for the 1600 *Second Booke of Songs*'s sympathetic tone and brooding aura intended to woo Essex's followers. The focus moves from the earl and solidly lands on the wise judgment and longevity of Elizabeth, who reigns over Cupid and is fashioned in the song "Say Love, if ever thou didst find" as "some Goddess or some Queen is she and only she, Queen of love and beauty."[31]

The second song in the *Third Booke*, "Time stands still with gazing on her face," also recalls a specific Elizabethan event. In a letter to Robert Sidney, William Browne includes a description of "A Dialogue of Time and Place," an entertainment presented to the queen at Harefield during her 1602 progress.[32] In the skit, two title characters note the agelessness of their goddess, one proclaiming, "I am her time, and time were very ungrateful if it should not ever stand still to serve, preserve, cherish, and delight her that is the glory of her time, and makes the time happy wherein she lives." Dowland's song "Time stands still" matches the entertainment nicely, highlighting the queen's *Semper eadem* motto with the words, "All other things shall change, but she remains the same."

> Time stands still with gazing on her face,
> Stand still and gaze for minutes, hours and years, to her give place.
> All other things shall change, but she remains the same,
> 'Til heavens changed have their course and Time hath lost his name.
> *Cupid* doth hover up and down, blinded with her fair eyes,
> And Fortune captive at her feet contemned and conquered lies.
>
> When Fortune, Love, and Time attend on
> Her with my fortunes, love, and time, I honor will alone.
> If bloodless envy say, duty hath no desert.
> Duty replies that envy knows herself his faithful heart,
> My settled vows and spotless faith no fortune can remove,
> Courage shall show my inward faith, and faith shall try my love.

This same theme of agelessness, certainly directed toward Elizabeth, reappears throughout the volume. Yet in the context of Essex's death, the book also provides a sort of resolution as the figures of Cupid and the queen interact again and again, with Love finally revealed as jest. Four songs before the end, "It was a time when silly bees could speak" sets a text most often attributed to Essex.[33] When the poem was first written, it stood as a negative commentary on the theatrics of the royal court. Yet in its place in Dowland's

Third Booke, the lyrics call for a new way forward as "The king replied but thus, peace peevish bee, thou art bound to serve the time, the time not thee."

Acting as the finale of one cohesive drama, the opening line of the book's final song reads like an encapsulation of the queen's relationship with the earl: "Come when I call, or tarry 'til I come. If you be deaf, I must prove dumb." In the form of a dialogue, the upper voice sings this sentiment. In answer, the bassus beseeches, "stay a while my heavenly joy, I come with wings of love," aurally sounding a conversation in a duet between male and female characters who are separated in earthly and heavenly realms. A few lines later the bass pleads, "O die not," a statement that could not be spoken aloud to an aging, yet ageless queen. Like so many apologetic texts, the sentiment is tempered within the context of musical verse. But it is the song's final lines that bring true closure. All voices join in, singing, "Then securely envy scorning, let us end with joy our mourning. Jealousy still defy, and love 'til we die," a clear call for movement forward from events that shook the nation. This last composition is written for five voices and lute, plus a second lute with tablature attached to the secunda voice part, a fitting culmination to what Dowland deemed his *Third and Last Booke*. Whether Dowland meant this label to mean the latest of his musical offerings or if he truly intended it to be his final collection remains unclear. In truth, the songbook remained his "last" vocal anthology only until 1612.

11

Lachrimae

(1604)

During the Renaissance, medical treatises held that one's being, whether psychological or physical, was affected by the balance of four "humors" within the body. These substances included blood, phlegm, and yellow and black bile, which were directly connected to the temperaments of sanguine, phlegmatic, choleric, and melancholic, respectively. An excess or lack of any one of the humors might temporarily affect personality, produce chronic illness, or even bring about death. The medical theory was adopted from ancient Greek writings and adapted into contemporary thought by physicians, scientists, philosophers, and artists alike.[1] Melancholy, which was thought to result from an overabundance of black bile, fit the aesthetic of Dowland's famous "Lachrimae" tune perfectly. The Latin title of "tears" provided a theme that was at once relatable and identifiable. In 1604, the lutenist used this melody as the basis of an incredible collection of consort music called *Lachrimæ, Or Seaven Teares Figured in Seaven Passionate Pauans, with diuers other Pauans, Galiards, and Almands, set forth for the Lute, Viols, or Violons, in fiue parts*. The anthology of twenty-one compositions for five bowed string instruments plus lute—with its thematic label that reads unambiguously Dowland—was the composer's most remarkable public offering, one that continues to entice with unspoken meaning.

A number of books related to melancholy were printed in England in the last decades of the sixteenth century. One of the first, Timothy Bright's *A Treatise of Melancholy*, describes the condition as "a certain fearful disposition of the mind altered from reason, or else an humor of the body, commonly taken to be the only cause of reason by fear in such sort depraved."[2] Robert Burton's popular *The Anatomie of Melancholie*, a pseudo-medical treatise examining the condition, described symptoms of the imbalance and provided cures.[3] Burton perceived melancholy as an epidemic, but he also believed writing about it could help cure his own disease. Perhaps Dowland followed the same course in making music about his tears?

Ex. 11.1 "Lachrimae" motive

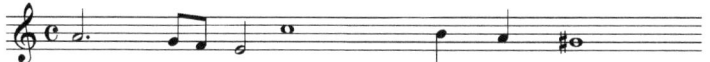

By the early seventeenth century, the descending four-note tetrachord that opens Dowland's tearful "Lachrimae" theme had long been recognized as a musical indicator of sorrow, despair, or lament, especially as applied to a bass line, over which new musical material or variations appeared within a single movement. Yet if ever a composer owned a musical emblem, it was John Dowland with his "Lachrimae" motive.[4] He certainly did not invent the opening descending four-note melodic subphrase, organized as two consecutive whole steps and a half, nor its sequenced answer, which immediately jumps up a sixth, moving downward in a half-whole-half step series (Ex. 11.1). Numerous examples of this pattern are found in other composers' music before and after Dowland. It was, however, the lutenist's realization of this musical gesture into a full composition that became one of the most well known tunes of his day. Subsequently, his composition was rearranged by other composers for a wide array of instruments, both in England and across Europe.

Dowland himself produced multiple versions of the piece, as a lute solo, for instrumental consort, and with added words as a song. The earliest surviving examples are found in a dozen lute manuscripts dated to the 1580s and 1590s, some with the solo piece titled and/or attributed and others not.[5] Holmes's consort books from the 1590s contain "Lachrimae," and the composition began to appear in manuscript keyboard arrangements around 1600.[6] Dowland included his own song version, "Flow my tears," in his *Second Booke* (1600), strengthening gloomy associations of his lachrymose tears through a text evoking the depths of melancholy, with words no doubt written specifically for this music.

> Flow my tears, fall from your springs,
> Exiled forever: Let me mourn
> where night's blackbird her sad infamy sings,
> there let me live forlorn.
>
> Down vain lights shine you no more,
> No nights are dark enough for those

that in despair their last fortunes deplore,
light doth but shame disclose.

Never may my woes be relieved,
Since pity is fled,
and tears, and sighs, and groans, my weary days,
of all joys here deprived.

From the highest spire of contentment,
My fortune is thrown,
and fear, and grief, and pain for my deserts,
are my hopes since hope is gone.

Hark you shadows that in darkness dwell,
Learn to contemn light,
Happy they that in hell
feel not the world's despite.

Prior to this official song version, Dowland's lute solo was printed in William Barley's unauthorized *A New Booke of Tabliture* (London, 1596) and Johannes Rude's volumes titled *Flores Musicae* (Heidelberg, 1598 and 1600). Soon afterward, the piece appeared in a consort version in Thomas Morley's *Consort Lessons* (London, 1599) and for lute solo in Joachim van den Hove's *Florida* (Utrecht, 1601) and Jean-Baptiste Besard's *Thesaurus Harmonicus* (Cologne, 1603). The song version even appeared with new Dutch words in Willem Swart's *Den Lust-Hoff der Nieuwe Musycke* (Amsterdam, 1603). Perhaps it was some of these volumes Dowland referenced when in his 1604 *Lachrimae* note to the reader he expressed:

Having in foreign parts met diverse lute lessons of my composition, published by strangers without my name or approbation, I thought it much more convenient that my labors should pass forth under mine own allowance, receiving from me their last foil and polishment.

Regardless, by 1604, Dowland's most famous piece was known far and wide. When he decided to create his own consort collection called *Lachrimae*, the musical entrepreneur knew the title alone would encourage sales.

Although written for the same set of five bowed strings and lute throughout, the music book is easily divided into two sections: an opening series of seven pavans, all based on Dowland's iconic "Lachrimae" tune, and a group of fourteen dances, each named for a specific individual. The most distinctive and intriguing aspect of Dowland's anthology is the first seven pavans, which are presented as a set of variations. Dowland individually titled them "Lachrimae Antiquae" (ancient tears), "Lachrimae Antiquae novae" (ancient tears anew), "Lachrimae Gementes" (moaning tears), "Lachrimae Tristes" (sad tears), "Lachrimae Coactae" (compelled tears), "Lachrimae Amantis" (lover's tears), and "Lachrimae Verae" (true tears). The first selection, "Lachrimae Antiquae," presents Dowland's original composition in consort form and serves as the theme for the six pavan variations that follow. These new renditions were likely written specifically for the 1604 *Lachrimae* consort collection.[7] None appears in any earlier source. Each develops the opening tear motive, clearly demonstrating the original theme while cultivating a unique character (Ex. 11.2). These movements are clearly meant for listening rather than dancing, for the composer deviates from typical pavan expectations in numbers of strains and phrases within each variation.[8] Dowland's titles add a programmatic element to the set, cluing performers to a specific mood for each.

Collectively, the seven "Lachrimae" pavans form a true cycle. Other English composers, starting with William Byrd, had presented song sequences in their music books and, while their music certainly imbues larger meaning through intentional choice of texts—a practice Dowland followed in his own song collections, *Lachrimae* proves that the same goal can be accomplished through musical means alone.[9] In essence, Dowland does musically what others had relied upon words to accomplish. The collective effect of the seven pavans must have been both unexpected and moving to those who first played and heard the works. Never before had an English composer put forth in print the equivalent of an extended multi-movement, cyclical instrumental suite of variations. Dowland's genius once again found a new outlet.

All of these different tears—old, new, sad, moaning, compelled, lover's, and true—immediately bring to mind early modern conceptions of melancholy. In this context, Dowland's *Lachrimae* cycle has perplexed scholars and performers for years. Many have attempted to determine the source of the individual "Lachrimae" titles and to interpret Dowland's program for each

Ex. 11.2 *Lachrimae*, pavan openings

Lachrimae antiquae   Lachrimae antiquae novae

Lachrimae gementes   Lachrimae Tristes

Lachrimae Coactae   Lachrimae Amantis

Lachrimae Verae

piece, as well as to prescribe larger meaning to the collective sequence. Most begin with Dowland's choice to set seven compositions. The number seven was marked as special in many religions, mythologies, and philosophies, in diverse places over time. The Greeks recognized seven heavenly bodies. There are seven days in a week, seven wonders of the world, seven deadly sins, and seven opposing virtues. Both Catholics and Protestants utilized the seven penitential psalms. Dowland himself wrote a set of seven psalms and prayers upon the death of Henry Noel. His *Lachrimae* was not, however, the only unified cycle of seven seemingly secular, tearful compositions printed in London in the early seventeenth century. Fellow lute song composer John Coprario wrote a set of seven *Funeral Teares* upon the death of Charles Blount, Earl of Devonshire, in 1606. Significantly, the volume of vocal works, dedicated to Blount's beloved, Penelope Devereux Rich, included the song text "In darkness let me dwell," which Dowland later reset for his son Robert's *A Musicall Banquet* (1610). Coprario later prepared another volume of seven *Songs of Mourning: Bewailing the vntimely death of Prince Henry* in 1613.[10]

More specific interpretations of the pavans, from those that embrace so-called cults of melancholy to ones associated with hermetical philosophy to theories heralding secret religious messages, cover a wide range of thought.[11] Most include elements of merit. A logical explanation for *Lachrimae*'s descriptive titles is that Dowland borrowed them from a single source defining seven different types of melancholy. He proved himself a borrower throughout his career, referencing popular tunes and the works of other composers within his own compositions. His one published theoretical treatise, *Micrologus* (1609), was fully a translation of an earlier writer. Yet no manuscript or print source has been discovered that aligns exactly with the *Lachrimae* sequence.

Burton's aforementioned *Melancholie of Anatomie* offers certain parallels. The massive book, which started with 900 pages and expanded throughout six editions printed during the author's lifetime, uses all of Dowland's Latin terms, although not always in the same manner, never together, and not necessarily as seven specific "kinds" of melancholy. Further, Burton's treatise was printed seventeen years after Dowland's anthology. Still, shared terminology may indicate that Dowland and Burton worked from a common body of literature.[12] Their editions certainly share a similar portrayal of the concept of melancholy, one that appeared among Elizabethan courtiers in many guises, both medical and fashionably emotive.

Another interpretation is a religious, rather than medico-philosophical, view of the sequence. Queen Anna, dedicatee of the volume, is the subject of much debate related to her conversion to Catholicism.[13] Thus, some have read the *Lachrimae* series as a secret offering to the new queen, embracing liturgical and confessional dogma from the Roman church.[14] The allusion to "passion" in the volume title *Lachrimæ, Or Seaven Teares Figured in Seaven Passionate Pauans* seems also to play upon the word's basic definition of "suffering." Some, but not all, of the terms Dowland borrows for his pavan titles are also used within Latin texts of the penitential psalms, their subject matter naturally turning toward tears and suffering. In 1604, however, Dowland showed no signs of any remaining allegiance to the Catholic church. In Christian IV's Protestant court there certainly was no opportunity for regular practice. Yet Dowland exhibited tendencies throughout his career to adapt to whatever circumstances aided him best and, more importantly, to flatter whoever was in his sight as an intended patron at any given moment. Thus, a religious inspiration aimed at the new queen is not out of the question. As educated and well-traveled as Dowland was, he surely understood scriptural matters and, if not outwardly religious, did move toward a more spiritual (if undefined) outlook as he aged.

Of course, Dowland might not have worked from any specific source at all, but simply created a series of compositions based on the types of tears discussed within his own intellectual circles of influence. Whether or not Dowland's *Lachrimae* pavans were intentionally endowed with religious, political, or philosophical meaning, they fully achieved a spiritual aesthetic. But until further primary source evidence is found that supports one particular reading of Dowland's *Lachrimae* cycle, we can never definitively ascertain what the musician was trying to convey with his seven instrumental pavans. No doubt Dowland would have wanted it this way, relishing the knowledge that his music might still be pondered, studied, and debated almost four hundred years after his death.

The second, larger portion of Dowland's *Lachrimae* consists of a series of dances, each associated with a named individual in the manner so often associated with his lute solos. The fourteen compositions include:

"Semper Dowland, semper dolens"
"Sir Henry Umpton's funeral"
"Mr. John Langton's pavan"
"The King of Denmark's galliard"

"The Earle of Essex's galliard"
"Sir John Souch, his galliard"
"Mr. Henry Noel, his galliard"
"Mr. Giles Hoby, his galliard"
"Mr. Nicholas Griffith, his galliard"
"Mr. Thomas Collier, his galliard" (with two trebles)
"Captain Piper, his galliard"
"Mr. Bucton, his galliard"
"Mrs. Nichol's almand"
"Mr. George Whitehead, his almand"

Some of these dances were first composed for other mediums, as evidenced by their inclusion in earlier manuscripts and prints. Ten of the pieces appear as lute solos in one or more of the first three Holmes manuscripts or the Euing lute book, all copied from the late 1580s through the first years of the 1600s.[15] The other four dances, those named for Unton, Griffith, Collier, and Whitehead, have no known earlier concordances. Three, those evoking Essex, Zouch, and Piper, appear with words in Dowland's *First Booke* as the songs "Can she excuse my wrongs," "My thoughts are winged with hopes," and "If my complaints could passions move." Dowland discloses this to his *Lachrimae* readers, verifying, "I have mixed new songs with old, grave with light, that every ear may receive his several content."

Collectively the persons evoked by the titles of the final fourteen dances in *Lachrimae* represent a wide range of social stations, from the King of Denmark and the Earl of Essex to a rough sea captain and several members of the gentry. When the volume was printed, Unton, Essex, Noel, and Piper were all dead. Some of those named had many more years to live. A few remain unidentified. One is a woman. While several of these people knew one another well (for instance, Henry Unton spent time traveling in France with Essex), they do not all fall together nicely into a common circle, except that perhaps they had some sort of relationship with John Dowland.[16]

In the first tribute, "Semper Dowland, semper dolens," Dowland places his own name within a composition title for the first time. The label clearly provided the musician with an opportunity to embrace his chosen artistic persona: "Always Dowland, always doleful." The title may also confirm pronunciation of the musician's surname, with the long "o" in Dowland matching that of the Latin term *dolens*. Versions of this composition appear in two manuscripts dated closer to 1600, one untitled and the other simply labeled

"Semper dolens."[17] Perhaps Dowland landed upon the composition's title after so many years of considering Elizabeth I's motto *Semper eadam,* which embodied her legendary ageless aura. The composer's self-portrayal as perpetually sullen then became one more way of uniting a theme throughout the larger volume.

This mournful focus is offered from the start, first with the Latin motto printed on *Lachrimae*'s title page. This time Dowland features the words *Aut Furit, aut Lachrimat, quem non Fortuna beauit* (Whom fortune does not favor, either rages or weeps). The allusion might or might not, however, have represented Dowland's true outlook. Thomas Fuller portrays Dowland in his posthumous *History of the Worthies of England* (1662) as "a cheerful person . . . passing his days in lawful merriment."[18] This sort of duality of sadness and positivity correlates precisely with the statement Dowland makes in his book dedication, that not all tears indicate melancholy. Regardless, "Semper Dowland, semper dolens" continues the anthology's musical mood from the previous *Lachrimae* variations, creating a sort of consistency in approaching "Sir Henry Umpton's funerall." The elegiac piece honoring Unton sonically replicates the "Lachrimae" opening tear motive, utilizing the first sustained cantus note and the subsequent descending notes in the altus (Ex. 11.3).

From thence forward, the pieces in *Lachrimae* feature more variety in terms of solemnity and joyfulness, rhythmic motion, and mode. Some have suggested that each piece reflects the personality of the person named.[19] While interpretations of instrumental music are inherently conjectural, it is pleasing to think Dowland afforded such thought to his friends.

The 1604 *Lachrimae* anthology is unique in a number of ways, but also builds upon previous conventions.[20] In addition to its novel introduction of an instrumental variation cycle, the volume s also stands as only the third English collection of music printed for instrumental ensemble, following Morley's *First Booke of Consort Lessons* and Holborne's *Pavans, Galliards, Almains,* both issued in 1599. Morley's collection consisted of twenty-five pieces by seven composers, including five Dowland compositions, all arranged for six-part mixed consort of treble and bass viols, flute (or recorder),

Ex. 11.3 "Sir Henry Umpton's funerall," cantus-altus opening

cittern, bandora, and lute.[21] None of the works provide a composer's name, including those arranged from Dowland compositions. Holborne's larger partbook collection features sixty-five short, self-composed, dance-like pieces. His five-voice instrumentation is less well defined, specified as "for viols, violins, or other musical wind instruments," thus providing flexibility for use with like or mixed consort.[22]

Consort music by Dowland first appeared long before *Lachrimae* and even before Morley's volume. Earlier, Mathew Holmes copied a set of partbooks for mixed consort of lute, bass viol, recorder, and cittern, each featuring four to ten Dowland works, including an early version of the "Lachrimae" pavan.[23] Violin and bandora parts surely also existed, but are since lost. Thus, the instrumentation matched Morley's 1599 set more closely than Dowland's 1604 *Lachrimae* print. Dowland, as a musical entrepreneur, likely had to perform his pieces in flexible combinations of instruments, depending on place, time, and personnel, and surely faced occasions when he performed his own music with instruments like the ones included in Holmes's and Morley's sets.

The types of dances included in the second section of Dowland's 1604 *Lachrimae*—pavans, galliards, and almains—are the same as those included in Morley's and Holborne's print volumes, but *Lachrimae* is distinctive in several ways. First, the collection follows the tablebook format of the composer's previous songbooks. The lute tablature, however, is now placed apart from the cantus and directionally separated with altus and tenor on the right page, while the cantus, quintus, and bassus parts appear on the left (Fig. 11.1). Unlike the earlier consort collections, Dowland's publication necessitated the purchase of only a single book rather than a whole set of partbooks, although a closely positioned duplicate volume might have allowed more comfort for six players than if all were crowded around a single tablebook.[24]

Dowland specifies only strings on his title page and implies his expectation of a consort of like instruments—either five viols or violins—always joined by lute. While England had a long tradition of music for viol consort, the addition of lute was uniquely Dowland. Further, typical English string quintets were often composed for one treble instrument, three middle-voiced instruments, and a bass, as was the case with Holborne's collection. Dowland writes some of his pieces for this combination, and others for two trebles, two inner voices, and bass, an arrangement more common in the German lands than in England.[25]

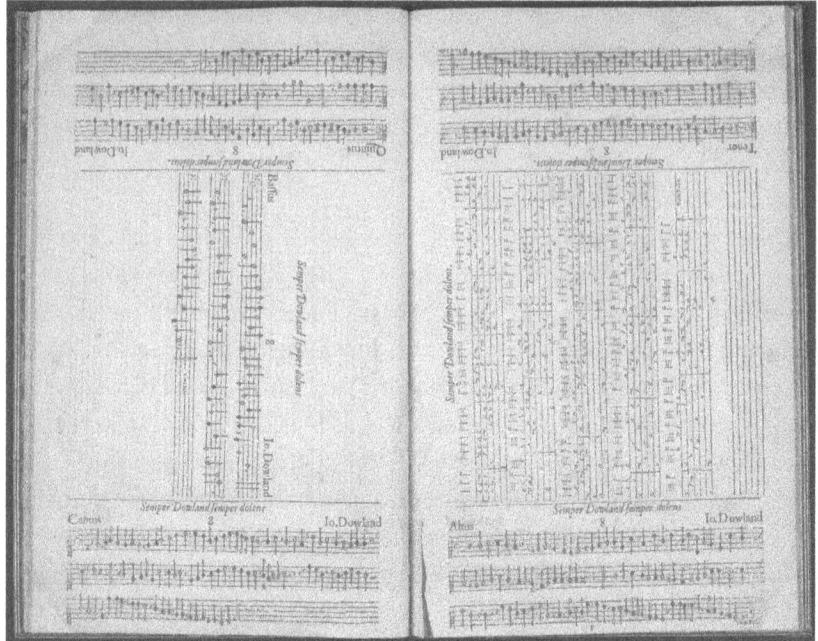

Fig. 11.1 "Semper Dowland, semper dolens," *Lachrimae*, E2v–F1r.
© The British Library Board, Music Collections K.2.i.16.

How Dowland's *Lachrimae* volume developed is not completely clear. Some of its works were certainly composed or arranged in Denmark and others in England, as his dedication to Christian IV's sister, the English Queen Anna, confirms, "I have presumed to dedicate this work of music to your sacred hands, that was begun where you were born, and ended where you reign."[26] If Dowland played with a consort as part of his duties for Christian IV, then perhaps he arranged his previously composed lute dances for practical Scandinavian use. Scholar Peter Holman noted that many of the dances in the second section of the volume are written at a slightly higher range and thus may have been intended for a violin consort in Denmark. The "Lachrimae" variations that open the book, as well as some of the lower dances, might then have been arranged later in a range favoring the viol, with English performers in mind.[27]

It seems Dowland originally planned for Thomas Adams, publisher of his *Third Booke*, to serve in that role once again. Adams registered *Lachrimae* with the Company of Stationers on 2 April 1604.[28] Adams's name, however, does not appear in the final volume, which was printed by John Windet. Further, the title page advertises the music book as being sold at Dowland's London home on Fetter Lane, implying the composer assumed production expenses himself and took possession of the printed pages for future sales. Perhaps he secured Adams's services simply for registration. Dowland also may have conceived the book while in Denmark but then felt he no longer needed an external publisher when he found himself delayed in England over the winter of 1603–1604.

Dowland's *Third Booke* was Adams's first venture into music publishing. Later, the publisher oversaw musical anthologies for John Danyel, Thomas Ravenscroft, and Dowland's son Robert. Likewise, although Windet had printed psalm books for patent holder Richard Day since 1591, Dowland's *Lachrimae* and Thomas Greaves's *Songes of Sundrie Kindes* (the only other music volume registered the same day as *Lachrimae*) marked the printer's first foray into commercial music printing.[29] This start put him in good stead for later lute song–air volumes by John Coprario, Thomas Ford, and Robert Jones. Intriguingly, *Lachrimae* stands as the only Dowland volume with no date printed on its title page, so chronological placement of printing might be questioned. However, ten other books were registered the same day that Adams entered *Lachrimae*. Of these, two are lost and one survives only in a posthumous version issued some years later. The other seven are printed with the date 1604, including Windet's print of Greaves's *Songes*. This information, combined with the timing of Dowland's presence in England and his prefatory remarks, supports 1604 as the date of issuance.

Lachrimae is dedicated to the new Queen Anna, whom Dowland met in Winchester in 1603. It may have been this meeting that inspired Dowland's creation of the "Lachrimae" variations, or even the whole volume, as a gesture to his new monarch. Ties to his employer, her brother Christian IV, must have remained at the forefront of his mind. How might it be possible to flatter the new regime without offending his current patron, who not only had been exceedingly generous to him, but was also a narcissistic authoritarian? Dowland needed to be savvy. In addition to "The King of Denmark's galliard," placed first among the dances of that type, Dowland extends the list of the lands over which Christian IV rules beyond those mentioned in his *Second* and *Third Booke*s. No longer is the ruler cited simply as "King of Denmark and Norway," but he is also recognized as King of the Vandals and the Goths. Further, his full honorifics of "Duke of Sleswicke, Holsten, Stormaria, and Ditmarsh" and "Earl of Oldenburg and Delmenhorst" are appended to the titular resume. Hence, Dowland demonstrated his musical abilities to the new English queen (and perhaps vicariously to King James via his wife), while recognizing Christian IV immediately on the first page and then centering the Danish monarch within the volume's contents.

Queen Anna was not denied her laudatory praises. A Latin poem, presumably penned by Dowland, praises his muse in sets of threes: "thrice blessed" Queen of Scotland, England, and Ireland; sister, spouse, and mother of kings; and bestower of wealth, wisdom, and beauty. As such, she is portrayed as one who holds valuable influence. In his subsequent dedication, Dowland reminds the queen of their meeting and recognizes her "most Princely Brother, the only patron and sunshine of my else unhappy fortunes," only then proceeding to cast Anna as recipient of the volume. He goes on to entrust the queen, his "worthy Goddess," with his music, always returning to the overarching tearful theme that remained his trademark.

> And though the title doth promise tears, unfit guests in these joyful times, yet no doubt pleasant are the tears which Music weeps, neither are tears shed always in sorrow, but sometime in joy and gladness. Vouchsafe then (worthy Goddess) your gracious protection to these showers of harmony, least if you frown on them, they be metamorphosed into true tears.

This concession, that not all tears are sorrow-filled, elevates the volume's proclaimed narrative to a place of accord and directly references the "true tears" found in the last of Dowland's *Lachrimae* variations. *Lachrimae* remains Dowland's only official offering of consort music, one unsurpassed in musical affect. It is hard to imagine that he could have improved upon this splendid musical treasure.

12

"Frozen in a colde and forreine country"

(Denmark, 1602–1606)

Dowland was employed in Denmark for more than seven years. During this time, he never lost contact with his homeland, as evidenced in the textual forewords of his musical prints. Conversely, those involved in English politics did not forget Dowland. Royal agent Stephen Lesieur traveled to Denmark multiple times on diplomatic matters as a representative of Queen Elizabeth. Born in Switzerland, the polyglot moved to England in 1575, eventually gaining citizenship. He worked closely on state matters, first with Elizabeth's spymaster Francis Walsingham, and later for Secretary Robert Cecil. Lesieur's diplomatic interests focused on ongoing trade issues between England and Denmark, a primary concern for Cecil. Denmark controlled both southern and northern shipping entry points to the East, and English merchants and sailors were forced to gain permissions and pay for passage rights, a constant aggravation (see Fig. 9.2). Other concerns involved fishing rights in Danish territories, the autonomy of sections of the North Sea and areas near Iceland, and the seizure of ships by both countries.[1]

Lesieur traveled to Copenhagen in 1599 and may have met Dowland during this visit. On a later May 1602 trip, he presented a letter to Christian IV from Queen Elizabeth. The English monarch maintained a measured relationship with her Danish peer, despite ongoing trade issues. In 1598, she sent a small portrait of herself to Denmark under the care of ambassador Lord Edward Zouche, who represented her as part of an envoy sent to congratulate the king on his recent marriage.[2] In 1602, Christian requested another portrait of the queen. The two, however, never developed the same close relationship that Christian would have with his brother-in-law James I. Dowland, dancing master Sandon, and harpist O'Reilly reached Copenhagen the same month that Lesieur provided Elizabeth's letter to Christian, so the musicians may have traveled with Lesieur on their return.[3] Lesieur and Dowland corresponded in September 1602 after the diplomat continued onto the German lands, but their letters have not survived. After a

September to December 1602 planned conference in Bremen, Lesieur again wrote to Dowland:

> Mr. Dowland. The 16th October I wrote unto you an answer upon your letter unto me of the 12th September. I doubt not but you have received my said letters in which I sent you one from your wife, also one for Mr. Antoine Waillant . . . and one from myself to Mr. Robert Flower. Then I gave you direction how you might speedily write unto me again by sending your letters unto Ruloff Pieterson, merchant in St. Ian's Street at Lübeck, who will send me all such letters as shall come to him for me, and by his means I sent you those letters. But hither unto I have not heard from you nor any else in Denmark.[4]

After complaining of a lack of diplomatic resolution, accentuated by details of the conference, Lesieur clearly asks Dowland to inform him as to Christian's stance on matters related to English sea trade: "Therefore I shall be very glad from time to time to hear from you of as much as may concern her majesty or her subjects that shall come to your knowledge." Such a request was not out of place, considering Dowland's intelligence-laden 1595 Cecil letter, especially since Lesieur worked directly for Cecil. Lesieur then intimates some sort of commendation to the queen:

> Spare not any reasonable charge to [send letters] for I will see you repaid. Besides that I will make your true heart and service to her majesty known to your good. Therefore, I pray satisfy me very particularly of what you shall think worthy my knowledge for her majesty's service.

Alongside indication of an accompanying letter from Dowland's wife, the request and its resultant possibilities may have been enticing for the musician. Still, Christian IV, whom Lesieur labels as "your king," certainly would not have looked kindly upon Dowland supplying the English court with any information at all. Thus, the appeal placed the lutenist in somewhat of an awkward position.

From Dowland's perspective, Elizabeth had disappointed him before. Why should he expect favor from her now? The letter's content ultimately reveals more about Lesieur's methods than Dowland's disposition. Regardless, the musician's Danish salary continued on its regular payment schedule and there are no indications of Christian's displeasure. The Lesieur document was preserved in the papers of Danish Secretary of State Jonas Charisius, indicating the missive was either intercepted in transit and copied, or that Dowland—in a show of loyalty or self-preservation—handed the inquiry over to Christian or his counselors. The letter was deemed important enough for Charisius to keep on file. No response from Dowland to Lesieur survives.

It would be easy to cast these considerations in a light that portrays Dowland as a spy and, indeed, musicians often found themselves in situations in which they could gather valuable information. There was quite a difference, however, between informing and actively spying.[5] Dowland had been privy to intelligence expectations since his days in Paris and was savvy enough to discern what he could pass on without angering his employer or endangering his life. What knowledge, if any, he provided Cecil via Lesieur, or anyone else for that matter, either from Denmark or during his travels back to England, remains purely conjectural.

Queen Elizabeth died in early 1603. James VI of Scotland ascended the English throne, becoming James I of England. His wife, Anna, sister of Christian IV of Denmark, assumed her role as queen consort. In spite of new familial connections, English-Danish trade and fishing issues did not immediately disappear. In fact, no treaty was reached until 1621. There was, however, a marked increase in cordiality between the countries' respective monarchs. In June 1603, Christian became the first foreign sovereign during James's reign to receive the Order of the Garter, England's highest chivalric accolade; the act was markedly reminiscent of when his father, Frederick II, was so honored by Elizabeth in 1578. James sent the Earl of Rutland, with Garter in hand for presentation, as representative for the baptism of Christian's son. Around the time of the 1603 christening, Dowland was advanced 125 daler and granted permission to travel to England once again. The day Rutland and his entourage left, Dowland was also reimbursed for expenses incurred two years earlier. Scholar Peter Hauge suggests that the English diplomats may have intervened on the musician's behalf and that Dowland perhaps traveled back with the English delegation that attended the Danish festivities.[6]

Dowland's 1603–1604 trip to England was seemingly to promote his own interests: delivering and overseeing production of his consort collection *Lachrimae* (1604) and perhaps advancing his cause with the new regime. Some scholars have implied, based on the timing of the 1604 volume, that perhaps Dowland initially intended to dedicate the anthology to Queen Elizabeth.[7] Lesieur's 1602 letter may have encouraged the musician to renew ties to the English monarch, seeking reward once again in the form of court employment. Supporting this theory, an opening Latin epigram compares eventual *Lachrimae* dedicatee Queen Anna to Juno, Minerva, and Venus of "the Judgement of Paris," evoking images that previously were applied to honor Queen Elizabeth in George Peele's *Araygnement of Paris* (1584), Barnfield's *Cynthia* (1595), and a 1569 painting by Joris Hoefnagel, among others.[8] If Dowland's plan was to flatter Elizabeth, the timing of her death was unfortunate for his cause. Dowland may have then made a hasty substitution, rededicating *Lachrimae* to Christian's sister Anna when it became advantageous to him. The timetable of Dowland's 1603 trip matches that of so many other English subjects who hoped to make an early impression on the new royal couple. But if Dowland truly wished to return permanently to England, the new rulers put him in an especially delicate position. He could not openly solicit for a role in the new English court without potentially offending his current employer, the new queen's brother. Even so, during his travel to England in the late summer or early fall of 1603, he met face to face with Anna.[9]

The plague raged in London in August 1603 and residents were ordered to lockdown. King James and Queen Anna relocated outside the city to Winchester from mid-September through early December. It was during this time that Dowland met with her majesty, and then that he may have decided to dedicate his latest musical offering to her. Although it is not clear through what channels Dowland secured this meeting, his *Second Booke* dedicatee, Lucy Russell, Countess of Bedford, had already assumed the role of first Lady of the Bed Chamber, and stood as Anna's closest associate. Robert Sidney was also in an advantageous position to set up an introduction. Sidney was appointed Lord Chamberlain to Queen Anna soon after Elizabeth's death, and was also created Baron Sidney of Penshurst, increasing his social and professional status. He used his sway more than once to advance individuals he supported.[10] Another Dowland associate, Robert Cecil, also seamlessly managed (or perhaps orchestrated) the transition to James I's court, remaining in his powerful office until his death in 1612.

Dowland was quite busy during this trip, meeting the queen and preparing *Lachrimae*. By early 1604, Dowland still had not returned to Denmark. On 9 May 1604, he signed the *album amicorum* of Hans von Bodeck, a young German visiting London as part of an international tour.[11] Christian went on progress in Denmark that spring. The king hired Hans Nielsen, a student of Gregory Howet, to fill a dedicated lute position on May 3. Dowland's long absence may have encouraged Christian, who had been without his main lutenist for quite some time. Dowland returned to Danish shores some time before 10 July. Because of his extended trip, he was paid in July 1604 for a full year. The Danish controller was not keen on the disbursement, for he notes:

> It depends on His Royal Majesty's gracious pleasure whether His Majesty will be pleased to grant him the said salary, in view of the fact that he has traveled to England on his own business and remained there for a long while, longer than His Royal Majesty had granted him leave of absence. And in case His Royal Majesty will not grant [part] of the said salary, he shall do future service therefore, or give satisfaction to His Royal Majesty therefore in other ways.[12]

Christian had no objection to paying Dowland for his time away, and the following November, the lutenist received his quarterly payment on the previously established schedule. He continued to receive regular compensation through May 1605.[13]

By 1604, Christian IV's focus was increasingly turning to international affairs. War was looming with Sweden over territorial claims and shipping issues. The king's council constantly blocked him from declaring war, one of the only actions in which they could override their monarch; they limited him solely to negotiations and mediations until 1610.[14] In July 1605, Christian granted Dowland an "advance payment with a view to his future service," noting that a boy apprentice was to be trained by the royal lutenist.[15] On 10 October, Hans Borckratz received an introduction letter to present to Dowland, stating the lutenist was to teach him and provide him board. As compensation, Dowland received 100 daler.

Throughout his time away, Dowland's reputation remained secure in England. As early as his departure in 1598, Francis Meres, an academic educated at both Cambridge and Oxford, confirmed Dowland's status in his *Palladis Tamia*. Meres's volume is perhaps best known as one of the earliest sources from which Shakespeare's early plays can be dated. The discourse, however, has a much larger scope, cataloguing significant figures throughout history. Meres included Dowland in a section titled "Music," where the author indexes great musicians from ancient Greece, followed by comparable ones from England, including "Master Dowland."

As *Mercury* by his eloquence reclaimed men from their barbarousness and cruelty: so *Orpheus* by his music subdued fierce beasts and wild birds. As *Demosthenes, Isocrates,* and *Cicero* excelled in oratory: so *Orpheus, Amphion,* and *Linus,* surpassed in Music. As Greece had these excellent musicians... so England hath these: *Master Cooper, Master Fairfax, Master Tallis, Master Taverner, Master Blithman, Master Byrd, Doctor Tye, Doctor Dallis, Doctor Bull, Mr. Thomas Mudd,* sometimes fellow of *Pembroke Hall* in *Cambridge, Mr. Edward Johnson, Master Blankes, Master Randall, Master Philips, Master Dowland,* and *Mr. Morley.*[16]

In a more eloquent rendering that same year, Richard Barnfield, a Brasenose, Oxford graduate with ties to the Inns of Court, also elevated Dowland in his *Poems: In diuers humors.* Barnfield portrays Dowland allegorically as a symbol of music mastery, the most superior in his field, comparing him to Edmund Spenser, who represented par excellence among early modern English poets. The oft-quoted sonnet reads:

> If Music and sweet Poetry agree,
> As they must needs (the sister and the brother)
> Then must the love be great, twixt thee and me,
> Because thou lov'st the one, and I the other?
> *Dowland* to thee is dear; Whose heavenly touch
> Upon the lute doth ravish human sense.
> *Spenser* to me, whose deep conceit is such,
> As passing all conceit, needs no defense.
> Thou lov'st to hear sweet melodious sound,
> That Phoebus lute (the Queen of Music) makes:
> And I in deep delight am chiefly drowned,
> When as himself to singing he betakes.
> One God is God of both (as poets feign)
> One knight loves both, and both in thee remain. [17]

Dowland is also mentioned in a 1603 English commonplace book belonging to John Ramsey.[18] Ramsey left his studies at Cambridge to pursue King James in his English entrance and was rewarded with acceptance as a courtier. In his manuscript, he names Dowland as "an excellent musician" on a page celebrating a wide variety of gentlemen chosen for skills in varied disciplines, including mathematics, logic, medicine, music, poetry, painting, law, and historiography.[19] Ramsey also instructs his wife that his son should learn to play the lute and "sing to it with the ditty," specifying "Dowland's books" as exemplar. Might Ramsey have heard Dowland play during the musician's 1603 sojourn to meet Queen Anna?

Toward the other end of Dowland's Denmark timeline, Joshua Sylvester offered up a full translation of Du Bartas's *Deuine Weekes & Werkes* (1605), in which Dowland's musical abilities are exalted. Sylvester had been releasing segments of the full work periodically since 1592. The volume opens with a direct plea to the newly established Jacobean court, with a primary dedication to James I, followed by lesser dedications to individual members of the royal family, Charles Blount (Baron Mountjoy), Sir Thomas Smith, and the children of the deceased Earl of Essex. *Divine Weeks* is a very Protestant tome that, in two volumes, verbosely expounds upon the creation story. In a chapter first released in 1595, the author proclaims in verse Dowland's musical superiority over the younger generation. The musician's name serves a utilitarian function but is still held up as a musical standard. A section explaining Satan's choice of the Serpent because of its facility compares:

> But this stands sure, however else it went,
> The old Serpent served as Satan's instrument
> To charm in *Eden* with a strong illusion
> Our silly Grandam to her self's confusion.
> For, as an old, rude, rotten, tuneless kit,
> *If famous* Dowland *deign to finger it*
> Makes sweeter music than the choicest lute
> In the gross handling of a clownish brute. [20]

By 1605, Dowland had been in the service of Christian IV for seven years. His *First Booke of Ayres* had gone through two reprints, and his second and third songbooks, as well as *Lachrimae*, were published in England. Sylvester's writing portrays the musician as an unsurpassed master. Confirming Sylvester's stance, the 1606 play called *Returne from Pernassus*, acted by students at St. John's College, Cambridge, presents one character incredulously asking another, "Have you never a song of master Dowland's making?"[21] It seems that while Dowland chased his courtly ambitions, the academic community kept his name and reputation alive in alternate public venues.

Dowland surely knew of and coveted the advancements of other English lutenists in the new Jacobean court. By 1605, the group of "lutenists in ordinary" had expanded beyond the three carried over from Elizabeth's reign.[22] Other members of the royal family such as Queen Anna and Prince Henry Frederick also created and maintained their own households with dedicated musicians. Especially notable, Robert Johnson and Philip Rosseter were granted replacement positions in the king's service in 1604. Dowland's musical prints of the Denmark years may have provided ongoing presence in bookshops, but his fellow lutenists were being recognized for their playing achievements in the form of court appointments.

From November 1605 through mid-February 1606, Christian IV traveled to Wolfenbüttel to aid his brother-in-law Heinrich Julius in defense of Brunswick rule. In spite of the military conflict, artistic performances and payments to musicians were recorded in the German location.[23] Christian likely brought musicians with him, as was his custom. If he was accompanied by a lutenist, either Dowland or Hans Nielsen might have been summoned for the journey. Considering Dowland's inability to fulfill Heinrich Julius's expectations in Wolfenbüttel in 1595, his appearance may have been uncomfortable. On the other hand, if Dowland was there, he may have seen potential in future German endeavors. Upon returning to Denmark, Christian released Dowland from service.[24]

In March 1606, Dowland received his final payment from the Danish court. He was not the only musician who left Christian's employ at that time, for William Brade's service ended as well. While it is possible that Dowland was dismissed for increasing absence and continued requests for additional funds, Christian may simply have realized that, after almost eight years of service, his prized lutenist was just not the right fit for his court, or not worth the large salary granted. Perhaps Dowland himself requested release, in order to pursue other interests. Throughout his Danish tenure, the lutenist acted as a valued employee, one close to his monarch, or at least as close as an employee could be to such a highly exalted sovereign. As late as October 1605, when the boy apprentice was placed with Dowland, there seem to have been no hard feelings, for Christian referred to him as "our well-beloved Jan Dulant the lutenist."[25] Yet it was only five months later that Dowland moved on from the place "forever lain hid in darkness, or at the least frozen in a cold and foreign country."[26]

Brade's next position was in the German court of Heinrich Julius. Might Dowland have traveled with his fellow musician, returning to the land that was such a turning point for him a decade earlier? Dowland's whereabouts from 1606 to 1609 remain elusive. A number of manuscripts and prints created in the German lands during Dowland's Denmark years and in the two decades following include arrangements of the composer's pieces. Is it possible that he played his way through some of the German courts during these years, building upon his fame as a noted, international lutenist? Whatever the circumstances, Dowland was facing an uncertain future. After so many years of a steady, guaranteed income, he eventually had to find his way home.

RETURNING HOME

13

"Old frend, thy yeares have made thee white"

(England, 1609–1612)

Micrologus

Dowland places himself back in London in his 1609 print, *Andreas Ornithoparcus His Micrologus*. This music theory translation was registered with the Company of Stationers for Thomas Adams on 20 January and issued sometime after 10 April, when Dowland signed his dedication to Secretary of State Robert Cecil.[1] By this time Dowland had known Cecil for many years. He may have used *Micrologus* as a return to grace after being gone from England for so long. More likely, he viewed the statesman, raised to Baron Cecil of Essendon by King James in 1603 and named Lord High Treasurer in 1608, as key to obtaining a permanent appointment to the King's Lutes.

A clue that the musician may have remained on the Continent past his 1606 parting with Christian IV in Denmark is found within his *Micrologus* dedication to Cecil. Dowland mentions a forthcoming work on lute playing (one that never materialized) and states that he is "being now returned home to remain." While he may have been referencing a homecoming years earlier, the wording seems to indicate otherwise. Another consideration is the origin of the treatise Dowland translated. Ornithoparcus's original *Micrologus* was first printed in Latin in Leipzig in 1519. The work stands as both a theoretical and practical guide to singing, although it may have appealed to Dowland because its focus moves beyond vocal music to commentary specifically directed toward instruments and instrumentalists. The treatise would have seemed old fashioned by 1609, echoing musical methods handed down over centuries, beginning with Greek theories of musical harmony that were later disseminated through so many early tomes reliant on interpretations of the sixth-century Boethian *De institutione musica*.

Ornithoparcus, the treatise's author (born Andreas Vogelberg), died almost thirty years before Dowland was born. In the original text, the theorist associates himself with the city of Lüneberg. This area held connections to Brunswick, and thus to Duke of Brunswick-Wolfenbüttel Heinrich Julius, who had issued Dowland an invitation to his court back in the 1590s. While Dowland may have first come across the Latin music instruction book at that time, or subsequently acquired it during his years with Christian IV, it is equally likely that he discovered the manual on a trip to the Continent after leaving Denmark, during those years from 1606 to 1609 when his activities cannot be traced. Regardless, his associations with the German courts seem even deeper than is readily apparent, especially when considering the number of Continental musicians he knew and the large number of German manuscripts and prints in which his music appeared in the early 1600s (see Tables 13.1 and 13.2).

Johannes Rude's *Flores Musicae*, a multivolume lute solo anthology printed in Heidelberg in 1598 and reissued in 1600, demonstrates such connections.

Table 13.1 Selected Continental manuscripts containing at least two Dowland works, c. 1603–1620

Manuscript	Archive	Medium	# arr.works	Year(s) created
Fabritius	DK-Kmk	lute	5	c. 1604–1608
Per Brahe	S-B	lute	7	c. 1610–1620
Eysbock	S-SKma	keyboard	6	c. 1600
Jena	D-Dl	lute	2	1603
Elisabeth-Montbuysson	D-Kl	lute	8	c. 1609–1611
Hainhofer	D-W	lute	5	1603
Romers	D-KNh	lute	2	late 16th/early 17th c.
Nauclerus	D-B	lute	6	c. 1607–1620
Thysius	NL-Lt	lute	12	c. 1610–1620
Königberg	LT-Vu	lute, bandora, consort	13	c. 1605–1625
Schmall	CZ-Pu	lute	2	c. 1608–1615
Eijsertt	A-LIb	lute	6	c. 1610

Table 13.2 Selected Continental prints with arrangements of Dowland works, 1600–1616

Compiler	Volume	Medium	#works	Publication
Besard	*Thesaurus Harmonicus*	lute	5	Cologne, 1603
Fuhrmann	*Testudo Gallo-Germanica*	lute	10	Nuremberg, 1615
Füllsack and Hildebrand	*Ausserlesener Paduanen und Galliarden*	consort	1	Hamburg, 1607
Francisque	*Trésor d'Orphée*	lute	1	Paris, 1600
Hagius	*Newe Künstliche Musicalische Intraden*	consort	2	Nuremberg, 1616
Haussmann	*Rest von Polnischen und andern Tänzen*	consort	1	Nuremberg, 1603
Hove	*Florida*	lute	5	Utrecht, 1601
Hove	*Delitiae Musicae*	lute	10	Utrecht, 1612
Mertel	*Hortus Musicalis Novus*	lute	3	Strasbourg, 1615
Praetorius	*Terpsichore*	consort	1	Wolfenbüttel, 1612
Rude	*Flores Musicae*	lute	2	Heidelberg, 1598
Simpson	*Opusculum neuwer Pavanen*	consort	3	Frankfurt, 1610
Swart	*Den Lust-Hoff der Nieuwe Musycke*	5 voices	1	Amsterdam, 1603
Vallet	*Secretum Musarum*	lute	3	Amsterdam, 1615, 1616

The second part of this collection is dedicated to Ernest and August, German brothers and Princes of Lüneburg. Ernest married Christian IV's aunt, Dorothea of Denmark. *Flores Musicae* contains versions of Dowland's "Lachrimae" and a solo elsewhere titled "Mrs. Bridget Fleetwood's pavan."[2] In Christoph Hunnich's commendatory verse found at the beginning of Rude's book, the poet begins with the line *Anglia Dulandi lacrymis moueatur* (England is moved by the tears of Dowland), revealing the lutenist's ongoing reputation in the region. Music by Dowland's fellow traveler from many years earlier in Germany, Gregory Howet, also finds concordance in *Flores Musicae*, as do pieces by other English composers.

In 1610, Dowland contributed a pedagogical essay to his son's *Varietie of Lute-Lessons*, in which he notes specific attributes of lute strings made in various places. While he may have been relying on advice given by others, or purchased strings made in these locations elsewhere, the statement implies he evaluated the products firsthand. Cities mentioned include Munich,

Meldorf, Nuremberg, Strasbourg, Frankfort, Leipzig, Livorno, Bologna, and Venice.[3] The lutenist's travels to Nuremberg and the Italian cities were cited in his 1595 letter to Cecil, but the other German locales suggest travel beyond what has been documented. At some time in the decade that Dowland served in Denmark, he signed the *album amicorum*—an autograph book of sorts—of Johannes Cellarius of Nuremberg.[4] The book contains signatures dated 1599 through 1606, but they do not appear chronologically, as if the owner simply handed over the album with instructions to "just sign anywhere" on the journal's interleaved blank pages. The entries include a diverse collection of signatures, epitaphs, hand-drawn coats of arms, and other illuminations. The folio Dowland signed is one of three featuring handscripted musical notation. The other two are dated 1600 and 1606. His creation is titled "fuga." The main theme opens with the first eight notes of Martin Luther's "Vater Unser," a chorale incorporated as the standard melody for the Lord's Prayer not only in German hymnals, but also in the *Whole Booke of Psalmes* in both its 1562 and 1592 formats.[5] Dowland then adapts the remainder of the theme as his own, creating an ingenious canon puzzle, solvable at a fourth above, that modulates around a circle of minor keys (Ex. 13.1).[6] He unambiguously identifies his entry with the signature "Jo: dolandi de Lachrimae, his own hande." The page, however, reveals no date. Falling between two 1603 entries, Dowland may have signed the book on travels during his tenure with Christian IV, but several other entries in the book, both before and after, are dated 1606. It is possible that his inscription was made in Germany in the months after he left the King of Denmark's service.

Whenever Dowland came back to England, he returned to his home on Fetter Lane. The byway was located in the Farrington Ward Without district in the heart of London. The neighborhood lay just beyond the city's official walls and was popular with artists and printers because there they could avoid certain city tariffs and regulations. The road itself connected two of the most important thoroughfares in the city, Fleet Street and Holborn. The Dowlands had resided there since at least 1604, even while John was abroad.[7] Sixteenth-century chronicler John Stow described the short road as

> Fewter lane, which stretcheth south into Fleet Street by the East end of St. Dunstans church, and is so called of Fewterers (or idle people) lying there as in a way leading to gardens: but the same is now of later years on both sides built with many fair houses.[8]

Ex. 13.1 "Fuga," based on "Vater Unser"

Dowland indicated he lived on the end of Fetter Lane nearest Fleet Street, the large crossroad notorious for its stench, crime, and overpopulation. Two prisons, Fleet and Bridewell, were located not too far away. In 1588, Jesuit priest Christopher Bales was executed—hanged, drawn, and quartered—in Fleet Street, at the corner that meets Fetter Lane. A block away, on the other side of Fleet Street, lay Ram's Alley, popularized in many plays of the day for its status as a refuge for debtors fleeing creditors.[9]

Yet Fleet Street was also home to many dining establishments and was known for the printers who set up presses in the area. A number of stationers and booksellers lived on or near Fetter Lane, including William Holme, John Hodgets, John Marriott, and John Wells. The Blackfriars Theatre was within easy walking distance, and the Whitefriars Theatre, which operated from circa 1605 to 1614, was even closer. Surrounded by churches, printers, and the Inns of Court—Lincoln's Inn to the west, Middle Temple to the south, and St. Paul's to the East—Dowland's location on Fetter Lane offered him close proximity to the city's hive of arts and print culture (Fig. 13.1).

That Dowland was in London when *Micrologus* appeared in print seems certain from his dedication. No longer able to rely on the steady income of an ongoing court position, the musician likely sought out performance and teaching opportunities whenever possible. *Micrologus*'s prefatory material,

Fig. 13.1 London, map by Augustine Ryther, with detail. © The British Library Board, Maps Crace Port. 1.32.

like that in so many of Dowland's prints, provides clues to the musician's circumstance. On the title page, he again portrays himself as "Bachelor of Music in both the Universities." With no surviving record of a degree from anywhere but Oxford, the statement's accuracy might be questioned. However, at the time, dedicatee Robert Cecil (Fig. 3.2) was Chancellor of Cambridge, the implied second university, and Dowland surely would not have declared credentials from both institutions had they had not been bestowed.

Fig. 13.2 Robert Cecil, unknown artist. NPG 107 © National Portrait Gallery, London.

Dowland's purpose for translating Ornithoparcus's book and putting it before the English public begs exploration. If taken at his word, Dowland translated *Micrologus* as an aid for lutenists, for in *Varietie of Lute-Lessons* the next year, he wrote:

> Wherefore I exhort all practitioners on this instrument to the learning of their pricksong, also to understand the elements and principles of that knowledge, as an especial great help, and excellent worker in this science, and soon attained, if the teacher be skillful to instruct aright: for which purpose I did lately set forth the work of that most learned *Andreas Ornithoparcus His Micrologus*, in the English tongue.[10]

Yet questions arise as to other motivations for pursuing the project. Might Dowland have been petitioning for a court or an academic position, necessitating a referral from Cecil? Was he simply appealing to the statesman's intellect? Or did he have another agenda altogether? His pointed allusion to Martin Luther in the dedication, which proclaims "you excellently understand, and royally entertain the Exercise of Music, which mind-tempering Art, the grave *Luther* was not afraid to place in the next seat to Divinity," provided assurance to Cecil that the musician was thoroughly versed in the ideals of Protestantism.

On his *Micrologus* title page, Dowland curiously calls himself both a lutenist and a lute player, perhaps paralleling the book's definitions separating "musicians" from singers. Such labels imply multiple levels of musicianship: those who play or sing well, as opposed to those who truly understand how music works—composers per se. This language marks the beginning of a trend in which Dowland disparaged waning music education standards in England, as evidenced by a lack of qualifications and understanding in contemporary musicians. Dowland had returned home to a different English musical establishment from that he had left, and he needed to find a way to fit into a musical culture that had moved in new directions without him.

In 1612, Henry Peacham afforded a new vision of John Dowland when he described him as living in these "ingrateful times, and worthless age of ours."[11] No longer do we see Dowland as the young go-getter who pursued his fortune and reputation through international travel, courtly connections, and entrepreneurial business opportunities. Rather, Peacham's words portray a man looking backward on his life—one who garnered an earned respect for his previous achievements but who sees his best days as in the past. This universal sentiment, one of wistful nostalgia mixed with regret for things left unfinished and indignation at accomplishments unrecognized, is in some ways reflective of what Sir Henry Lee must have felt when he stepped down as the queen's champion in 1590, the event preserved in Dowland's song "His golden locks," or of Queen Elizabeth as she approached her later years in that same decade, certain that her long reign irrevocably changed the course of England, but also cognizant that the question of succession loomed large.[12]

Dowland's own son Robert foreshadowed Peacham's allusion in his 1610 *Varietie of Lute-Lessons* introduction when he described his forty-something-year-old father as "being now gray, and like the Swan, but singing towards his end."[13] In modern times, this declaration seems a bit premature, but in the Tudor-Stuart era, old age was considered to onset as early as age forty-five, a time when a shift in humors was thought to decrease physical strength, but could accelerate thoughtfulness, relaxation, and wisdom.[14] Although this view advantaged men of a more mature age for placement in important offices, it was also accompanied by a great deal of anxiety related to a loss of manhood.

Peacham included more words reflecting his friend Dowland's place in English music history, in more separate volumes, than did any other author of the Elizabethan-Jacobean era. The writer, who was some fifteen years younger than Dowland, held a Bachelor of Arts degree from Trinity College, Cambridge. Comfortable with both courtiers and scholars, he was an especially respected author of his time. His 1622 volume *The Compleat Gentleman* argues humanistic sentiments directed initially at members of the royal court, in an effort to convince them of the benefits of earlier philosophies related to well-roundedness obtained through formal, classical education. His earlier 1612 book of emblems, *Minerva Britanna*, is dedicated to Henry Frederick, eldest son of James I. At the time, the princely heir was seen as the hope for a continuation of Elizabethan courtly ideals. Sadly, the teenaged royal died later that same year.[15] *Minerva* contains emblems dedicated to King James, Queen Anna, Princess Elizabeth, Princes Henry and Charles, other members of the royal family, and the Kings of France and Spain. Robert Cecil received first nod after the royals, followed by assorted peers, knights, and ladies. In all, the book reads as a virtual "Who's Who" of the early Stuart regime. After a number of undedicated emblems evoking classical figures and moral gestures, images and verses reach out to Peacham's academic acquaintances. Among them is an extended emblem heralding John Dowland.

In this 1612 depiction, Peacham moves from a simple Latin dedication, *Ad amicum suum Iohannem Doulandum Musices peritissimum* (To his friend John Doulandus, most skilled musician), to an anagram of Iohannes Doulandus—*Annos ludendo hausi* (years used up in playing), before offering up a much more personal English emblem (Fig. 13.3).

The image depicts a nightingale standing tall on a thorn bush in the rain, next to a house bordered by a dilapidated fence. Its accompanying text reads:

> Here *Philomel*, in silence sits alone,
> In depth of winter, on the bared briar.
> Whereas the Rose had once her beauty shown,
> Which Lords, and Ladies, did so much desire:
> > But fruitless now, in winter's frost and snow,
> > It doth despised, and unregarded grow.
>
> So since (old friend), thy years have made thee white,
> And thou for others, hast consumed thy spring,
> How few regard thee, whom thou didst delight,
> And far, and near, came once to hear thee sing:
> > Ingrateful times, and worthless age of ours,
> > That lets us pine, when it hath cropped our flowers.[16]

The image, which references Dowland's former glory, no doubt recognizes the lutenist's own perceived lack of appreciation in his later years, after he had left Denmark and prior to his appointment as a regular lutenist in James's court, which took place later that same year. At not yet fifty years old, the musician says as much in the introduction to his 1612 songbook, *A Pilgrimes Solace*. Peacham's portrayal followed Dowland, for in Henry Hawkins's 1633 emblem book *Partheneia Sacra,* the author describes the nightingale:

> Sometimes again will [the nightingale] be in a melancholy dump, and strike you such notes, as *Dowland* himself never struck, in all his Plaints and Lachrimaes. It is then perhaps, when he feels so the prickle at his breast, in the midst of his nocturnes.[17]

Not only did Peacham mention Dowland in three of his books, but he also wrote about or dedicated emblems to a number of figures with whom the composer made acquaintance throughout his career. It seems clear that Dowland provided vivid descriptions of particular individuals to his London friend. In addition to the late Earl of Essex and to Cecil, the author also created a *Minerva*

HEERE *Philomel*, in silence sits alone,
In depth of winter, on the bared brier,
Whereas the Rose, had once her beautie showen;
Which Lordes, and Ladies, did so much desire:
  But fruitles now, in winters frost, and snow,
  It doth despis'd, and vnregarded grow,

So since (old frend,) thy yeares haue made thee white,
And thou for others, hast consum'd thy spring,
How few regard thee, whome thou didst delight,
And farre, and neere, came once to heare thee sing:
  Ingratefull times, and worthles age of ours,
  That let's vs pine, when it hath cropt our flowers.

Fig. 13.3 Peacham, Dowland emblem, *Minerua Britanna*, STC 19511, M1r. Used by permission of the Folger Shakespeare Library.

emblem for Moritz, Landgrave of Hesse, Dowland's old friend and sponsor in Kassel. Peacham calls Moritz "Most Illustrious and Most Powerful Prince and Lord," before noting his "languages, and learning in all arts, that gain you millions of remotest hearts."[18] Peacham describes the prince in even more detail ten years later in his *Compleat Gentleman*. While Dowland, through publication of Moritz's pavan in Robert's 1610 *Varietie of Lute-Lessons* and through the associated writings of Peacham, helped to keep Moritz's presence fresh in the minds of Englanders, those associated with Moritz's court were doing the same for Dowland in Germany. In 1620, Johann Daniel Mylius, who served Moritz, published a lute collection titled *Thesaurus gratiarum* that includes at least seven pieces by Dowland, including the volume's opening piece, "Farewell," labeled "Grammatica illustris Douland."[19]

In *The Compleat Gentleman*, Peacham also wrote about Giovanni Croce, maestro di cappella at St. Mark's in Venice whom Dowland met in Italy and singled out in his *First Booke*, as well as Luca Marenzio, whom Dowland had hoped to meet in Italy but had to be content with written correspondence.[20] Peacham and Dowland's friendship was steadfast, for the author returns to the composer again and again in his writings. That the two lived in close proximity, both on Fetter Lane, surely helped maintain their closeness.[21] In addition to his writing skills and a declared aptitude for art, it seems that Peacham also tried his hand at musical composition. In his drawing treatise *Graphice*, he revealed that he set Petrarch's "Zefiro torna," a favorite in English madrigal translations, as a "ditty in my songs of 4 and 5 parts."[22] Almost ten years later in *Thalia's Banquet*, he once again noted that he had a set of four- and five-voice ayres ready for print. Although no collective trace of these songs remains, a four-voice composition celebrating the new King James appears in a manuscript emblem book drawn by Peacham in the early 1600s.[23] If this was one of a number he hoped someday to publish, he no doubt showed them to his master musician friend, seeking Dowland's musical guidance and evaluation.

Peacham again honored Dowland in his 1620 *Thalia's Banquet*, the first place in which Dowland is referred to as "Doctor" in print. The same honorific appears the following year in Thomas Lodge's *A Learned Summary upon the Famous Poeme of William of Saluste Lord of Bartas*. Near the end of the voluminous treatise, a statement on musical affects expresses the author's admiration for Doctor Dowland, with the addition "an ornament of Oxford," implying the advanced degree came from the same university where the lutenist was granted his bachelor degree more than thirty years before.[24] In *Thalia's Banquet*, Peacham dedicates epigram 99, the one referencing a Venice lute, to "Master Doctor Dowland."[25]

Peacham's *Compleat Gentleman* (1622) concluded the writer's celebration of his friend and neighbor. Peacham replicated the same earlier Latin epitaph from *Minerva* and adds this statement:

> Of my good friend M. *Doct. Dowland*, in regard he had slipped many opportunities in advancing his fortunes, and a rare Lutenist as any of our Nation, beside one of our greatest Masters of Music for composing: I gave him an Emblem with this.[26]

The treatise, written at the height of Peacham's career, is another courtier's guide. The volume was quite successful and reissued in 1626 and 1627. A new edition was offered in 1634, as well as posthumously in 1661. G. S. Gordon suggested the purpose of the book was to "protest against slovenliness in the education of his time, and by precept and example, to supply a remedy."[27] Dowland apparently was not the only one who felt educational standards had declined. The musician, however, was becoming a nostalgic figure in an age, not unlike our own, when academics felt the need to fight for the importance of critical thought as a continued tradition within the humanities.

Peacham, as Dowland's friend, knew his heart. He first presented him in *Minerva* as the most pitiful Philomel, the beautiful creature who lost her voice. This entry stands as the only representation of the time that moves beyond heralding Dowland as one of the foremost musicians of his generation to consider his personal anguish. And yet, a decade later the *Compleat Gentleman* treats Dowland in the same manner as earlier lists by Case, Meres, and others that name Dowland as one of England's most esteemed musicians. After a statement on great English composers of the past in a section titled "Of Music," Peacham proclaims:

> I willingly, to avoid tediousness, forbear to speak of the worth and excellency of the rest of our English composers, Master Doctor Douland, Thomas Morley, Mr. Alphonso, Mr. Wilbye, Mr. Kirby, Mr. Weelkes, Michael East, Mr. Bateson, Mr. Deering, with sundry others, inferior to none in the world (how much soever the Italian attributes to himself) for depth of skill and richness of conceit.[28]

Peacham placed Dowland in an honored position of respect at the front of his list, reflecting a new order, even as the emblem of 1612 was now himself an object of nostalgia.

14

Varietie of Lute-Lessons and *A Musicall Banquet*

(1610)

If *Micrologus* was Dowland's theoretical reintroduction to England's press, his compositional presence was realized soon afterward. The following year, his son Robert was credited with compiling two musical anthologies, the only prints connected to the younger Dowland: *Varietie of Lute-Lessons* and *A Musicall Banquet*. Both volumes include music composed by his father, John, who no doubt paved the way for publication through his own connections and who certainly provided advice on dedications, content, assemblage, and production. The first of Robert's books featured lute solos in tablature by various composers, while the second contained vocal airs. Although the collections were quite different in content, commonalities abound.

Both anthologies were published by Thomas Adams and printed by Thomas Snodham, the same combination responsible for *Micrologus* (see Table 14.1). Robert was only about nineteen years old in 1610, but the opening letters to the reader in each book suggest the younger Dowland received a fine education. His references to Greek mythology demonstrate a depth of general knowledge and his prose flows neatly. It seems the young man understood established literary tropes, theatrical scenarios, and courtly allusions well, or else he had careful direction from one who did. The lute volume appeared first, for in *A Musicall Banquet* Robert states, "my collected lute-lessons which I lately set forth," placing the songbook afterward.[1] *Varietie of Lute-Lessons* was one of only a handful of surviving lute solo anthologies printed in England in the era, following two translations of Le Roy's *A Briefe and Plaine Instruction* (1568 and 1574), Barley's *New Booke of Tabliture* (1596), and Thomas Robinson's *The Schoole of Musicke* (1603). As the largest printed set of John Dowland's lute solos in England, one offered by his own son and no doubt created with his own careful guidance, the collection's importance cannot be overstated.

Table 14.1 Publishers and printers of volumes by John and Robert Dowland

Volume	Year	Publisher	Printer	Patent Holder
First Booke	1597	—	Peter Short	—
Second Booke	1600	George Eastland	Thomas East	Thomas Morley
Third Booke	1603	Thomas Adams	Peter Short	Thomas Morley
Lachrimae	1604	—*	John Windet	[Thomas Morley]
Micrologus	1609	Thomas Adams	[Thomas Snodham]	—
Varietie of Lute-Lessons	1610	Thomas Adams	[Thomas Snodham]	[William Barley]
A Musicall Banquet	1610	Thomas Adams	[Thomas Snodham]	[William Barley]
A Pilgrimes Solace	1612	Matthew Lownes John Browne Thomas Snodham	[Thomas Snodham]	William Barley

Information in brackets not specified on original print
* Registered with Stationers' Company by Adams, sold by Dowland

Varietie provides insight into Robert's training while his father was abroad. The young lutenist was sponsored by the book's dedicatee, Sir Thomas Monson (spelled Mounson), a Member of Parliament for Castle Rising and a chancellor for Queen Anna. The gentleman also held a number of important positions for King James, including master falconer. In his dedication, Robert recalls "the grateful remembrance of your bounty to me, in part of my education, whilst my Father was absent from England." Monson was pursued as patron by a number of musicians and must have held a special interest in the lute. In addition to *Varietie of Lute-Lessons*, he was also dedicatee of Philip Rosseter and Thomas Campion's *Booke of Ayres* (1601) and Campion's *Third and Fourth Booke of Ayres* (1617), both songbooks featuring lute tablature. Campion was an intimate part of Monson's circle, as evidenced in his prefatory comments in his books. Thus, while under Monson's care, Robert Dowland may have interacted with other important lute song composers of his time.

The cosmopolitan nature of *Varietie of Lute-Lessons* is immediately apparent in its complete title: *Varietie of Lute-Lessons: Viz. Fantasies, Pauins, Galliards, Almaines, Corantoes, and Volts: Selected out of the best approued*

Avthors, as well beyond the Seas as of our owne Country. Robert's note to the reader at once draws upon John Dowland's reputation:

> I am bold to present you with the first fruits of my skill, which albeit it may seem hereditary unto me, my father being a lutenist, and well known amongst you here in England, as in most parts of Christendom beside.

By the end of the following sentence Robert educes, "but I trust without danger, because we find it true in Nature that those who have loved the Father, will seldom hate the Son." He continues,

> But whatsoever I have here done (until my father hath finished his greater work, touching the art of lute-playing), I refer it to your judicious censures, hoping that that love which you all generally have born unto him in times past, being now gray, and like the swan, but singing towards his end, you would continue the same to me his son.[2]

Highlighting his patrimonial legacy might underlie a solid marketing ploy, but Robert had to approach the matter carefully if he was also trying to establish a professional reputation in his own right.

Varietie of Lute-Lessons is organized in three primary sections—two instructional essays followed by forty-two lute solos grouped in sets of seven by the genres indicated in the volume's title: fantasies, pavans, galliards, almains, corrantes, and voltas. The book's short opening instructional manual by Jean-Baptiste Besard is titled "Necessary observations belonging to the lute and lute-playing." Besard was a Burgundian-born physician trained in Rome who settled in the German lands. His essay is essentially a translation of the 1603 Latin *De Modo in testudines libellus* that he appended to his own 1603 *Thesaurus Harmonicus*, a collection of more than 400 lute pieces by the best lutenists of the day.[3] Besard's 1603 anthology offers at least seven versions of Dowland works, including three based on "Lachrimae." The pedagogical tract recreated in *Varietie* addresses choosing and holding a lute, reading tablature, and the mechanics of fingering and plucking.

Following the Besard tutorial is a John Dowland essay titled "Other necessary observations belonging to the lute." The tract advises on choosing and maintaining strings, setting frets, and tuning the lute. This commentary is the only place in which the internationally famous lutenist directly addresses the mechanics of his instrument. The essay was written, or at least revised, not long before it was printed, for Dowland declares, "I did lately set forth the work of that most learned *Andreas Ornithoparcus* his *Micrologus*," referring to his recent 1609 print.[4] A savvy entrepreneur, Dowland surely inserted the reminder as a means to inspire *Varietie* purchasers to consider buying *Micrologus* as well. His content closely follows that of Hans Gerle's *Tabulatur auff die Laudten* (1533), an instruction manual Dowland mentions in his essay. The only living practitioner singled out in this section is Mathias Mason, "Lutenist, and one of the Grooms of his Majesty's most honorable Privy Chamber."[5] Mason had been employed in Elizabeth's court since 1577 and was granted a permanent position as one of the queen's lutenists in 1579. When James took the throne, Mason continued in service as one of three "lutenists in ordinary," acting as group leader.[6] The isolated mention seems a bit random, but Mason died the same year that *Varietie* was printed. If the older lutenist was showing signs of age or illness, Dowland may have set his sights on Mason's position in the Jacobean court. Recognizing the musician's skills in print provided a way of linking himself to the lutenist, while bringing attention to his own knowledge of courtly activities and qualifications as one who might easily take over the post.

The remainder of *Varietie* consists of lute music in tablature. The organizational groupings of seven of each type of composition, from fantasias through various dance forms, is modeled on Continental lute anthologies printed in the previous several decades.[7] Composers featured in *Varietie* represent a disperse group of individuals. The opening seven fantasias include pieces by professional lutenists who worked for nobles across the Continent, including those who had served the Kings of Poland and France and lutenists who worked in Rome and Bologna. Such references to foreign musicians serving other monarchs provided a direct allusion to Dowland's international experience and place among the best performers in the world.

The final two fantasias in the opening section were composed by Gregory Howet, Dowland's traveling companion during his German years, and John Dowland himself. Side by side, they provide a remarkable print parallel to the 1595 playing competition that Moritz, Landgrave of Hesse, described in his apologetic letter to the Duke of Brunswick the same year. In that correspondence, Howet was declared a fine, experienced player and Dowland a good composer. This second sentiment is reinforced in the title of the next work in *Varietie*, a pavan "made by the most magnificent and famous Prince *Mauritius*, Landgrave of Hessen, and from him sent to my father, with this inscription following, and written with his grace's own hand: *Mauritius*

Landgrauius Hessiae fecit in honorem Ioanni Doulandi Anglorum Orphei."[8] Moritz's portrayal of Dowland as the English Orpheus surely reassured the lutenist that, in his princely mind, the English musician was not only a great composer but the superior player as well. The introductory label also suggests an ongoing correspondence between the two men. The pavan's placement immediately after the Howet and Dowland fantasias cannot be coincidental, recalling Dowland's time at the Kassel court in the 1590s. By 1610, Moritz was a vocal advocate for a marriage match between James I's daughter, Princess Elizabeth, and Frederick, Elector Palatine, with the hope of creating a stronger network between England and the German Protestant league.[9] The German prince's presence in *Varietie of Lute-Lessons* helped keep his name current in the minds of English court members, with Dowland in close sight.

If the fantasias present a world view of excellent lutenists, the pavanes that follow place the lute, like our lutenist, solidly back on English soil. The section consists of works with music by contemporaneous English composers Anthony Holborne and Daniel Bacheler, as well as the deceased Thomas Morley and Alfonso Ferrabosco, who had served Elizabeth for many years. Dowland contributes just one, titled "Sir John Langton, his pavan." The final pavan in the set then provides the first public offering of a composition by the younger Dowland. Robert, in the manner of so many of his father's lute solos, named his pavan specifically for his dedicatee, "Sir Thomas Monson, his pavan."

The subsequent galliard section acts as a full tribute to John, with six of seven pieces contributed by him. The final unattributed galliard is dedicated once again to volume honoree Monson, creating a sort of matched set, with the implication that the dance was also composed by Robert. The personalized titles of John Dowland's galliards represent people the musician had encountered throughout his career, ordered by hierarchical status of decreasing magnitude: Christian IV of Denmark, Queen Elizabeth I, the Earls of Essex and Derby, and Ladies Rich and Clifton. The first five pieces are all clearly attributed to "John Dowland, Bachelor of Music." Robert then claims credit for the sixth. However, a concordance of "The right honorable, the Lady Clifton's spirit," titled "K. Darcy's spirit" (referring to Clifton's maiden name), is found in the first Mathew Holmes lutebook of the 1590s, attributed to "J. Dowl." This earlier volume was compiled when Robert was still a child, and so the composition was surely John's. Perhaps Robert was instead claiming this particular arrangement.

Varietie then moves on to a set of almains, with at least one composed by John Dowland, "Sir John Smith, his almain." Four unattributed dances used in Ben Jonson's 1609 *The Masque of Queenes* are also included in this group.[10] Sets of corantos and unattributed voltas conclude the volume. The combination of international and English composers, music in both older fantasia and dance styles, newly in-fashion French and Italian dances, and inclusions from a recently performed masque by the leading court playwright of the time gives the anthology a wonderfully sophisticated and fresh essence, worthy of notice by those who were in positions to advance the careers of both Dowlands.

Robert Dowland's second musical anthology of 1610, *A Musicall Banquet*, also suggests the influence of his father. The global nature of the volume follows that of *Varietie of Lute-Lessons* and closely matches parts of John's lifelong international itinerary with songs in English, French, Italian, and a few in Spanish. While Robert Dowland does not draw attention to his musical heritage as he had in *Varietie*, John's presence is first felt in the words of the volume's single Latin commendation, contributed by Dowland friend and neighbor Henry Peacham. Although the tribute is addressed to Robert, John is mentioned in Peacham's title, *Ad Robertum Doulandum Joannis filium de Musico suo convivio* (A musical banquet for Robert, son of John). Peacham portrays Robert in verse as "continuing the quill" of his "divine" father and then styles him as Linus, son of Apollo and Calliope. He then returns to Orpheus, the musician Peacham most often associated with John in his later writings.

The dedication in *A Musicall Banquet* honors Robert's godfather and namesake, Robert Sidney (Fig. 14.1), who rose considerably in James's court, by this time receiving the titles Baron of Penshurst and Viscount Lisle. Although Sidney stood much higher in social rank and political circles than John Dowland, many parallels are found in the two mens' lives. They were exact contemporaries with birthdates circa 1563 and death dates in 1626. Both experienced Paris through the English embassy in early adulthood, gaining diplomatic training and potential connections to the French court. Both had a history at Christ Church, Oxford, Robert studying there in the 1570s and John receiving his Bachelor of Music degree in 1588. Sidney was granted an honorary Master of Arts degree from Oxford the same year. Dowland and Sidney each held close associations with members of both sides of the competing Essex and Cecil court circles during Elizabeth's reign. Both men worked for an extended number of years on the Continent, John in Denmark and the German lands and Sir Robert in Flushing, each

Fig. 14.1 Robert Sidney, unknown artist. NPG 1862 © National Portrait Gallery, London.

separated from his wife and family. Each man was also survived by a son named Robert.

Sidney biographer Millicent Hay commented:

> Sidney's ambitions were not unreasonable in light of his background and training. He desired four things: a secure, prestigious position, influence,

money, and an office that would keep him in England. These he sought to obtain by seeking employment that would show his worth, by bringing himself to the queen's attention, and by associating himself with members of the ruling court factions, who he hoped would use their influence to help him.[11]

She also notes:

All his requests for advancement were denied, his military achievements scorned or ignored, his personal initiative discouraged, and his aspirations frustrated.... [Elizabeth] never raised him to the position at the court for which his inheritance and service qualified him.[12]

Dowland's name might easily be substituted for Sidney's in the first quotation and the word "musical" for "military" in the second.

Sidney first met King James on a diplomatic mission to Scotland in 1588, and the impression he made on the monarch stood firm. While both Sidney and Dowland finally received placements within the Jacobean court, Sidney's hopes were fulfilled almost immediately upon the new king's accession, with bestowment of promotions and titles. Dowland had to wait almost a decade for his own court appointment, in which he took a step backward in career status. A recognized supporter of the arts, Sidney received other printed music dedications before *A Musicall Banquet*. For example, Robert Jones, another lute song composer, presented his *First Booke of Songs or Ayres* to Sidney in 1600, prior to the statesman's elevation to baron, viscount, and ultimately earl. In a not so subtle gesture, the first piece appearing in *A Musicall Banquet* is a direct nod to its dedicatee.

"The right honorable, the Lord Viscount Lisle, Lord Chamberlain to the Queen's Most Excellent Majesty, his galliard" by "John Dowland, Bachelor of Music," recognizes Sidney's new titles and sets the tone for the entire volume that follows. The composition is the only lute solo among the slate of songs by various composers that make up the rest of the collection. The galliard, a set of variations on the popular tune "Susanne du Jour," was not wholly original. A similar lute solo by Dowland, without the variations, appears in the 1590s Holmes manuscript with the title "Suzanna galliard," as does a version titled "Mr. Bucton's galliard" in Dowland's 1604 *Lachrimae*, arranged for viol consort with lute.[13] Dowland seemingly recycled his previous arrangements for the Sidney volume, perhaps choosing the piece for French associations with its well-known source tune, a gesture acknowledging Sidney's interest in Parisian affairs.

Scholar Gavin Alexander describes the *Musicall Banquet* galliard as a sequence of strains that present the original French melody with responding divisions, which serve as English answers.[14] This practice parallels Sidney's poetry, which relied on English verse constructed on Continental models. More intimately, the "Susanna" musical source material served as a reminder to Sidney that Dowland was in the employ of the Parisian embassy when he first visited the city back in the 1580s. In spite of the composition's form as a sprightly dance, this galliard, like others composed by Dowland, exhibits a somewhat restrained mood, matching the lutenist's self-styled downtroddenness, as well as the ambiance of much of Sidney's poetry written during the time he longed to leave his post in Flushing in the 1590s, dreaming of a permanent return to England.

The ten English songs following Sidney's galliard in *A Musicall Banquet* were no doubt intended to enhance the volume dedicatee's appreciation. They are entrenched in a bygone Elizabethan courtly ethos, with poems attributed to Earl of Cumberland George Clifford, Robert's slain brother Sir Philip Sidney, the executed Earl of Essex Robert Devereux, and Elizabeth's former champion Sir Henry Lee. All were important courtier-poets in the final decades of Elizabeth's rule who knew each other well. The verses written by these men are set to music by composers Anthony Holborne, Richard Martin, Robert Hales, Daniel Bacheler, Dowland's French acquaintance Guillaume Tessier, and Dowland himself.

Bacheler worked for Philip Sidney's wife, Frances Walsingham, before moving to the household of her second husband, Essex. Hales also worked for Essex. Both Bacheler and Hales went on to serve Queen Anna during the time Robert Sidney served as her Lord Chamberlain. Tessier was also closely connected to the Essex circle. Tessier's son Charles dedicated his first songbook, published in London in 1597, to Essex's sister Penelope Rich. One of Dowland's galliards in *Varietie of Lute-Lessons* was labeled "The right honourable, the Lady Rich" and another "The right honorable Robert, Earl of Essex, high Marshall of England, his galliard." Holborne composed two songs in other volumes named for Robert Sidney's sister Mary Sidney Herbert, a fine poet in her own right. And, of course, the Dowlands had a close connection with Sidney, as documented by the *Musicall Banquet* dedication identifying Sidney as Robert's godfather. Collectively, *A Musicall Banquet*'s composers make up a sort of musical circle equivalent to the one represented by the poets they set.[15] The force that bound them all together? Robert Sidney.

The first song in *A Musicall Banquet*, "My heavy spirit oppressed with sorrow's might" by Holborne, presents Cumberland's words in a setting for solo voice, lute, and bass viol, the same instrumentation used in the first five songs of Dowland's *Third Booke*. The work is the only English song in *A Musicall Banquet* with no text attached to the bass until John Dowland's setting of Lee's "Far from triumphing court" seven songs later. Thus, the two pieces form a distinct connection, reminding those who remembered that it was Cumberland who replaced Lee as Queen Elizabeth's tiltyard representative. The two-voice texted songs with lute accompaniment placed in between are comprised mainly of songs with settings of verses by Philip Sidney and the Earl of Essex, again a shrewd choice for a volume dedicated to Robert Sidney. The lyrics certainly evoked memories of the viscount's brother and his niece's husband, who was heralded as Philip's successor. The three Philip Sidney texts used ("Go my flock," "O dear life," and "In a grove," the first two marked "uncertain" as to composer and the last set by Tessier) all derive from *Astrophel and Stella*, the courtier's sonnet sequence inspired by Essex's sister Penelope.

Unpublished during Philip's lifetime, these poems were well known by 1610. After first finding notice in circulating manuscripts, they were then released in print in 1591, but not realized in an authoritative version until 1598, printed alongside Sidney's weighty *Arcadia*. Production was overseen by Robert and Philip's sister, Mary Sidney Herbert. The last Sidney-texted song presented, "In a grove," sets Sidney's *Astrophel and Stella* poem to music borrowed from Tessier's *Premier Livre d'airs*, a volume released in France in 1582 during the time Dowland was serving in the English embassy in Paris.[16] The piece is immediately followed by three John Dowland songs that complete the section of English songs.

Dowland's simple, dramatic, and declamatory "Far from triumphing court," a sequel to the *First Booke*'s "His golden locks," serves well as the opening song of the trio. The first verse ends with the words "in darkness left to moan," foreshadowing the title of his final inclusion, "In darkness let me dwell." "Lady, if you so spite me" separates the other two Dowland pieces, providing a lighter musical contrast. The text used is an English translation of an Italian madrigal by Ferrabosco that first appeared in Nicholas Yonge's *Musica Transalpina* (1588), printed not long after Philip Sidney died. Unlike his other two songs, Dowland provides words for the bassus parts. He also delivers greater clarity to the text, now far removed from Ferrabosco's five-voice imitative, contrapuntal setting.

The final Dowland work, "In darkness let me dwell," is perhaps the most disconsolate and evocative of all of Dowland's more than eighty lute songs. The composition stands as an exquisite climax to the melancholic persona the composer spent years cultivating. As if he were building toward the moment, Dowland alluded to the text multiple times over the years. "Flow my tears," his most famous song, introduced the idea in its 1600 lyric, "hark you shadows that in darkness dwell." In the same *Second Booke*, the listener is compelled to "mourn, mourn, day is with darkness fled" and "in darkness learn to dwell."[17]

The full "In darkness let me dwell" text was previously set by another composer. English lutenist-composer John Coprario used the verse prominently in his 1606 sequential tribute *Funeral Teares*, written to commemorate the death of Charles Blount, Baron Mountjoy. If Coprario's original musical setting was mournful and touching, Dowland's is downright heartbreaking. The song's text may have first been offered to the memory of Mountjoy, but in a section filled with so many compositions associated with Sir Philip Sidney and the Earl of Essex, Dowland's song tenders a living lament for Robert Sidney. The statesman's professional aspirations were finally being fulfilled in 1610, but he had overcome many struggles earlier in his career, including the deaths of many who were close to him. These losses left him alone to navigate his way through a complex English hierarchy. Thus, two themes interlace throughout both *Varietie of Lute-Lessons* and *A Musicall Banquet*: John Dowland's music and Robert Sidney's associations of the previous generation.

Songs in other languages make up the remainder of *A Musicall Banquet*. A mid-volume French *air de coeur* recalls other songs by Tessier. In fact, the entire volume might have been modeled on Tessier's *Premier Livre*, which featured French, Italian, and Spanish songs, albeit in partbook format. Robert Sidney, of course, had a great interest in French affairs. He even indicated that one of his own poems, found in a manuscript penned in late 1598, should be sung "To a french tune, *Ou estes vous allez mes belles amourettes*," referencing the refrain of the popular song "Puis que le ciel."[18] Continuing a narrative following Dowland's travels, two works in the section of Italian songs introduce the book's English audience to Giulio Caccini, whom Dowland may have met in 1595. Finally, although there is no record of Dowland journeying to Spain, the nation did maintain control of regions of

Tuscany he visited. Even so, were the Spanish pieces at the end of the volume substituted with Danish ones, the book might well serve as a travelogue accompaniment, retelling the highlights of Dowland's career.

So while Robert Dowland's two collected anthologies may have been issued to place the younger lutenist in the minds of those who might advance his professional development, they served equally well as a reminder of the musical abilities of his father. Close Sidney-Essexian associations in both books are surely not coincidental, for individuals connected to that group found new life in James's regime. In fact, the faction took on an especially influential and rewarded stance. Dowland had reached out directly to Cecil, one of the most powerful statemen in James's court, in *Micrologus* to no avail. *Varietie of Lute-Lessons* and *A Musicall Banquet* subsequently publicized the lutenist-composer's outstanding musical achievements to Robert Sidney, who stood second in line only to Cecil in Queen Anna's household. In 1610, an opening for a royal lutenist once again became available with the death of Mathias Mason. While Dowland's *First Booke* may have been a bid for such a position in the Elizabethan court following the death of John Johnson, the 1609 and 1610 books seem to have been intended to gain support for permanent placement in the employ of James I. If so, the musician was once again frustrated. Simon Merson was added to the King's roster of lutes in place of Mason.

15

A Pilgrimes Solace

(1612)

Dowland's final printed anthology of English songs, *A Pilgrimes Solace*, was released in London in 1612. The songbook collectively surpasses all of the composer's previous efforts in terms of complexity, both musically and textually. Organized in three distinctly contrasting sections, the volume's twenty-two musical works include secular partsongs about love and despair, devotional songs focusing on death and redemption, and a group of works appropriate for dramatic presentation. Perhaps some were used as such. Standing alone, a final galliard for lute solo completes the volume.

In his prefatory note to the reader, Dowland addresses his previous time away from his homeland, as well as his reputation abroad.

> Worthy Gentlemen, and my loving Countrymen: moved by your many and foretasted courtesies, I am constrained to appear again unto you. True it is, I have lien long obscured from your sight, because I received a kingly entertainment in a foreign climate, which could not attain to any (though never so mean) place at home, yet have I held up my head within this horizon, and not altogether been unaffected elsewhere. Since some part of my poor labors have found favor in the greatest part of Europe, and been printed in eight most famous cities beyond the seas, *viz. Paris, Antwerp, Cologne, Nuremberg, Frankfort, Leipzig, Amsterdam*, and *Hamburg* (yea and some of them also authorized under the Emperor's royal privilege), yet I must tell you, as I have been a stranger: so have I again found strange entertainment since my return, especially by the opposition of two sorts of people that shroud themselves under the title of musicians.[1]

In spite of his international renown and the appearance of his works in at least a half-dozen London collections outside his own, the lutenist remained dissatisfied with his reception at home. In his *Pilgrimes Solace*

Table 15.1 Select musical anthologies printed prior to 1612 featuring arrangements of Dowland works. Cities listed in *A Pilgrimes Solace*

Compiler	Volume	Medium	Publication Info
Antoine Francisque	*Trésor d'Orphée*	lute	Paris, 1600
Jean-Baptiste Besard	*Thesaurus Harmonicus*	lute	Cologne, 1603
Valentin Haussmann	*Rest von Polnischen und andern Tänzen*	consort song	Nuremburg, 1603
Willem Swart	*Den Lust-Hoff der Nieuwe Musycke*	Dutch songbook	Amsterdam, 1603
Valentin Haussmann	*Neue Intrade mit sechs und fünff Stimmen*	instrumental consort	Nuremburg, 1604
Zacharias Füllsack and Christian Hildebrand	*Ausserlesener Paduanen und Galliarden*	instrumental consort	Hamburg, 1607
Thomas Simpson	*Taffel Consort*	instrumental consort	Frankfurt, 1610

dedication, Dowland decisively laments the lack of respect he has received within London's musical community and condemns several specific types of musicians. He rails first at church vocalists, who seem not to have achieved the foundational learning of previous generations.

> The first are some simple cantors, or vocal singers, who though they seem excellent in their blind division-making, are merely ignorant, even in the first elements of music, and also in the true order of the mutation of the *hexachord* in the *system*, (which hath been approved by all the learned and skillful men of Christendom, this 800 years), yet do these fellows give their verdict of me behind my back, and say, what I do is after the old manner: but I will speak openly to them, and would have them know that the proudest cantor of them, dares not oppose himself face-to-face against me.

To support the notion, Dowland includes a piece of music in the middle of his songs titled "Lasso vita mia," the only song of all those he composed that fully features a foreign text. The composition provides a direct connection back to his comments on the younger generation's lack of understanding of the proper use of the hexachord system, which had been taught in choir schools for generations. The song's lyrics are filled with syllables such as "la," "sol," "fa," "mi," and "re," matching those used in standard hexachords, but are disguised within an Italian verse.

> *La*sso vita *mi*a, *mi fa* mori*re,*
> Crudel amor *mi*o cor consume,
> Da *mi*lle ferite, Che *mi fa* morir,
> Ahi me, Deh, che non *mi fa* mori*re,*
> Crudel amor, *mi fa so*frir *mi*lle marti*re.* (emphasis added)

Throughout the song, Dowland musically guides his singer through a number of hexachordal mutations, a sort of "in joke" hidden from those without formal musical training.[2]

The book's dedication continues on to assess young "professors of the lute" and comments on foreign musicians who have arrived recently in England, insinuating to readers that his own experienced musical manners qualify him to make such judgments.

> [They] vaunt themselves, to the disparagement of such as have been before their time (wherein I myself am a party), that there never was the like of them... Moreover that here are and daily doth come into our most famous kingdom, diverse strangers from beyond the seas, which aver before our own faces that we have no true method of application or fingering of the lute.

He then works in examples of his own learned abilities, quoting a Latin proverb, *Cucullus non facit Monachum* (the cowl does not make the monk), thereby warning readers that musical imposters are in their midst. A generation gap in the musical world was fully evident.

Dowland also derides "a book in defense of the viol de gamba, wherein not only all other the best and principal instruments have been abased, but especially the lute by name." Here he refers to Tobias Hume's *The First Part of Ayres* of 1605, which addresses its readers with the statement: "From henceforth, the stateful instrument gamba viol shall with ease yield full various and deviceful music as the lute."[3] Dowland's fury that his own instrument should be demoted from a primary position may have become known to Hume soon after publication, for in *Captain Humes Poeticall Musicke* (a shorter 1607 book of viol chamber music with some pieces repeated from the earlier volume), the author reprints the sentence but changes the words "as the lute" to "as any other instrument." Whether or not Dowland knew of the change, he obviously held a grudge.

When *A Pilgrimes Solace* was completed, Dowland was in the employ of Theophilus Howard, Lord Walden, to whom the larger volume is dedicated. Walden, twenty years younger than Dowland, descended from a long-established noble family. He was granted a slew of political appointments from 1606 onward, including Lieutenant for the Gentleman Pensioners, the same group in which Dowland's supporter Henry Noel had participated many years earlier. In 1610, Walden was granted a seat in the House of Lords through writ of acceleration. A learned courtier, he was known for his support of artistic endeavors, and he participated in a number of masques. Dowland's dedication gives the nobleman his due:

> To the Right Honorable *Theophilus*, Lord Walden, son and heir to the most noble *Thomas*, Baron of Walden, Earl of Suffolk, Lord Chamberlain of His Majesty's household, Knight of the Most Noble Order of the Garter, and one of his Majesty's most Honorable Privy Council.
>
> Most Honored Lord:
> As to excel in any quality is very rare, so is it a hard thing to find out those that favor Virtue and Learning. But such being found, men of judgment are drawn (I know not by what sympathy) to love and honor them, as the saints and sovereigns of their affections and devices. Wherefore (most worthy Lord) your Honor being of all men noted (as natural borne heir of your most renowned father and mother) to be the only and alone supporter of goodness and excellency, known to none better (unless I should be the most ungrateful of all others) than myself, who am held up only by your gracious hand. For which I can show no other means of thankfulness then these simple fruits of my poor endeavors which I most humbly present as a public pledge from a true and devoted heart, hoping hereafter to perform something, wherein I shall show myself more worthy of your honorable service. In the meantime you shall have a poor man's prayers for your Lordship's continual health and daily increase of honor.

Dowland sought patronage where he could, but his words to Walden, that he was "held up only by your gracious hand," sound as if the lord was his primary means of support in the years after he returned to England. Of course, the typical loquacious, obsequious nature of the dedication may have amplified Dowland's meaning.

A Pilgrimes Solace transcends the composer's previously adopted melancholic persona and reaches toward a personal resolution with God. When the musical anthology was registered in October 1611, it was not yet titled, but listed as "A book of ayres made and set forth both for the lute and bass viol with voices to sing to, by John Dowland."[4] *A Pilgrimes Solace*, as the book was called in print, then became the first and only one of Dowland's songbooks to embrace a metaphorical label. The title conjures up images of a traveler near the end of his journey, looking backward upon the hardships of life and accepting a restful end.

The lyrics of the opening song, "Disdain me still, that I may ever love," seem to be full of hidden meaning. Although the musical style might fit any song of unrequited love, its poetic words, which were later printed with slight variants in the verse anthology *The Harmony of the Muses* (1654), present a microcosm of the emotional toll of aging.

> Disdain me still, that I may ever love,
> For who his love enjoys, can love no more.
> The war once passed with ease men cowards prove:
> And ships returned, do rot upon the shore.
> And though thou frown, I'll say thou art most fair:
> And still I'll love, though still I must despair.
>
> As heat to life, so is desire to love,
> And these once quenched, both life and love are gone.
> Let not my sighs nor tears thy virtue move,
> Like baser metals do not melt too soon.
> Laugh at my woes although I ever mourn,
> Love surfeits with reward, his nurse is scorn.

Especially evocative is the line "and ships returned, do rot upon the shore," seemingly mirroring Dowland's own experience of receiving adulation beyond his homeland, only to be overlooked at home. As the poem continues, the image of a very depressed and bitter individual emerges. The verse is elsewhere attributed to William Herbert, third Earl of Pembroke, the son of Mary Sidney Herbert and nephew to Robert Sidney.[5] Pembroke was an important figure in James's court. He was also the patron to whom Tobias Hume's 1605 viol treatise was dedicated. Dowland's choice to begin

Table 15.2 Contents of *A Pilgrimes Solace* (1612)

(songs to four voices and lute)
I. Disdain me still, that I may ever love
II. Sweet stay a while
III. To ask for all thy love
IV. Love those beams that breed
V. Shall I strive with words to move
VI. Were every thought an eye
VII. Stay Time awhile thy flying
VIII. Tell me true Love

(voice, lute, and two viols)
IX. Go nightly cares, the enemy to rest
X. From silent night, true register of moans
XI. *Lasso vita mia, mi fa morire*

(songs to four voices and lute)
XII. In this trembling shadow
XIII. If that a sinner's sighs be angels' food
XIV.–XVI. Thou mighty God
XVII. Where sin sore wounding
XVIII. My heart and tongue were twins

(tenor-bass dialogue, lute, four-part chorus)
XIX. Up merry mates, to Neptune's praise

(voice, lute, four-part chorus)
XX. Welcome black night

(voice, lute, bass, four-part chorus)
XXI. Cease these false sports

(lute)
XXII. A Galliard to *Lachrimae*

his collection with a setting of this verse thus reflects back upon his own opening words.

The lyrics of the remaining songs revel in their inclusion of words like "die," "perish," "tears," and "anguish," but musically, the first eight four-voice songs do not all sound as dour as one might imagine. In fact, song number 6, "Were every thought an eye," might even be described as sprightly, providing contrast to the preceding plea, "Shall I strive with words to move," and the hymn-like "Stay time awhile thy flying" that follows. A marked musical change occurs in the next three compositions, which make up the true songs of despair. The lyrics of these entries are drenched in sorrow and death. Dowland reduces the number of musical forces to just three parts (cantus, altus, and bassus) with lute, dropping the tenor voice. In "Go nightly cares" and "Lasso vita mia," Dowland places a single singing part in the altus, while the cantus and bassus are scored for instruments only. This lower tessitura adds to a desolate ambience. All three of the works, the two previously mentioned plus "From silent night," carry an old-fashioned consort song feeling with instrumental openings followed by phrases that alternate voice with instrumental response. These pieces also feature Dowland's most apparent text painting. For example, "From silent night" uses downward stepwise motion on the word "sighs," and a drooping lowered note to begin "heavy moans" that adds weight (Ex. 15.1). Fast repeated notes on the word *mille* in "Lasso vita" provide breadth (Ex. 15.2).

The dreary text of "From silent night" is attributed variously to the Earl of Essex (written as his final poem while awaiting execution in the Tower) and to Nicholas Breton (as a reflection on Essex's final thoughts).[6]

From silent night, true register of moans,
From saddest soul consumed with deepest sins,
From heart quite rent with sighs and heavy groans,
My wailing muse her woeful work begins.
And to the world brings tunes of sad despair,
Sounding naught else but sorrow, grief, and care.

Sorrow to see my sorrows cause augmented,
And yet less sorrowful were my sorrows more:
Grief that my grief with grief is not prevented,
For grief it is must ease my grieved sore.
Thus grief and sorrow cares but how to grieve,
For grief and sorrow must my cares relieve.

If any eye therefore can spare a tear,
To fill the wellspring that must wet my cheeks,
O let that eye to this sad feast draw near.
Refuse me not my humble soul beseeks.
For all the tears mine eyes have ever wept
Were now too little had they all been kept.

Ex. 15.1 "From silent night," text painting

Ex. 15.2 "Lasso vita," text painting

Regardless of authorship, associations of the poem with Essex were well known, as evidenced in manuscript copies in which Essex's name is attached. Allusions to the earl's preparation for death were no doubt recognized by those purchasing Dowland's book, even a decade after Essex's downfall. Modern lutenist-scholar Anthony Rooley noted that Dowland's setting "is a sublime example of 'Inspired Melancholy,' where a text could hardly be conceived to be blacker, yet the effect in performance is one of wholly cleansing catharsis."[7]

A set of devotional songs follow that stand as the heart of the volume. In this group, the composer returns to four voices, all texted, but the feeling of these pieces remains in the realm of consort song. They are especially effective when performed by a single solo voice with viols, for although Dowland offers the option for four-part singing, overlapping words obscure the depth of text when all parts are sung. In the first devotional song, Dowland leaves no doubt as to his purpose. The first verse of "In this trembling shadow" begins:

> In this trembling shadow, cast
> From those boughs which thy wings shake,
> Far from humane troubles placed.
> Songs to the Lord would I make.
> Darkness from my mind then take.
> For thy rites none may begin,
> 'Til they feel thy light within.

Not only does Dowland demonstrate the power of music to cleanse the soul, but he also clearly specifies that it is the Lord to whom those songs should be directed.

With a single verse, "If that a sinner's sighs" is noticeably shorter than the devotional songs surrounding it, but the pithy sentiment resounds.

> If that a sinner's sighs be angels' food,
> Or that repentant tears be angels' wine,
> Accept, O Lord, in this most pensive mood,
> These hearty sighs, and doleful plaints of mine,
> That went with *Peter* forth most sinfully,
> But not as *Peter* did, weep bitterly.

Here Dowland links his angel tears to his own infamous "Lachrimae" motive, with an opening sighing chromatic movement in the bass that is immediately followed by an idiomatic descending tetrachord in "Lachrimae" rhythm, cutting through the texture of accompanying parts. His tears not only now embrace a personal dissatisfaction, but also take on a distinctly religious hue. The song's text, opening with references to angels' food and wine, immediately transports the setting to a eucharistic realm. Midway through the song, Dowland places a rare intraphrasal rest in all parts, allowing a brief silence to set up the word "sighs." Then, to complete his aural tale, he repeats the word "weep" in the cantus, as if sobbing, setting the word in syncopation against the other parts. This becomes the one spot in these devotional songs in which four-part singing creates an especially profound moment, for in that final line of weeping, with all voices singing the word in imitation, the song provides a sonic downpour of tears (Ex. 15.3).

The mention of the disciple Peter at the end of "If that a sinner's sighs" sets up the next extraordinary three songs, which provide three distinctive parts of complementary texts written by Nicholas Breton, each focused on a biblical character's woes and resultant virtues: Job's patience, David's forgiveness, and the cripple by the pool's hope and faith.

Ex. 15.3 "If that a sinner's sighs," weeping

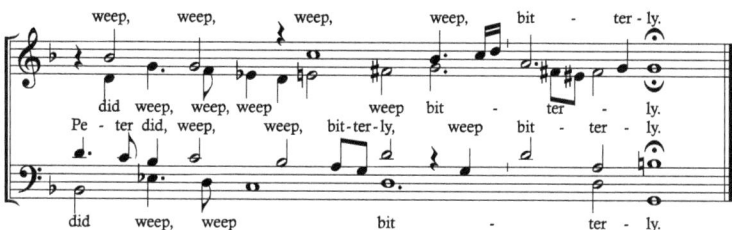

(The first part)
Thou mighty God, that rightest every wrong,
Listen to patience in a dying song.
When *Job* had lost his children, lands, and goods,
Patience assuaged his excessive pain,
And when his sorrows came as fast as floods,
Hope kept his heart 'til comfort came again.

(The second part)
When *David*'s life by *Saul* was often sought,
And worlds of woes did compass him about,
On dire revenge he never had a thought,
But in his griefs, hope still did help him out.

(The third part)
When the poor cripple by the pool did lie,
Full many years in misery and pain,
No sooner he on Christ had set his eye,
But he was well and comfort came again.
No *David*, *Job*, nor Cripple in more grief,
Christ give me patience, and my hopes relief.

Breton's lyrics were first presented as the conclusion to his 1602 *The Soules Harmony* and they anchor a message that perfectly aligns with *A Pilgrimes Solace*'s aesthetic, priming the reader/singer for Dowland's final devotional song. "When sin sore wounding" provides a Protestant message of grace through faith through reminders of hope and repentance.

Where sin sore wounding, daily doth oppress me,
There grace abounding freely doth redress me:
So that resounding still I shall confess thee,
    Father of mercy.

Though sin offending daily doth torment me,
Yet Grace amending, since I do repent me.
At my life's ending will I hope present me,
    clear to thy mercy.

The wound sin gave me was of death assured,
Did not grace save me, whereby it is cured:
So thou wilt have me to thy love inured,
    free without merit.

Sin's stripe is healed, and his sting abated,
Death's mouth is sealed, and the grave amated,
Thy love revealed, and thy grace related,
    gives me this spirit.

It is the word "grace"—the crux of the Protestant faith—that also serves as the first word proper of Breton's *The Soules Harmony*, as the poet acknowledges God the Trinity. His earlier words provide the overarching theme of both his and Dowland's volumes:

Grace in all glory's height,
On whom all glories wait,
Describes my joy's conceit.[8]

That Dowland looked to Breton's text for inspiration in his own time of self-reflection reveals much about his psychological state.

After this extraordinary group of devotional songs, *A Pilgrimes Solace* unexpectedly shifts toward a final cluster of compositions structured for use in celebratory, dramatic events. The lyrics to the first in this set, "My heart and tongue were twins," were sung at Sudeley Castle in an entertainment presented during Queen Elizabeth's 1592 progress.[9] "Up merry mates," a jovial sea-themed dramatic song for tenor voice and lute follows, with dialogue implied through interjections by the bass. The cantus and altus voices join only on concluding couplets, abruptly changing the metrical feel while evidencing the early Baroque operatic convention of a chorus reacting and providing commentary after a featured character's aria. The second verse text indicates that the tenor and bass voices belong to characters with the initials M. and S., hinting that the piece was intended for some specific drama (Fig. 15.1).[10]

The final two songs of the volume, "Welcome black night" and "Cease these false sports," are treated similarly, as solo works with commenting chorus at the end. They unambiguously feature wedding texts, calling upon the marriage god Hymen to "bless this night," in a rather patriarchal tone. It is quite likely these songs were included in a masque staged for the March 1612 nuptial activities of Elizabeth Home and Dowland's employer Lord Walden, to whom the songbook is dedicated.[11] As such, the songs provide symmetry to the dedication at the volume's start.

The songs in *A Pilgrimes Solace* single out two individuals beyond its dedicatee. "From silent night" is addressed to "To my loving countryman Mr. John Forster the younger, merchant of Dublin in Ireland."[12] "Sweet stay awhile," the second song in the collection, is labeled "To my worthy friend Mr. William Jewel of Exeter College in Oxford," once again tying Dowland to

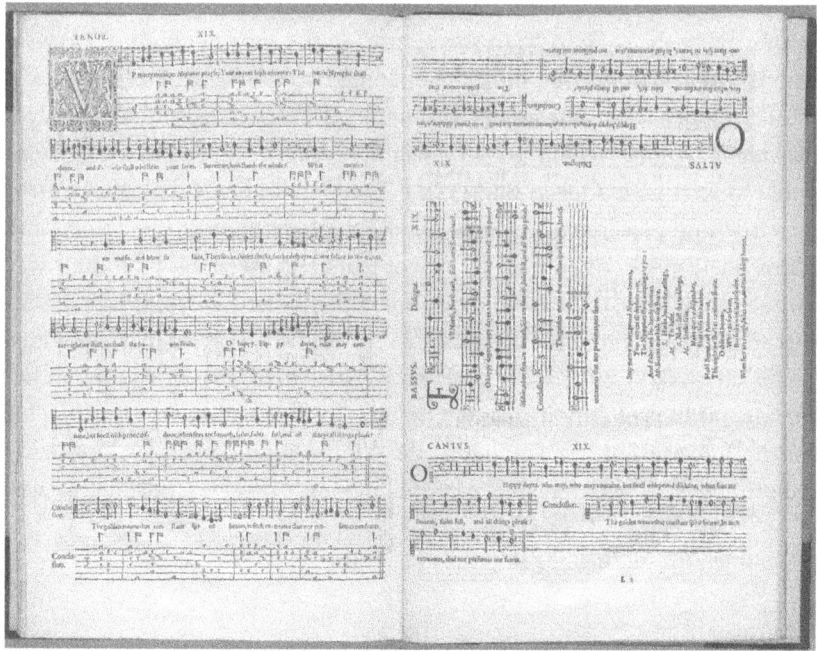

Fig. 15.1 "Up merry mates," from *A Pilgrimes Solace*. RB59103, The Huntington Library, San Marino, California.

the learned academies. When Jewell was granted a fellowship at the college in 1607, he sent a letter expressing his thanks to Robert Cecil, who died the same year *A Pilgrimes Solace* was printed.[13] A philosophical treatise written by Jewell and printed that same year encapsulates the sentiment portrayed in Dowland's anthology in one of only two places mentioning music:

> Sadness, sullenness, melancholy, despair, doleful pensiveness, and all other kinds of woeful discontents, are not these the choicest flowers and godliest shady trees of thy voluptuous paradise? Are not the crystal tears, that trickle from thine eyes, and crimson drops of blood distilling from thine heart, the pleasant bubbling fountains of the same? Are not thy griefs, thy groans, thy sobs, thy sighs, thy lamentations, the ear-enchanting tunes, the warbling melody, and sweetest shrilling music of the pleasant groves?[14]

For Dowland, not only do the songs included in *Pilgrimes Solace* move through a downtrodden journey from love to redemption to final celebration, but individual pieces also reflect back on the composer's previous work. "My heart and tongue were twins" conveys Dowland's early career, looking backward upon the days when he first hoped to join the queen's retinue. The second verse of "Love those beams that breed" places the narrator in the woods, tying the song to "Can she excuse" in the *First Booke* and "O sweet woods" in the *Second*. Similarly, the opening lyrics of "Shall I strive" aurally recall "Shall I sue," also from the *Second Booke*. "Stay time awhile" embraces the theme of time, which pops up again and again throughout the *Third Booke* in relation to Queen Elizabeth I. The final dramatic dialogues mirror the structural placement of single dialogues at the ends of the *Second* and *Third Bookes*. And of course, themes of tears and weeping wind their way through all of Dowland's anthologies, including the wordless *Lachrimae* consort collection. Poignantly, the musician concludes *A Pilgrimes Solace* with a single lute solo, "A galliard to *Lachrimae*." This offering presents yet another version of his most famous melody, in his favorite dance form, honoring his beloved musical instrument. Thus, the composition concludes Dowland's last printed work with one final personal signature on a heartfelt pilgrimage.

16

"Maister Doctor Dowland"

(England, 1612–1626)

Although Dowland's *A Pilgrimes Solace* was dedicated to Theophilus Howard, introductory remarks in the music anthology include several passing gestures to the gentleman's father, Thomas Howard, first Earl of Suffolk and Baron Walden. Dowland initially declares the elder Howard "the most noble," with an attached list of honorifics, and later dubs him "renowned." These tributes may have paid off well, for in October 1612, Dowland finally received a long-coveted position as a musician in the English court. Suffolk was acting as James I's Lord Chamberlain at the time and perhaps played a part in lobbying for Dowland's advancement, an action that Cecil, who died earlier that same year, never brought to fruition. Thus, King James ultimately granted the musician that which Queen Elizabeth would not.

Dowland's name first appears in court registers on 28 October 1612 in a list of payments to six lutenists, "And to John Dowland, one other of his Majesty's Musicians for the Lutes in the room and place of Richard Pyke, deceased."[1] Dowland was paid for a full half year, suggesting he had filled the long-vacant role before it was officially registered. Dowland's payment of £23. 5s. 5d. for a partial year is understandably lower than other lutenists who served the entire term. His original contract provided a pay rate of 20 pennies a day and a yearly livery of £16. 2s. 6d., which never varied thenceforth, as subsequent registers show Dowland receiving a consistent payment of £46. 10s. 10d. per annum.[2] Positions in the "Musicians for the Lutes" were granted for life. The amount Dowland received was equal to that paid to Robert Johnson, son of the lutenist whom Dowland had hoped to replace back in 1594, who was appointed in 1604. Still, Dowland's salary was a bit higher than that of Robert Hales, Simon Merson, and Philip Rosseter, who received £40, £40, and £36 2s. 6d., respectively. The difference may have reflected an estimation of Dowland's talent but more likely was simply a symptom of salary compression, for when Hales was replaced after his January 1616 death, Nicholas Lanier received yearly payments of just over £56, higher than that of both

Dowland and Johnson. Likewise, when Timothy Collins took over Merson's spot two years later, he received the same.

As a member of the king's lutes, Dowland received no special acclaim for his international reputation and certainly was not revered in the same way he had been when serving the king of Denmark fifteen years prior. In fact, all English court lutenists, five of whom served as regular lutes for the king, were each paid less than half the amount of a sixth musician, the queen's lutenist John Maria Lugario; he received a whopping £100 per year.[3] Further, the lute was an expensive instrument to play, and musicians were compensated only occasionally for their required tools and upkeep. One record shows a payment "To John Dowland, one of his Majesty's Musicians, upon a warrant dated 3 December 1624, for a lute: £10, and for strings to be used at such times as he should wait: 100s: in all £ 15. 0s. 0d."[4] This expenditure alone cost more than half his annual salary before livery.

In 1614, Dowland's previous employer Christian IV visited England, leaving Copenhagen on 4 July and arriving in London on 22 July.[5] He returned to Denmark in early August, a seemingly short stay for such an arduous journey. Christian brought with him a large entourage, including musicians. Surely the English court met Queen Anna's brother with a reception befitting his royal status. As a regular member of the king's lutes, Dowland likely stood before his former employer in performance, somehow coming to terms with the fact that he was now a lutenist for his king, but not *the* lutenist to a king.

Dowland, like most court musicians, supplemented his position with activities beyond his official duties, as his yearly wage would never cover London living expenses. In February 1613, he acted as contractor for a group of musicians hired to play for an event at Middle Temple, a receipt stating,

> Received by me John Dowland for myself and my fellow musicians, upon Candlemas Day, 1612, for the consort performed before the judges and reverent benchers, of the Honorable Society of the Middle Temple, by the hand of Mr. Richard Baldwinn, Undertreasurer of the said Middle Temple, the sum of five pounds sterling, I say by me received.
>
> Jo: dowlande
> Lutenist to the King's Majesty [6]

That same month, an extraordinary masque presented by Middle Temple and Lincoln's Inn celebrated the marriage of Princess Elizabeth, James I's daughter, to Frederick V, Elector Palatine. This happy occasion provided some salve to the recent death of Crown Prince Henry Frederick. The production was beyond extravagant. An account of the opening procession alone awes the reader:

> Fifty gentlemen, richly several and as gallantly mounted, with footmen particularly attending, made the noble *vant-guarde* of these nuptial forces.
>
> Next (a fit distance observed between them) marched a mock-masque of baboons, attired like fantastical travellers, in Neapolitan suits and great ruffs...
>
> After them were sorted two cars triumphal, adorned with great mask heads, festoons, scrolls, and antique leaves, every part enriched with silver and gold. These were through-varied with different invention, and in them advanced the choice musicians of our kingdom, six in each, attired like Virginian priests, by whom the Sun is there adored, and therefore called the Phoebades. Their robes were tucked up before, strange hoods of feathers and scallops about their necks, and on their heads turbans, stuck with several-colored feathers, spotted with wings of flies of extraordinary bigness like those of their country. And about them marched two ranks of torches.[7]

The description continues on for four more pages, each paragraph topping the spectacle that came before. A number of musicians were involved in the production, as documented in payment records. Dowland's colleague Robert Johnson earned an impressive £45 "for music and songs," equaling almost a year's wage. Dowland, Rosseter, and Cutting each received £2. 10s. for their performance. Several lutenists outside the king's service also participated, including Robert Dowland, who had the opportunity to play in the same event as his father, receiving £2. Musicians were also provided with a meal, "gloves, ribbon, and other things."[8] A Lincoln's Inn register names nine lutenists, including those mentioned above, as well as three musicians without instrument indication, an unspecified number of pipe and tabor players and trumpeters, and eight singers. Perhaps Dowland was among the twelve "choice musicians of our kingdom...attired like Virginian priests."

In 1614, Dowland wrote commendations for two music volumes printed in London. The resultant congratulatory poems speak to Dowland's ability to compose verse as well as music. The first appears in a curious treatise called *A Briefe Discourse* authored by Thomas Ravenscroft and published by Thomas Adams, who had handled Dowland's *Micrologus*. The book explains basic music fundamentals before offering up a number of four-voice songs extolling such aristocratic leisure activities as hunting, hawking, dancing, drinking, and "enamoring."[9] Dowland's approval appears as the third of nine verse commendations preceding the text. The volume is also one of the first places in print in which Dowland heralded his newly appended title, "Bachelor of Music, and Lutenist to the King's Sacred Majesty." His verse again jabs at younger musicians who lacked the level of training Dowland felt necessary, in the same manner his *A Pilgrimes Solace* had done two years earlier.

> *Figurate Music* doth in each *Degree*
> Require it *Notes,* of several *Quantity*;
> *By* Perfect, or *Imperfect Measure* changed:
> And that of *More,* or *Less,* whose *Marks* were ranged
> By *Number, Circle,* and *Point*; but various use
> Of unskilled *Composers* did induce
> Confusion, which made muddy and obscure,
> What first *Invention* framed most clear, and pure.
> Those, (worthy *RAVENSCROFT*) are restrained by *Thee*
> To one fixed *Form*: and that approved by *Me.*[10]

Dowland later contributed a new harmonization for Psalm 100 to Ravenscroft's 1621 edition of the *Whole Booke of Psalmes*.[11] In the psalm-book, Ravenscroft noted twenty-one contributing composers. Dowland heads the list of his musical contemporaries, marked as a "Doctor of Music," in contrast to all the Bachelors of Music who immediately follow. The only name preceding his is that of Thomas Tallis, the venerable figurehead of Tudor music who had died all the way back in 1585. Dowland's wide range of musical talent is made evident, with his inclusion in a list of composers heavily weighted by those known for their vocal works, a clear contrast to his current court position as an instrumental specialist. In print at least, Dowland was receiving the esteem he deserved.

Dowland's second commendation of 1614 appears in William Leighton's *Teares or Lamentacions of a Sorrowfull Soule*, to which Dowland also contributed two musical works. The music book sets devotional texts

Leighton penned while in debtors' prison in 1613.[12] In Leighton's original textual collection, the opening verse draws upon the same pilgrimage theme that Dowland's *A Pilgrimes Solace* took on two years earlier.

> Like a poor Pilgrim, all alone I stand,
> Taking my journey to the holy land:
> And fain would have, since thus transported hither,
> All sorts and sects, associate me thither,
> But all (alas, woe worth) do me disdain,
> & on my Palmers' weeds, with scorn complain.

In his "Declaration by the Author," Leighton reveals that his poetry was intended for musical setting and, true to his word, his verses appeared in a new volume the following year, this time in a musical edition. Dowland's textual verse commendation stands as the first one newly appended to those previously included in the 1613 volume.

> If that be true the Poet doth aver,
> Who loves not Music and the heavenly Muse,
> That man God hates, why may we not infer?
> Such as that skill unto his praise do use,
> Are heavenly favored, when (as Angels) breathe,
> High Mysteries in lowly tunes beneath.
>
> Such was that sweetest singer Israel's King,
> Whom after his own heart the Lord did choose,
> And many more that did divinely sing,
> To whom be added thy devotest Muse,
> Who while she sounds her great Creator's praise,
> Doth her own fame next his high glory raise.[13]

The two Dowland compositions included in the musical anthology share little in common with each other beyond their sacred penitential tone, as provided by Leighton's words. "An heart that's broken and contrite" is found in an opening group of consort songs, the first one following eight songs composed by compiler Leighton. This work—like others in the section (and presumably at the request of Leighton)—is scored for four voices that are doubled and accentuated by a broken consort of treble and bass viols, flute, treble lute, bandora, and cittern.[14] The lyrical topic is redemption, and the song's words, "An heart that's broken and contrite to God is a sweet sacrifice. Repentant sinners him delight, far more than just men in their sight," musically reflect the original 1613 petition titled:

> A prayer wherein the distressed, humbly confesseth his sins, and the vanities of his former times lewdly misspent, desiring others to take example by him, and to return to God by repentance before it be too late. And at the last preparing to die, commendeth his soul to God, with whom after death he hopeth to live forever.[15]

The voices move in a simple, reverent, and mostly homorhythmic texture, allowing amateur singers and players to easily conquer the three-stanza lyric (Ex. 16.1).

By contrast, Dowland's second composition, "I shame at mine unworthiness," included in the songs for five voices, is written in a much more complex style (Ex. 16.2). The song features one of the most densely woven textures of all of Dowland's compositions, with ongoing dissonances created as notes clash unexpectedly. Because of this, the work might better achieve its intended affect if performed in a consort setting for solo voice and instruments, rather than the multi-voice texting that matches others in the

Ex. 16.1 "An heart that's broken and contrite," opening

Ex. 16.2 "I shame at mine unworthiness," opening

section. Dowland sets only four lines of Leighton's original thirty-six-line, four-and-a-half-stanza text for "the second part of the ninth Lamentation":

> I shame at mine unworthiness,
> yet fain would be at one with Thee.
> Thou art a joy in heaviness,
> a succor in necessity.

A musical tension continues throughout, a reminder of the complicated emotions the lutenist must have experienced in his new court-appointed lifestyle.

Once Dowland began his English royal employ, he never again offered up a collection of his own music for public dissemination. Instead, he settled into his London position, perhaps finally content to live out his life in the comfort of the one location that truly felt like home. Performing at court and for selected outside occasions seems to have been enough. Yet even as he was ensconced in England, his reputation continued to spread elsewhere throughout the 1610s and into the 1620s. Johannes-Philippus Mendelius contributed a Latin poem of commendation to Elias Mertel's

Hortus Musicalis Novus, printed in Strasbourg in 1615, that names the most admired musicians from Italy, France, and the German lands. Dowland is singled out, described as England's foremost musician: *Musica testatum facit hoc: namq Anglia summè Artem Doulandi suspicit, ornat, amat* (Music testifies to this: in England Dowland is supreme, they honor, adorn, and love his art).[16] The lutenist's 1595 traveling companion Gregory Howet receives a similar honor for Germany. Mertel then includes three Dowland fantasias in his collection.[17] No doubt Dowland dreamed of this international recognition, especially in those waning days of 1612. Perhaps his English court appointment brought him closer to the respect he coveted but, as in so many cases, artists are often best appreciated beyond their homelands.

Still, by this time, Dowland's music had also fully woven its way into the broader English consciousness. His *First Booke* received its fifth printing in 1613, officially marking it as the most popular volume of English secular songs of the age. Specific pieces of Dowland's music served as popular culture references, most especially "Lachrimae." Philip Massinger's drama *The Maid of Honour* of the early 1620s offers one such example. The play is set in Italy but calls for Dowland's tune to be played in a dramatic moment of national pride. In the first act, the protagonist Bertoldo muses about an impending battle:

> Or with the hilts thunder about your ears
> Such music as will make your worship's dance
> To the doleful tune of *Lachrymae*.[18]

In 1622, Thomas Tomkins dedicated the seventh of his *Songs of 3. 4. 5. and 6. parts* to "Doctor *Douland*."[19] On initial examination, the piece, titled "O let me live for true love," seems an odd choice. A love song made up of a plethora of "tra-la-la"s, the lyrics are far removed from the courtly verse Dowland set in his own volumes of ayres. Yet Tomkins brilliantly references the "Lachrimae" theme in his song's musical line, opening with the same two four-note descending melodic-rhythmic subphrases as "Flow my tears" (Ex. 16.3). The song also mimics the shape and harmonic support of "Lachrimae," creating a tribute tinged with a touch of humor.

Two years later, William Webb contributed a commendatory sonnet to Francis Pilkington's *Second Set of Madrigals*. In it, Dowland is listed among the greatest English composers of his lifetime:

Ex. 16.3 Tomkins, "O, let me live" (1622), opening based on "Lachrimae"

Those great Achievements our Heroic Spirits
Have done in England's old or later Victories,
Shall we attribute wholly to the Merits,
Of our Brave Leaders? And fair Industries
Which their not-named Followers have expressed
Lie hid? And must the Matchless Excellencies
Of *Bird*, *Bull*, *Dowland*, *Morley*, and the rest
Of our rare Artists, (who now dim the lights
Of other lands) be only in Request?
Thyself, (and others) losing your due Rights
To high Desert? nay, make it (yet) more plain,
That thou canst hit the Ayres of every vain.

> Their praise was their Reward, and so 'tis thine:
> The Pleasure of thy pains, all men's—and mine.[20]

About this same time, Dowland's son Robert was exploring career possibilities on the Continent, as his father had done three decades earlier. In the 1620s, Robert worked in the court of Duke Philip Julius of Pomerania-Wolgast in Northern Germany, alongside English musicians Richard Farnaby and Richard Jones. John's connections likely advanced Robert's career, for Philip Julius was brother-in-law to Heinrich Julius, Dowland's European sponsor back in 1594. On 30 August 1623, Robert, with Jones and Johan Kostressen, requested permission to leave the Duke's service and return to England, where Robert found performance opportunities with his father.[21]

In March 1625, England once again saw a new king take the throne, predicated by the death of James I. After more than two decades of strengthened foreign policy and relative peace, the Anglo-Scottish monarch's son Charles assumed one of the most powerful positions in Europe. James was interred at Westminster Abbey on 5 May. Dowland and other musicians of "The Consort," including the other four court lutenists, were provided a mourning livery allowance in preparation for the solemn occasion, as were all servants of the household.[22]

It was the final royal funeral in which the musician would participate. John Dowland, England's most skilled and renowned lutenist, died in London in early 1626, leaving behind a legacy like none other. His pay from the Jacobean court ended 20 January 1626, likely the day of his death, and he was buried at London's St. Ann Blackfriars one month later on 20 February 1626.[23] On 26 April, Charles I granted Robert his father's position in the King's Lutes at the same salary his father received more than a decade earlier.[24] The following Michaelmas, John's estate was paid for one quarter of the year and Robert the remainder.[25] Back in 1622, Henry Peacham noted Dowland's "slipped opportunities." Even in death, a few remained for the musical giant, for John Dowland did not live to see the marriage of his son Robert to Jane Smally that summer, or the births of his grandchildren, John in 1627 or Mary in 1629.[26] He was spared some heartbreak, for his grandson did not live long. On 22 December 1627, "John, Son to Robert and Jane Dowland" was buried in the same parish, no doubt near his grandfather and namesake, the man now recognized as the greatest English lutenist of his generation: *Dowland*.

Epilogue

Dowland's lute song–airs, along with those of contemporaries like Campion, Coprario, and Pilkington, emanate from a trendy, short-lived, early-seventeenth-century favor, following a similar trajectory as the English madrigals composed by Morley and others. In lute song print realization, the two forms were regularly conflated for commercial reasons. From another vantage, Dowland's songs solidly reflect a practice already taking place on the Continent, one that moved away from the contrapuntal, multi-voice vocal pieces that made up so many of the era's printed songbooks, toward accompanied solo song. The earliest dedicated basso continuo lines printed in England would not show up until the next generation, in the songs of Walter Porter, but one needs only to look back to the lute and bass viol parts in Dowland's *A Pilgrimes Solace* to see that a model was already in place. In England, however, a mid-century Civil War loomed that would temporarily slow secular music production and change its direction. Dowland was not alive to see these events, but when English music and theatre returned full-scale, they did so with a decidedly Baroque flair, one for which Dowland was instrumental in setting a foundation.

In the centuries that followed, Dowland's music was not forgotten, although it was often reinterpreted in ways that fit the needs of new musical communities. His music circulated in manuscript for a quarter century after his death, especially on the Continent, where arrangements appear in more than two dozen copied collections. Late-eighteenth-century authors John Hawkins and Charles Burney knew enough about the lutenist and his music to include him in their music histories, but it was Dowland's music that propelled his legacy forward. Four-part choral arrangements of his songs came into fashion in the mid-nineteenth century, and when an early music revival blossomed at the beginning of the twentieth century, interest in the lutenist and his compositions found new life.

Since that time, Dowland has served as a beacon for singers and lutenists alike and is embraced by the guitar community as a rich source of repertoire. Twentieth-century composers such as Granville Bantock, Benjamin Britten, Peter Maxwell Davies, and George Crumb, among others, looked back to

Dowland's music, incorporating his themes into compositional settings of their own. Thus, in hindsight, Dowland's final words to the reader in his *Third Booke* seem prophetic in an age when long-lasting legacy was reserved for but a few, belying his faith in his own abilities: "My labors for my part I freely offer to every man's judgement, presuming that favor, once attained, is more easily increased then lost." More poignantly, his last printed word to the reader in his final anthology, *A Pilgrimes Solace*, puts forth a simple "Farewell."

APPENDIX A

John Dowland, Letter to Robert Cecil, 10 November 1595

Hatfield House Archives, Cecil Papers, 172:91–93

Right honorable, as I have been most bound unto your honor, so I most humbly desire your honor to pardon my boldness and make my choice of your honor to let you understand my bounden duty and desire of God's preservation of my most dear sovereign queen and country, whom I beseech God ever to bless and to confound all their enemies what and whomsoever. Fifteen years since, I was in France, servant to Sir Henry Cobham who was Ambassador for the Queen's Majesty, and lay in Paris, where I fell acquainted with one Smith a priest, and one Morgan sometimes of her majesty's Chapel, one Verstigan who brake out of England being apprehended and one Morris a Welshman that was our porter, who is at Rome. These men thrust many idle toys into my head of religion, saying that the papists' was the truth and ours in England all false, and I being but young their fair words overreached me and I believed with them. Within two years after I came into England where I saw men of that faction condemned and executed, which I thought was great injustice, taking religion for the only cause, and when my best friends would persuade me I would not believe them. Then in time passing one Mr. Johnson died and I became an humble suitor for his place (thinking myself most worthiest) wherein I found many good and honorable friends that spake for me, but I saw that I was like to go without it, and that any might have preferment but I, whereby I began to sound the cause, and guessed that my religion was my hindrance. Whereupon my mind being troubled, I desired to get beyond the seas, which I durst not attempt without license from some of the Privy Council, for fear of being taken and so have extreme punishment, and according as I desired there came a letter to me out of Germany from the Duke of Brunswick, whereupon I spake to your honor and to my Lord of Essex, who willingly gave me both your hands (for which I would be glad if there were any service in me that your honors could command). When I came to the Duke of Brunswick he used me kindly, and gave me a rich chain of gold, £23 in money with velvet and satin and gold lace to make me apparel, with promise that if I would serve him he would give me as much as any prince in the world. From thence I went to the Landgrave of Hessen (who gave me the greatest welcome that might be for one of my quality), who sent a ring into England to my wife valued at 20£ sterling, and gave me a great standing cup with a cover gilt, full of dollars with many great offers for my service. From thence I had great desire to see Italy and came to Venice and from thence to Florence where I played before the Duke and got great favors. And one evening I was walking upon the piazza in Florence, a gentleman told me that he espied a English priest and that his name was Skidmore and son and heir to Sir John Skidmore of the court. So I being intended to go to Rome to study with a famous musician named Luca Marenzio stepped to this Mr. Skidmore the priest and asked him if he were an Englishman, and he told me yea, and whose son he was, and I telling him my name he was very glad to see me. So I told him I would go to Rome and desired his help for my safety, for said I, if they should mistake me there, my fortune were hard, for I have been thrust off of all good fortunes because I am a Catholic at home. For I heard that her majesty being spoke to for me said I was a man to serve any prince in the world, but I was an obstinate papist. Whereunto he answered, "Mr. Dowland if it be not so make her words true," so in further talk we spake of priests, and I told him that I did not think it true that any priests (as we said in England) would kill the queen or one go about to touch her finger, and said I, "Whatsoever my religion be I will neither meddle nor make with anything there done so that they do not anything against the queen." Whereunto he answered that I spake as a good subject to her majesty, but said he "in Rome you shall hear Englishmen, your own countrymen, speak most hardly of her and wholly seek to overthrow her and all England, and those be the Jesuits," said he "who are of the Spanish faction." Moreover said he, "we have many jars with them," and withal wished to God the queen were a Catholic. And said he, "to defend my country against the Spaniards I would come into England and bear a pike on my shoulders." Among our talk he told me that he had order to attach diverse English gentlemen, and that he had been three years [from] England. So I brought him to his lodging door, where he told me that there was nine priests come from Rome to go for England. He came but the day before to Florence, and I think they came all together. He told me that he would stay there in the town and study in an abbey called Sancta Maria Novella, and that he must keep in for a month, and that he would write letters of me to Rome, which I should receive very shortly, but I heard not of him in a month after, and then there came two friars to my lodgings, the one was an Englishman named Bailey, a Yorkshireman. The next day after my speech with Skidmore, I dined with my Lord Gray and diverse other gentlemen, whom I told of my speech with Skidmore giving them warning. Whereupon my Lord Gray went to Siena, and the rest dispersed themselves. Moreover I told my Lord Gray howsoever I was for religion, if I did perceive anything in Rome that either touched her majesty or the State of England, I would give notice of it though it were the loss of my life, which he liked well and bade me keep that secret. This Friar Bailey before named, delivered me a letter which I have here sent unto your honor, which letter I brake open before Mr. Josias Bodley, and showed what was written in it to him and diverse other[s]. After this, this Friar Bailey told me he had received letters from Rome to hasten me forward, and told me that my discontentment was known at Rome, and that I should have a large pension of the pope, and that his holiness and all the cardinals would make wonderful much of me. Thereupon I told him of my wife and children, how to get them to me. Whereunto he told me that I should have acquaintance with such as should bring them over if she had any willingness or else they would lose their lives, for there came those into England for such purposes. For quoth he, "Mr. Skidmore brought out of England at his last being there seventeen persons both men and women, for which the Bishop weeps when he sees him for Joy." After my departure I called to mind our conference and got me by myself and wept heartily, to see my fortune so hard that I should become servant to the greatest enemy of my prince, country, wife, children, and friends, for want, and to make me like themselves. God knoweth I never loved treason nor treachery nor never knew of any, nor never heard any mass in England, which I find is great abuse of the people, for on my soul I understand it not, wherefore I have reformed myself to live according to her majesty's laws, as I was born under her highness, and that most humbly I do crave pardon, protesting if there were any ability in me, I would be most ready to make amends. At Bologna I met with two men, the one named Pierce an Irishman, the other named Dracot. They are gone both to Rome. In Venice I heard an

Italian say that he marveled that King Philip had never a good friend in England that with his dagger would dispatch the Queen's Majesty, but said he, God suffers her, in the end to give her the greater overthrow. Right honorable, this have I written that her majesty may know the villainy of these most wicked priests and Jesuits, and to beware of them. I thank God I have both forsaken them and their religion which tendeth to nothing but destruction. Thus I beseech God night and day to bless and defend the queen's majesty, and to confound all her enemies and to preserve your honor and all the rest of her majesty's most honorable Privy Council. I think that Skidmore and the other priests are all in England, for he stayed not at Florence as he said he would to me, and Friar Bailey told me that he was gone into France to study the law. At Venice and all along as I come into Germany say that the King of Spain is making great preparation to come for England this next summer, where if it pleased your honor to advise me by my poor wife I would most willingly lose my life against them. Most humbly beseeching your honor to pardon my ill writing, and worse indicting, and to think that I desire to serve my country and hope to hear of your good opinion of me. From Nuremberg this 10th of November 1595.

Your honor's most bounden
forever
Jo: Dowlande

APPENDIX B

Calendar

1563	Dowland is born, according to personal statements in *Varietie of Lute-Lessons* and *A Pilgrimes Solace*.
c. 1579–1583	Employed in Paris by Henry Cobham, English Ambassador to France. Dabbles with Catholicism.
c. 1583–4	Returns to England.
1588	Receives Bachelor of Music degree from Christ Church, Oxford.
1592	Six psalm harmonizations appear in Thomas East's *Whole Booke of Psalmes*.
1594	John Johnson dies. Dowland unsuccessfully petitions for Johnson's lutenist position in the Elizabethan court.
1594–1595	Travels to German courts in Wolfenbüttel and Kassel.
1595	Tours Italian lands. Meets English papists in Florence. Returns to Germany.
	Writes to Robert Cecil from Nuremburg.
1596	Receives letter from Henry Noel at Kassel. Returns to England.
1597	Composes *Mr. Henry Noell, his funerall Psalmes*.
	The First Booke of Songes or Ayres receives the first of five printings.
1598	Contributes a commendatory verse to Giles Farnaby's *Canzonets*.
	Receives Kassel court employment offer from Moritz, Landgrave of Hesse.
	Named Royal Lutenist to Christian IV of Denmark.
1599	Contributes commendatory verse to Richard Alison's *Psalmes*.
1600	*Second Booke of Songs or Ayres* printed in London.
1601	Travels to England from Denmark to buy instruments and secure musicians for Christian IV.
1602	Stephen Lesieur requests Danish intelligence.
1603	Queen Elizabeth I dies.
	Returns to England on personal business.
	Third and Last Booke of Songs or Aires printed in London.
1604	*Lachrimae, or Seaven Teares* printed in London. The title page attests to Dowland's residence on Fetter Lane.
	Meets with Queen Anna at Winchester.
	Returns to Denmark.
1606	Leaves Christian IV's service and the Danish court.
1609	*Ornithoparcus His Micrologus* printed in London.
1610	*Varietie of Lute-Lessons* and *A Musicall Banquet*, both compiled by Robert Dowland and containing works by John Dowland, are printed in London.
1612	*A Pilgrimes Solace* released.
	Henry Peacham includes a Dowland emblem in *Minerva Britanna*.
	Hired into the service of James I of England.

1613 Receives payment for Middle Temple concert.
Performs in Lincoln's Inn masque celebrating the wedding of Princess Elizabeth to Frederick, Elector of Palatine.
1614 Contributes prefatory commendations for Thomas Ravenscroft's *A Briefe Discourse* and William Leighton's *Teares or Lamentacions*.
1621 Provides new harmonization for Psalm 100 for Thomas Ravenscroft's *Whole Booke of Psalmes*.
1625 Participates in funerary activities for James I.
1626 Buried at St. Ann Blackfriars in London.

APPENDIX C

Select List of Works

This works list was created to guide readers to select Dowland compositions in primary sources and in modern editions. Each composition is listed with its most authoritative source and assigned catalog number in *RG*.

Source abbreviations

FB	*First Booke of Songes or Ayres* (1597)
SB	*Second Booke of Songs or Ayres* (1600)
TB	*Third and Last Booke of Songs or Aires* (1603)
PS	*A Pilgrimes Solace* (1612)
	(Modern edition: *Ayres for Four Voices*, Musica Britannica 6, ed. Greer)
LHN	*Lamentatio Henrici Noel* (manuscript, GB-NO)
WBP-E	*Whole Booke of Psalmes* (East, 1592/1594)
WBP-R	*Whole Booke of Psalmes* (Ravenscroft, 1621)
	(Modern edition: *Complete Psalms*, ed. Poulton)
LST	*Lachrimae, or Seaven Teares*
	(Modern edition: *Complete Consort Music*, ed. Hunt)
MB	*A Musicall Banquet* (R. Dowland, 1610)
	(Modern edition: English Lute Songs 16, ed. Stroud)
TL	*Teares or Lamentacions of a Sorrowfull Soule* (Leighton, 1614)
	(Modern edition: Early English Church Music 11, ed. Hill)
VLL	*Varietie of Lute-Lessons* (R. Dowland, 1610)
m	miscellaneous lute manuscripts and prints (see *RG* for source information)
	(Modern edition: *CLM*, ed. Poulton and Lam)

Lute Song–Airs

"All ye whom love or fortune hath betrayed," *FB* (D134)
"Awake sweet love, thou art returned," *FB* (D24)
"Away with these self-loving lads," *FB* (D139)
"Behold a wonder here," *TB* (D162)
"Burst forth my tears," *FB* (D128)
"By a fountain where I lay," *TB* (D171)
"Can she excuse my wrongs," *FB* (D42)

"Cease these false sports," *PS* (D198)
"Clear or cloudy, sweet as April show'ring," *SB* (D158)
"Come again, sweet love doth now invite," *FB* (D60)
"Come away, come sweet love," *FB* (D138)
"Come heavy sleep," *FB* (D138)
"Come when I call, or tarry 'til I come," *TB* (D180)
"Come ye heavy states of night," *SB* (D151)
"Daphne was not so chaste as she was changing," *TB* (D163)
"Dear if you change, I'll never choose again," *FB* (D127)
"Die not before thy day," *SB* (D143)
"Disdain me still, that I may ever love," *PS* (D181)
"Faction that ever dwells in court," *SB* (D155)
"Far from triumphing court," *MB* (D199)
"Farewell, too fair," *TB* (D160)
"Farewell unkind, farewell," *TB* (D173)
"Fie on this feigning, is love without desire," *TB* (D175)
"Fine knacks for ladies," *SB* (D149)
"Flow my tears, fall from your springs," *SB* (D15)
"Flow not so fast, ye fountains," *TB* (D167)
"From silent night, true register of moans," *PS* (D189)
"Go crystal tears," *FB* (D129)
"Go nightly cares, the enemy to rest," *PS* (D188)
"His golden locks Time hath to silver turned," *FB* (D137)
"Humor, say what mak'st thou here," *SB* (D159)
"I must complain, yet do enjoy my love," *TB* (D176)
"I saw my lady weep," *SB* (D141)
"If floods of tears could cleanse my follies past," *SB* (D148)
"If my complaints could passions move," *FB* (D19)
"If that a sinner's sighs be angels' food, " *PS* (D192)
"In darkness let me dwell," *MB* (D201)
"In this trembling shadow," *PS* (D191)
"It was a time when silly bees could speak," *TB* (D178)
"Lady, if you so spite me," *MB* (D200)
"Lasso vita mia, mi fa morire," *PS* (D190)
"Lend your ears to my sorrow good people," *TB* (D170)
"Love stood amaz'd at sweet Beauty's pain," *TB* (D169)
"Love those beams that breed," *PS* (D184)
"The lowest trees have tops," *TB* (D178)
"Me, me, and none but me," *TB* (D164)
"Mourn, mourn, day is with darkness fled," *SB* (D144)
"My heart and tongue were twins," *PS* (D195)
"My thoughts are winged with hopes," *FB* (D26)
"Now cease, my wandering eyes," *SB* (D150)
"Now, O now I needs must part," *FB* (D23)
"O sweet woods, the delight of solitariness," *SB* (D147)
"O, what hath overwrought my all amazed thought," *TB* (D172)
"Praise blindness eyes, for seeing is deceit," *SB* (D146)
"Rest awhile you cruel cares," *FB* (D132)

"Say Love, if ever thou didst find," *TB* (D166)
"Shall I strive with words to move," *PS* (D34)
"Shall I sue, shall I seek for grace," *SB* (D156)
"A shepherd in a shade," *SB* (D154)
"Sleep wayward thoughts," *FB* (D133)
"Sorrow stay, lend true repentant tears," *SB* (D142)
"Stay Time awhile thy flying, " *PS* (D186)
"Sweet stay awhile, why will you rise," *PS* (D182)
"Tell me true Love," *PS* (D187)
"Then sit thee down," *SB* (D145)
"Think'st thou then by thy feigning," *FB* (D130)
"Thou mighty God," *PS* (D193)
"Time stands still," *TB* (D161)
"Time's eldest son, old age the heir of ease, " *SB* (D145)
"To ask for all thy love," *PS* (D183)
"Toss not my soul," *SB* (D157)
"Unquiet thoughts," *FB* (D125)
"Up merry mates, to Neptune's praise," *PS* (D196)
"Weep you no more sad fountains," *TB* (D174)
"Welcome black night," *PS* (D197)
"Were every thought an eye," *PS* (D185)
"What if I never speed," *TB* (D168)
"What poor astronomers are they," *TB* (D179)
"When David's life," *PS* (D193)
"When others sing *Venite exultemus*," *SB* (D145)
"When Phoebus first did Daphne love," *TB* (D165)
"When the poor cripple," *PS* (D193)
"Where sin sore wounding," *PS* (D194)
"White as lilies was her face," *SB* (D152)
"Whoever thinks or hopes of love for love," *FB* (D126)
"Wilt thou unkind, thus reave me of my heart," *FB* (D135)
"Woeful heart with grief oppressed," *SB* (D153)
"Would my conceit that first enforced my woe," *FB* (D136)

Psalm Harmonizations and Sacred Music

"All people that on earth do dwell" (Ps. 100), *WBP-E/WBP-R* (D206/D211)
"Behold and have regard" (Ps. 134), *WBP-E* (D209)
Fuga, GB-Lbl (D124)
"An heart that's broken and contrite" (Ps. 51), *TL* (D203)
"The humble complaint of a sinner," *LHN* (D216)
"The humble suit of a sinner," *LHN* (D215)
"I shame at mine unworthiness," *TL* (D204)
"The Lamentation of a Sinner," *LHN* (D212)
"Lord hear my prayer, hark the plaint" (Ps. 143), *LHN* (D218)
"Lord in thy wrath reprove me not" (Ps. 6), *LHN* (D213)
"Lord to thee I make my moan" (Ps. 103), *WBP-E/LHN* (D208/D217)

"My soul praise the Lord" (Ps. 104), *WBP-E* (D207)
"O God of power omnipotent," *WBP-E* (D210)
"O Lord consider my distress" (Psalm 51), *LHN* (D214)
"Praise God upon the lute and viol" (Ps. 150), *SB* (D140)
"A prayer before evening prayer"/"A prayer before morning prayer"/"Praise the Lord all ye Gentiles all," *WBP-E* (D206)
"A prayer for the Queen's most excellent Majesty," *WBP-E* (D210)
"A Thanksgiving"/Psalms 2, 5, 10, 13, 17, 20, 26, 28, 32, 35, 38, 47, 51, 53, 56, 60, 64, 71, 75, 80, 84, 85, 86, 95, 98, 101, 106, 109, 114, 118, 138, 142, *WBP-E* (D205)

Consort music

All printed in *LST*.

Captain Piper, his galliard (D19)
Earl of Essex galliard (D42)
King of Denmark's galliard (D40)
Lachrimae amantis (D118)
Lachrimae antiquae (D15)
Lachrimae antiquae novae (D114)
Lachrimae coactae (D117)
Lachrimae gementes (D115)
Lachrimae pavan (D15)
Lachrimae tristes (D116)
Lachrimae verae (D119)
Mr. Bucton, his galliard (D38)
Mr. George Whitehead, his glmand (D123)
Mr. Giles Hoby, his galliard (D29)
Mr. Henry Noel, his galliard (D34)
Mr. John Langton's pavan (D14)
Mr. Nicholas Griffith, his galliard (D121)
Mr. Thomas Collier, his galliard (D122)
Mrs. Nichol's almand (D52)
Semper Dowland, semper dolens (D9)
Sir Henry Umpton's funeral (D120)
Sir John Souch, his galliard (D26)

Lute music

Note: A single representative title is chosen for each composition, as many title variants exist in manuscripts. Titles referring to specific individuals are standardized by last name and dance. Most are found in modern edition in *CLM*.

Aloe, m (D68)
Aria, m (D200)
Candish's Gallard, Captain, m (D21)
Case's Pavan, m (D12)

APPENDIX C   223

Clifton's Almain, Mrs., m (D53)
Come away, m (D60)
Complaint, m (D63)
A Coy Toy, m (D80)
Darcy's Galliard, K. (*aka* Do. Re. Ha.), m (D41-*see also* Queen Elizabeth)
Darcy's/Clifton's Spirit, Lady, *VLL* (D45)
Derby Galliard, Earl of, *VLL* (D44)
Dowland's adieu for Master Oliver Cromwell, *SB* (D13)
Dowland's Midnight, m (D99)
A Dream, m (D75)
Essex Galliard, Earl of *VLL* (D42)
Farewell, m (D3/D4)
Fleetwood's Pavan, Mrs. Brigide, m (D11)
Forlorn Hope, m (D2)
Fortune my foe, m (D62)
Frog Galliard, m (D23)
Galliard for Two to Play Upon One Lute, *FB* (D37)
Galliard on a galliard by Daniel Bacheler, m (D28)
Galliard on Gregory Huet's Galliard, m (D108)
Galliard to *Lachrimae*, *PS* (D46)
Go from my window, m (D64)
Guilford's Almain, m (D111)
Hasellwood's Galliard, m (D84)
Hoby's Galliard, Giles, m (D29)
Hunsdon's Allmande/Puffe, Lady, m (D54)
King of Denmark's Galliard, *VLL* (*aka* Battle Galliard, m) (D40)
Knight's Galliard, Mr., m (D36)
La mia Barbara, m (D95)
Lachrimae, m (D15)
Laiton's Almain, Lady, m (D48)
Langton's Galliard, Mr., m (D33)
Langton's Pavan, John, *VLL* (D14)
Leighton's Choice, Mrs. Jane, m (D112)
Loth to depart, m (D69)
Melancholy Galliard, m (D25)
Mildmay's Delight, My Lady, m (D83)
Monsieur's Almain, m (D113)
My Lord Willoughby's Welcome Home, m (D66)
Nichol's Almain, Mrs., m (D52)
Noel's Galliard, Mr. Henry/Mignarda, m (D34)
Norrish's Delight, Mrs., m (D77)
Orlando Sleepeth, m (D61)
Piper's Galliard, Captain Digorie, m (D19)
Piper's Pavan, Captain, m (D8)
Queen Elizabeth's Galliard, *VLL* (D41)
Queen's Galliard, m (D97)
Resolution, m (D13)
Rich's Galliard, Lady, (*aka* Dowland's Bells), *VLL* (D43)

Robin, m (D70)
Round Battle Galliard, m (D39)
Russell's Pavan, Lady, m (D17)
Semper dolens, m (D9)
The Shoemaker's Wife, a Toy, m (D58)
Sidney's Galliard, Sir Robert (*aka* Bucton's), m (D38)
Smith's Almain, Sir John, *VLL* (D47)
Solus cum sola, m (D10)
Souch's Galliard, Sir John, m (D26)
Strang's March, Lord, m (D65)
Tarleton's Jig, m (D81)
Tarleton's Resurrection, m (D59)
Une jeune filette, m (D93)
Vaux's Galliard, Mrs., m (D32)
Vaux's Jig, Mrs., m D57
Walsingham, m (D67)
What if a day, m (D79)
White's Choice, Mrs./White's Thing, m (D50)
White's Nothing, Mrs., m (D56)
Winter's Jump, Mrs., m (D55)

Plus various almains, courantes, fantasias, galliards, jigs, pavans, preludes, and voltas. Please note that some may be arrangements of Dowland works and many variants are present. Many of these pieces were also arranged for other instruments and ensembles and several are of questionable authorship.

APPENDIX D

Personalia

Adams, Thomas (c. 1566–1620) English publisher and member of the Stationers' Company. Registered Dowland's *Lachrimae* (1604) and published *The Third and Last Booke of Songes or Aires* (1603), *Andreas Ornithoparcus His Micrologus* (1609), and Robert Dowland's *Musicall Banquet* and *Varietie of Lute-Lessons* (both 1610).
Anna of Denmark (1574–1619) Queen of England, Scotland, and Ireland. Wife of James I of England and sister of Christian IV of Denmark. One of England's greatest patrons of the arts during her reign (r. 1603–1619). Dedicatee of Dowland's *Lachrimae* (1604).
Barley, William (c. 1565–1614) English publisher who assumed the royal patent on music publishing in 1606. Issued a book of instrumental pieces in 1596 featuring seven unauthorized arrangements of Dowland works.
Besard, Jean-Baptiste (c. 1567–after 1616) Burgundian lawyer-physician-lutenist who taught and composed for lute. Responsible for two collated volumes of lute music, *Thesaurus Harmonicus* (Cologne, 1603) and *Novus Partus* (1617), which include pieces based on Dowland compositions. Robert Dowland printed a section from the former in English translation in *Varietie of Lute-Lessons* (1610) that addressed basic lute instruction.
Campion, Thomas (1567–1620) English poet, composer, lutenist, physician, and gentleman associated with the Inns of Court. Issued lute song anthologies and a counterpoint treatise. Wrote a commendation for the *First Booke* and included an epigram lauding Dowland in his *Poemata* (1595).
Carey, Elizabeth Spencer (1552–1618) Wife of George Carey, 2nd Baron Hunsdon. Honored in "Lady Hunsdon's Allemande," which is copied and signed in the composer's hand in the *Folger-Dowland Lutebook*.
Carey, George, 2nd Baron Hunsdon (1547–1603) Statesman. Lord Chamberlain for the Royal Household and Captain of the Gentlemen Pensioners (1596–1603). KG 1597. MP for Hampshire. Patron of Shakespeare and the Lord Chamberlain's Men. Dedicatee of Dowland's *First Booke* (1597).
Cecil, Robert, 1st Earl of Salisbury (1563–1612) Privy Councillor (from 1591), Secretary of State (1596–1612) and Lord Privy Seal (1598–1608) under Elizabeth I and James I, and Lord High Treasurer for James (1608–1612). KG 1601. Provided permission for Dowland's travels to the German lands in 1594, and recipient of an important 1595 letter written by Dowland. Dedicatee of Dowland's *Andreas Ornithoparcus His Micrologus* (1609).
Christian IV (1577–1648) King of Denmark and Norway and Duke of Holstein-Schleswig (r. 1588–1648). Built up one of the most spectacular, powerful, and artistic courts in all of Europe. Employed Dowland as "Royal Lutenist" (1598–1606).
Cobham, Henry (1537–1592) Elizabethan stateman. Resident ambassador to France (1579–1583). Dowland was in his employ in Paris at this time.
Croce, Giovanni (1557–1609) Italian composer, known especially for madrigals. Assistant and then *maestro di cappella* at St. Mark's Cathedral in Venice. Dowland met Croce while touring in 1595 and describes him in his *First Booke* as "that great master."

Devereux, Robert, 2nd Earl of Essex (1565–1601) Elizabethan Privy Councillor, poet, and favorite. Married the daughter of Francis Walsingham/widow of Philip Sidney. Led military expeditions against the Spanish Armada, in the Low Countries, and in Ireland. KG 1588. Executed in 1601 for treason after an alleged plot to overthrow Elizabeth I. Dowland asked the earl's permission for German travel in 1594 and named a galliard for Essex that appears as a lute solo in *Varietie of Lute-Lessons* and as a consort arrangement in *Lachrimae*.

Dowland, Robert (c. 1591–1641) English lutenist. Son of John Dowland. Took his father's place in James I's court. Compiler of *A Musicall Banquet* and *Varietie of Lute-Lessons*, which include multiple John Dowland compositions.

East, Thomas (c. 1540–1609) Printer who worked closely with music monopolist William Byrd. Compiled four-part harmonizations by important English composers for a 1592 edition of the *Whole Booke of Psalmes*, including some by Dowland. Printed Dowland's *Second Booke*.

Eastland, George (dates unknown) Publisher of Dowland's *Second Booke*, which resulted in litigation related to printing conventions.

Elizabeth I (1533–1603) Queen of England and Ireland (r. 1558–1603). A galliard is renamed in her honor in *Varietie of Lute-Lessons*.

Hales, Robert (d. 1616) Singer-lutenist. Groom of Privy Chambers for Elizabeth I and Queen Anna. Sang "My golden locks" at Sir Henry Lee's 1590 retirement. Only known composition is included in *A Musicall Banquet*.

Heinrich Julius, Duke of Brunswick-Lüneburg (1564–1613) North German nobleman. Married Elisabeth of Denmark, sister of Christian IV and English Queen Anna. Invited Dowland to his court in 1594.

Holborne, Anthony (c. 1545–1602) English lutenist and composer. Served Robert Cecil and received support from Mary Sidney Herbert, sister of Robert Sidney. His *Cittarn Schoole* was printed in 1597 by Peter Short. Dowland dedicated a song to Holborne in the *Second Booke*.

Holmes, Mathew (d. 1621) Singer and Precentor at Christ Church, Oxford from 1588, and at Westminster Abbey from 1597. Compiled four manuscripts that together contain more Dowland lute compositions than any other source. Also copied Dowland consort arrangements.

Howard, Theophilus, Lord Walden (1584–1640) Jacobean courtier and regular masque participant. Captain of the Gentlemen Pensioners (1626–1635). 2nd Earl of Suffolk after 1626. KG 1627. Dowland patron and dedicatee of *A Pilgrimes Solace*.

Howet, Gregory (c. 1550–c. 1616) Flemish lutenist. Served Heinrich Julius, Duke of Brunswick-Lüneburg. Traveled to Kassel with Dowland in 1594–1595. A Howet fantasia is included in *Varietie of Lute-Lessons*.

James I (1566–1625) King of England and Ireland (r. 1603–1625) and King of Scotland (James VI, r. 1567–1625). Succeeded Elizabeth I to the English throne, uniting England and Scotland. Dowland served James from 1612 until the king died.

Johnson, John (d. 1594) English court lutenist and composer. Appointed as a "musician for the three lutes" in 1579. Father of Robert Johnson. Dowland unsuccessfully petitioned for John Johnson's post upon his death.

Johnson, Robert (c. 1583–1633) Lutenist-composer. Son of John Johnson. Apprenticed in the household of George Carey in 1596. Joined the court of James I in 1604. Also served Princes Henry Frederick and Charles. Provided music for multiple Shakespearan plays and court masques.

Le Roy, Adrian (c. 1520–1598) French lutenist-composer. Partner in the printing firm Ballard and Le Roy, which held the French royal music printing patent. His lute tutorial was issued in two English translations in 1568 and 1574.

Lee, Henry (1533–1611) Elizabethan courtier, statesman, and poet. MP for Buckinghamshire. KG 1597. Served as "Knight of the Crown" at ceremonial tilts (1570–1590). Three Dowland songs with texts attributed to him commemorate his retirement from this honorary position.

Leighton, William (c. 1565–1622) English writer, composer, and politician. Gentleman Pensioner. Sentenced to debtors' prison in 1610, where he wrote the text *Teares and Lamentations* (1613). A year later, he issued a musical version that includes two settings by Dowland.

Lesieur, Stephen (d. c. 1640) Swiss-born English diplomat. Corresponded with Dowland in Denmark.

Marenzio, Luca (c. 1553–1599) Italian singer and composer who produced twenty-four volumes of printed music. Especially known for madrigals. Dowland hoped to meet Marenzio during his Italian travels in 1595.

Monson, Thomas (1565–1641) MP from Lincolnshire, Castle Rising, and Cricklane. Chancellor for Queen Anna, Keeper of the Armories at Greenwich and the Tower. Master Falconer for James I. Made Baronet in 1611. Sponsor of Robert Dowland and dedicatee of *Varietie of Lute-Lessons* (1610).

Moritz (1572–1632), Landgrave of Hesse (r. 1592–1627) North German Lutheran prince who later embraced Calvinism. Sponsored musicians and actors. Dowland visited his court in 1595 and 1596 and was invited to return. A lute pavan by Mortiz is included in *Varietie of Lute-Lessons*. Dowland's music is included in a later lute manuscript belonging to Moritz's daughter, Elisabeth.

Morley, Thomas (1557–1602) Norwich-born English musician-composer known for his embrace of Italian and English madrigals and his theoretical treatise *A Plaine and Easie Introduction to Practicall Musicke* (1597). BMus Oxford 1588. Singer and organist at St. Paul's. Gentleman of the Chapel Royal. Held the royal patent for music prints from 1598.

Noel, Henry (d. 1597) Elizabethan courtier. Gentleman pensioner. Participant in Accession Day tilts. Wrote to Dowland in 1596, summoning the lutenist back to England. Dowland composed *Mr. Henry Noell, his funerall Psalmes*, a set of seven psalm settings that survive only in manuscript.

Orologio, Alessandro (c. 1550–1633) An Italian trumpeter-composer who served the court of Rudolf II in Prague from 1580 through 1613. He met Dowland in Kassel in 1594–1595 and dedicated madrigal and instrumental collections to the Landgrave of Hesse and Christian IV in 1595 and 1597, respectively.

Peacham, Henry (1578–1644) English gentleman writer, poet, and artist. Fetter Lane neighbor and friend of John Dowland. Included references to Dowland in his volumes *Minerva Britanna* (1612), *Thalia's Banquet* (1620), and *The Compleat Gentleman* (1622).

Ravenscroft, Thomas (c. 1590–c. 1635) English theorist and composer. Trained as chorister at St. Paul's. BMus Cambridge. Wrote *A Briefe Discourse*, one of only a few English theoretical treatises of the era. Compiled a set of *Whole Booke of Psalmes* harmonizations in 1621, including one contributed by Dowland.

Rosseter, Philip (1568–1623) English lutenist-composer. Court lutenist for James I from 1604. Associated with Inns of Court entertainments and Jacobean children's theatre. Collaborated with Thomas Campion and served in the King's Lutes with Dowland.

Russell, Elizabeth (1528–1609) Elizabethan-Jacobean patroness. Puritan. Daughter of Anthony Cooke, tutor to Edward VI. Married Thomas Hoby and then John, Lord Russell, son of the 2nd Earl of Bedford. Aunt to Robert Cecil. Entertained Elizabeth I at Bisham Abbey in 1592. Named in a Dowland pavan.

Russell, Lucy Harington, Countess of Bedford (1581–1627) Elizabethan-Jacobean artistic patroness and poet. Performed in Jacobean court masques. Married Edward Russell, 3rd Earl of Bedford. Member of the Sidney-Essex Circle. Queen Anna's Lady of the Bedchamber. Dedicatee of Dowland's *Second Booke*.

Scudamore, John (1567–c. 1635) English priest. Dowland met Scudamore in Florence and obtained from him a letter of recommendation for travel to Rome in July 1595.

Short, Peter (d. 1603) Elizabethan printer and sometime publisher. Printed Dowland's *First Booke*, its first two reprints, and the *Third and Last Booke*.

Sidney, Robert, 1st Earl of Leicester (1563–1626) English statesman. Governor of Flushing. Created Baron of Penshurst and Viscount Lisle. Educated at Christ Church, Oxford. Nephew of Robert Dudley, Earl of Leicester, and of Henry Hastings, Earl of Huntingdon. Brother to Philip Sidney and Mary Sidney Herbert. Father of Lady Mary Wroth, poet and patroness. Lord Chamberlain for Queen Anna from 1603. Godfather of Dowland's son Robert. Named in the title of a Dowland galliard for lute solo in *A Musicall Banquet*, for which he is dedicatee.

Stafford, Edward (1552–1605) Elizabeth I's Ambassador to France (1583–1590), whom Dowland may have served.

Tessier, Charles (b. c. 1550) French lutenist-composer. Presumed son of Guillaume Tessier, who petitioned Henry Cobham for English travel in 1580. Patronized in England in the 1590s by members of the Essex circle, most especially foreign secretary Anthony Bacon. His *Premier livre de chansons et airs de cour* was printed in London in 1597, the same year as Dowland's *First Booke*.

Zouch, John (c. 1564–c. 1639) Knighted at Belvoir Castle 1603. Dedicatee of Dowland's *Third and Last Booke*, where he is addressed as "my honorable good friend." Honored in "Sir John Souch's galliard" in *Lachrimae*.

Notes

Chapter 1

1. *VLL*, D2r; *PS*, A2v. Hans Gerle's lute treatise *Tabulatur auff die Laudten* was released in 1533. Gerle (c. 1500–1570) spent his entire life in Nuremberg, where Dowland wrote an important letter to Robert Cecil in 1595.
2. John Nichols, *The Progresses and Public Processions of Queen Elizabeth* (London: Nichols and Son, 1823), 1:147; "London Plagues 1348–1665" (pdf), www.museumoflondon.org.uk.
3. Thomas Fuller, *The History of the Worthies of England, Who for Parts and Learning have been eminent in the several Counties* (London, 1662), 244.
4. W. H. Grattan Flood, "New Facts about John Dowland," *Gentleman's Magazine* 301 (1906): 287–91.
5. University of Nottingham, Pw V 77; *CL*.
6. *JD*, 22–25.
7. Edward Arber, ed., *A Transcript of the Registers of the Company of Stationers of London, 1554–1640, A.D.* (London: Privately Published, 1875), 1:42; Cecil Hill, "John Dowland: Some New Facts and A Quatercenterary (*sic*) Tribute," *MT* 104, no. 1449 (1963): 785.
8. *LB*, 64–65.
9. David G. T. Harris, "Musical Education in Tudor Times (1485–1603)," *Proceedings of the Musical Association* 65 (1938–1939): 120–25; A. F. Leach, *Educational Charters and Documents* (Cambridge: Cambridge University Press, 1911), 502–5.
10. Edward Doughtie, introduction to *Liber Lilliati: Elizabethan Verse and Song* (Newark: University of Delaware Press, 1985), 25.
11. For example, see Ian Payne, "Instrumental Music at Trinity College, Cambridge, c. 1594–c. 1615: Archival and Biographical Evidence," *ML* 68, no. 2 (1987): 128–40.
12. "An Acte towching dyvers Orders for Artificers Laborers Servantes of Husbandrye and Apprentises," *The Statutes of the Realm* (London: Eyre and Strahan, 1819), 4:414–22, cited in Lynn Hulse, "Music Apprenticeship in Noble Households," in *John Jenkins and His Time: Studies in English Consort Music*, ed. Andrew Ashbee and Peter Holman (Oxford: Clarendon Press, 1996), 76. Also see O. Jocelyn Dunlop, *English Apprenticeship & Child Labor* (New York: Macmillan, 1912), 45–93.
13. Dunlop, *English Apprenticeship*, 69–71.
14. *LB*, 105–6 includes a facsimile of the indenture (NA E 40/12979) and describes many connections between musicians and elite patrons. The most complete biography of Bacheler is found in Anne Batchelor, "Daniel Bacheler: The Right Perfect Musician," *JLS* 28 (1988): 3–12.
15. A facsimile and transcript of the Johnson indenture is provided in *DM*, 88–89. The original indenture is housed at Berkeley Castle, Select Charter 822.
16. Hulse, "Music Apprenticeship," 85.
17. *LB*, 48, 73–76.
18. See Donald Gill, "The Elizabethan Lute," *The Galpin Society Journal* 12 (1959): 60–62.
19. Peter Holman, *Dowland: Lachrimae (1604)* (Oxford: Oxford University Press, 1999), 22–23; Michael Gale, "John Dowland, Celebrity Lute Teacher," *EM* 41, no. 2 (2013): 206; *LB*, 101.
20. John Ward, *Music for Elizabethan Lutes* (Oxford: Clarendon Press, 1992), 1:25; *LB*, 68–69.

Chapter 2

1. *CL*. The Cecil letter is fully transcribed in Appendix A.
2. Sara Warneke, *Images of the Educational Traveller in Early Modern England* (Leiden: Brill, 1995), 4. For a representative primary source related to early English travel recommendations,

see Thomas Palmer, *An Essay of the Meanes how to make our Trauailes, into forraine Countries, the more profitable and honourable* (London, 1606).
3. Jeanice Brooks, *Courtly Song in Late Sixteenth-Century France* (Chicago: University of Chicago Press, 2000), 396–406.
4. *FB*, dedication.
5. For examples see NA SP 78/4A/7; SP 78/6/42; SP 78/6/69.
6. On Cobham, see Gary McClellan Bell, "The Men and Their Rewards in Elizabethan Diplomatic Service, 1558–1585" (PhD Diss., University of California, Los Angeles, 1974); and F. Jeffrey Platt, "Sir Henry Cobham's Embassy to France 1579–1583" (MA Thesis, Brigham Young University, 1968).
7. William A. Shaw, *The Knights of England* (London: Sherratt and Hughes, 1906), 2:76.
8. BL Cotton, Galba E. VI, ff. 1–2.
9. One of these exiles was George Vaux (the second son of Lord Vaux), who was smuggled out of England in 1582. Cobham made note of his arrival in Paris (NA SP 78/8/71). Jessie Childs suggests that Dowland's pieces "Mrs. Vaux's galliard" and "Mrs. Vaux's jig" celebrate George's wife, Eliza (née Roper). Childs, *God's Traitors: Terror and Faith in Elizabethan England* (London: The Bodley Head, 2014), 97. George Vaux's uncle Sir Thomas Tresham was one of four gentlemen knighted alongside Cobham in 1575.
10. NA SP 78/3/54; NA SP 78/11/111. The lease was continued from the previous ambassador, Sir Amias Paulet.
11. Henry W. Meikle, James Craigie, and John Purves, eds., *Nouveau Larousse illustré*. In *The Works of William Fowler: Secretary to Queen Anne, Wife of James VI* (Edinburgh: Blackwood and Sons, 1940), 3:37n25.
12. Described in *DM*, 15.
13. On the academy, see D. P. Walker, "The Aims of Baïf's 'Académie de Poésie et de Musique,'" *Journal of Renaissance and Baroque Music* 1, no. 2 (1946): 91–100; Frances A. Yates, *The French Academies of the Sixteenth Century* (London: Warburg Institute, 1947); Brooks, *Courtly Song*, 293–315.
14. Brooks, *Courtly Song*, 11–12, from which much information on musicians in Henri's court is gathered.
15. Paris, Bibliothèque nationale de France, Fr. 7007 (1575), Dupuy 127 (1580), and Dupuy 489 (1584), as transcribed in Brooks, *Courtly Song*, 396–98, 402–6. Musicians were also employed in the *chappelle* and the stables.
16. Brooks, *Courtly Song*, 77.
17. NA SP 78/8/71. Quoted in David Potter and P. R. Roberts, "An Englishman's View of the Court of Henri III, 1584–1585: Richard Cook's 'Description of the Court of France,'" *French History* 2, no. 3 (1988): 324.
18. FSL MS V.b.41, ff. 117–24. Reproduced in Potter and Roberts, "Englishman's View," 341.
19. NA SP 78/4A/7.
20. Yates, *French Academies of the Sixteenth Century*, 237; Wilfrid Mellers, "Absolute Values," *MT* 142, no. 1874 (2001): 43–44.
21. NA SP 78/6/40. Noted in Yates, *French Academies of the Sixteenth Century*, 239.
22. Balthasar de Beaujoyeulx, *Balet comique de la Royne* (Paris, 1581). On the event, see Yates, *French Academies of the Sixteenth Century*, 236–74; Thomas M. Greene, "The King's One Body in the *Balet Comique de la Royne*," *Yale French Studies* 86 (1994): 75–93; and Edward J. Dent, "Music and Drama," in *The Age of Humanism 1540–1630*, ed. Gerald Abraham (London: Oxford University Press, 1968), 806–11. Also see New York Public Library, Drexel 5995; Anne Daye, "The Role of *Le Balet Comique* in Forging the Stuart Masque: Part 1," *Dance Research: The Journal of the Society for Dance Research* 32, no. 2 (2014): 185–207. A facsimile of Beaujoyeulx's print with commentary is available as *Le balet comique by Balthazar de Beaujoyeulx, 1581: A Facsimile with an Introduction*, ed. Margaret M. McGowan (Binghamton, NY: Center for Medieval and Early Renaissance Studies, 1982), and in translation as *Le Balet Comique de la Royne 1581*, ed. Carol and Lander MacClintock (Rome: American Institute of Musicology, 1971).
23. NA SP 78/4B/153. Quoted in John M. Ward, "Tessier and the 'Essex Circle,'" *Renaissance Quarterly* 29, no. 3 (1976): 379.
24. See Jeanice Brooks, "Tessier's Travels in Scotland and England," *EM* 39, no. 2 (2011): 185–94; Jeremy L. Smith, "The Dilatory Space of *While that the sun*: Byrd, Tessier, and the English Sequence," *Early Music* 40, no. 4 (2012): 672–73.

25. On Charles Tessier, see Gustav Ungerer, "The French Lutenist Charles Tessier and the Essex Circle," *Renaissance Quarterly* 28, no. 2 (1975): 190–203. Ward, "Tessier and the 'Essex Circle,'" questions Ungerer's logic.
26. Brooks, *Courtly Song*, 21–22.
27. Adrian Le Roy, *A Briefe and easye instrution* [sic] *to learne the tableture to conducte and dispose the hande vnto the Lute englished by I. Alford Londenor* (London, 1568). Reissued in 1574 as *A briefe and plaine Instruction to set all Musicke of eight diuers tunes in Tableture for the Lute with a briefe instruction how to play on the Lute by tablature, to conduct and dispose thy hand vnto the Lute, with certaine easie lessons for that purpose. And also a third Booke containing diuers new excellent tunes* (London, 1574).
28. Brooks, *Courtly Song*, 20; Frank Dobbins, "Les Airs pour luth de Charles Tessier, luthiste et compositeur en Angleterre à l'époque de Dowland," in *Luths et luthistes en Occident: Actes du colloque organisé par la Cité de la musique, 13–15 mai 1998* (Paris: Cité de la Musique, 1999), 169–70.
29. CL.
30. Richard Verstegan was known in England as Richard Rowlands. See *The Letters and Despatches of Richard Verstegan 1550–1640*, ed. Anthony G. Petti (London: Catholic Record Society, 1959); and Benjamin Charles Watson, "Recusant Literature" (2003), Gleeson Library Librarians Research, http://repository.usfca.edu/librarian/2.
31. A 1591 Privy Council arrest warrant describes Morgan as an "obstinate and seditious papist." Edward F. Rimbault, ed., *The Old Cheque-Book, or Book of Remembrance, of the Chapel Royal from 1561 to 1744* (London: Camden Society, 1872), 2. See also Andrew Ashbee et al., *A Biographical Dictionary of English Court Musicians 1485–1714* (Aldershot: Ashgate, 1998), 2:806–7.
32. See *JD*, 420–21; Ashbee et al., *Biographical Dictionary*, 2:810–11; W. H. Grattan Flood, "Morgan of the Queen's Chapel," *The Month* 140, no. 697 (122): 67.
33. NA SP 78/12, f. 371. Quoted in *JD*, 27.
34. *Calendar of State Papers, Foreign Series, of the Reign of Elizabeth: Aug. 1584–Aug. 1585* (London: HMSO, 1916), 216.
35. See André Nieuwlaat, "John Dowland in Parijs," *Geluit-Luthinerie Yearbook* (2021): 16. Nieuwlaat suggests Dowland may have returned with Cobham and remained in his employ.
36. NA SP 78/6/47.
37. David Potter, ed., *Foreign Intelligence and Information in Elizabethan England: Two English Treatises on the State of France, 1580–1584* (Cambridge: Cambridge University Press, 2004), 7–8.

Chapter 3

1. Anthony Munday, *A Banquet of Daintie Conceits. Furnished with verie delicate and choyse inuentions, to delight their mindes, who take pleasure in Musique, and there-withall to sing sweete Ditties, either to the Lute, Bandora, Virginalles, or anie other Instrument* (London, 1588), G4v–H1r. Cited in Ashbee et al., *Biographical Dictionary*, 2:354. Among the twenty-two verse sets in Munday's anthology, only Dowland, Johnson, and Munday are specifically named in tune indications.
2. See Keith Wrightson, "Estates, Degrees, and Sorts: Changing Perceptions of Society in Tudor and Stuart England," in *Language, History and Class*, ed. Penelope J. Corfield (Oxford: Oxford University Press, 1991), 30–52; David Cressy, "Describing the Social Order of Elizabethan and Stuart England," *Literature and History* 3 (1976): 29–44; Lawrence Stone, "Social Mobility in England, 1500–1700," *Past and Present* 33 (1966): 15–55.
3. Harris, "Musical Education in Tudor Times," 109–39.
4. A few honorary doctoral music degrees were granted in the fifteenth century. C. F. Abdy Williams, *A Short Historical Account of the Degrees in Music at Oxford and Cambridge with a Chronological List of Graduates in That Faculty from the Year 1463* (London: Novello, 1893), 15–16.
5. Anthony à Wood, *Athenæ Oxonienses. An Exact history of All the Writers and Bishops Who have had their Educaton in The most ancient and famous University of Oxford* (London, 1691), 760; Joseph Foster, *Alumni Oxonienses: The Members of the University of Oxford, 1500–1714* (Oxford: Parker, 1891), 1:418, 3:1034; Williams, *Short Historical Account of the Degrees in Music*, 72–73.

6. Thomas Whythorne, *The Autobiography of Thomas Whythorne*, ed. James M. Osborn (London: Clarendon Press, 1961), 300–303. The original is housed at the Bodleian Library, Oxford, MS. Eng. misc. c. 330.
7. Wood, *Athenæ Oxonienses*, 762; "Mystris Norrishis Delight," Dublin, Marsh's Library, Z.3.2.13, 382; "Sir Robert Sidney's Galliard," *MB*, B1r; "The Earle of Essex Galiard," *LST*, H1v–H2r. Another MA recipient that day was Thomas, Lord Clinton. During his later German travels, Dowland may have known Clinton's father, the Earl of Lincoln.
8. On Lee, see Sue Simpson, *Henry Lee (1533–1611): Elizabethan Courtier* (London: Routledge, 2014).
9. William Segar, *Honor, Military, and Ciuill, contained in foure Bookes* (London, 1602), 197–98.
10. *FB*, I2v–K1r.
11. George Peele, *Polyhymnia Describing, The honourable Triumph at Tylt, before her Maiestie, on the 17. of Nouember, last past, being the first day of the three and thirtith yeare of her Highnesse raigne. With Sir Henrie Lea, his resignation of honour at Tylt, to her Maiestie, and receiued by the right honorable, the Earle of Cumberland* (London, 1590). Segar's version sets the verse in first person: "My golden locks . . . My helmet." Dowland's lyrics match Peele's with a few minor variants. The lyrics also appear in manuscripts BL Add. MS 33963, f. 109, Add. MS. 28635, f. 88v, and Stowe MS 276, f. 2.
12. On the authorship of "His golden locks," see Thomas Clayton, "'Sir Henry Lee's Farewell to the Court': The Texts and Authorship of 'His Golden Locks Time Hath to Silver Turned,'" *English Literary Renaissance* 4, no. 2 (1974): 268–75.
13. Lilliat's miscellany also includes poetry ascribed to the Earl of Essex, Philip Sidney, Walter Raleigh, and Edward Dyer. Oxford, Bodleian Library, Rawlinson MS Poet 148, fol.75v. See Doughtie, *Liber Lilliati*, 77, 165; and Max W. Thomas, "Reading and Writing the Renaissance Commonplace Book: A Question of Authorship?," in *The Construction of Authorship*, ed. Martha Woodmansee and Peter Jaszi (Durham: Duke University Press, 1994), 401–15.
14. Lilliat, f. 20. Quoted in Doughtie, *Liber Lilliati*, 77.
15. *MB*, E2v–F1r.
16. Simpson believes this poem was written for the new Queen Anna, with whom Lee dined in 1603, but the poem consistently adheres to the idea of a goddess/saint in heaven. Simpson, *Sir Henry Lee*, 179.
17. Numerous authors have discussed both the 1590 tilt and the 1592 entertainment, including Winifred Maynard, *Elizabethan Lyric Poetry and Its Music* (Oxford: Clarendon Press, 1986), 67–68, 118–19; *JD*, 237–39; Anthony Rooley, "Time Stands Still: Devices and Designs, Allegory and Alliteration, Poetry and Music and a New Identification in an Old Portrait," *EM* 34, no. 3 (2006): 443–64; Kirsten Gibson, "John Dowland and the Elizabethan Courtier Poets," *EM* 51, no. 2 (2013): 241–42.
18. CUL Dd.2.11, f. 38v. On Lady Russell, see Chapter 4.
19. *Speeches Delivered to Her Majestie This Last Progresse, at the Right Honourable the Lady Rvssels, at Bissam, the Right Honorable the Lorde Chandos at Sudley, at the Right Honorable the Lord Norris, at Ricorte* (Oxford, 1592), B2r.
20. *Speeches Delivered to Her Majestie*, B4r.
21. LMA DL/A/D/002/MS10091/011, f. 34.
22. CL.
23. Detailed in Chapter 10.
24. *MB*, A2r.
25. CL. Unless otherwise noted, subsequent quotations in this chapter are excerpted from this same source.
26. See Katherine Duncan-Jones, *Philip Sidney: Courtier Poet* (London: Hamilton, 1991), 124–27, 215–19. On musical connections between Sidney and Campion, see Jeremy L. Smith, *Verse & Voice in Byrd's Song Collections of 1588 and 1589* (Woodbridge, UK: Boydell, 2016), 125–33.
27. Charles Edward Mallet, *A History of the University of Oxford* (New York: Barnes and Noble, 1924), 2:104. The oath swore allegiance to the monarch as supreme governor and spiritual leader.
28. On Dowland's psalm settings, see Chapter 7.
29. John Ward places Johnson's death on 21 June 1594. *DM*, 107.
30. Tessa Murray, *Thomas Morley: Elizabethan Music Publisher* (Woodbridge, UK: Boydell Press, 2014), 16–20.
31. Rimbault, *Old Cheque-Book*, 4–5.

32. Walter Woodfill, *Musicians in English Society from Elizabeth to Charles I* (New York: Da Capo Press, 1969), 243.
33. *DM*, 107–12.
34. *LB*, 103.
35. John Case, *Apologia Musices Tam Vocalis Quam Instrumentalis et Mixtæ* (Oxford, 1588), 44; John Johnson, *Collected Lute Music*, ed. John W. J. Burgers (Lübeck: Tree, 2001), 1:263–65; FSL MS. V.b.280. On the Folger-Dowland lute manuscript, see Chapter 4.

Chapter 4

1. For examples of Dowland's lute solos in modern notation, see *CLM*.
2. CUL Dd.5.78.3, 43v–44r. See Levi Sheptovitsky, "Mastery of Sorrow and Melancholy: Expressivity in Two Chromatic Fantasias by John Dowland," *LN* (April 2007): 20–32.
3. CUL Dd.9.33, 16v–17r.
4. CUL Dd.9.33, 67v–68r. A shorter intabulation is available in New Haven, Yale University Music Library, Music Deposit 1, 17r. Versions are also found in several later Continental manuscripts, including the Königsberg manuscript housed at the Central Library of the Lithuanian Academy of Science. Full transcription in *CLM*, 204–8. Also see James Meadors, "Dowland's 'Walsingham,'" *JLSA* 14 (1981): 59–68.
5. John M. Ward, "Apropos *The British Broadside Ballad and Its Music*," *Journal of the American Musicological Society* 20, no. 1 (1967): 79–83.
6. CUL Dd.9.33, ff. 67v–68r.
7. See Alan Brown, "Pavan" and "Galliard," in *Grove Music Online*, http://www.oxfordmusiconline.com.
8. Thoinot Arbeau, *Orchesography*, ed. Mary Stewart Evans (New York: Dover, 1967), 59.
9. Arbeau, *Orchesography*, 78.
10. Lambeth Palace Library, Talbot Papers, *olim* MS.3201, f. 67. Quoted in Edmund Lodge, ed., *Illustrations: British History, Biography and Manners, in the Reigns of Henry VIII, Edward VI, Mary, Elizabeth, and James I* (London, 1791), 2:411.
11. André Hurault, *A Journal of All That Was Accomplished by Monsieur de Maisse Ambassador in England from Henry IV to Queen Elizabeth, Anno Domini, 1597*, ed. G. B. Harrison (Bloomsbury: Nonesuch, 1931), 95; Martin A. S. Hume, ed., *Calendar of Letters and State Papers Relating to English Affairs Preserved in, or Originally Belonging to, the Archives of Simancas* (London: Eyre and Spottiswoode, 1899), 4:650.
12. *VLL*, M1v.
13. CUL Dd.2.11, 59r; CUL Dd.5.20, 5v (bass viol); Dd.5.21, 6r (recorder); Dd.14.24, 20r (cittern).
14. CUL Dd.2.11, f. 62; London, Royal Academy of Music MS 603, f. 24r.
15. *PS*, M2v; BL Royal Music 23.l.4, 7v–8v; BL Sloane MS 1021, 44v–45r; CUL Dd.2.11, 82v; Dd. 5.78.3, 37r.
16. CUL Dd.5.78.3, 35v–36r.
17. For an in-depth probe of the dance, see Ian Payne, *The Almain in Britain, c. 1549–c. 1675* (London: Routledge, 2017).
18. Arbeau, *Orchesography*, 125.
19. Le Roy, *A Briefe and easye instrution* [sic], E3v–4r, G4v–H1r, H2v–3r, I2v–3r.
20. Anthony Rooley, "John Dowland and English Lute Music," *EM* 3, no. 2 (1975): 118.
21. Robert Spencer, "Dowland's Dance Songs: Those of his Compositions which Exist in Two Versions, Songs and Instrumental Dances," in *Le concert des voix et des instruments a la Renaissance: Actes du XXXIVe Colloque International d'Etudes Humanistes, Tours, Centre d'Etudes Supérieures de la Renaissance, 1–11 juillet 1991: Arts du spectacle*, ed. Jean-Michel Vaccaro (Paris: CNRS, 1995), 587–99.
22. See Christopher Goodwin, "Some Recent Dowland Discoveries," *LN* 68 (December 2003): 17–18.
23. London, Royal Academy of Music Library, MS 603; BL Egerton MS 2046; Kassel, Landesbibliothek und Murhardsche Bibliothek der Stadt Kassel, MS 4° mus. 108.1.
24. CUL Dd.5.78.3, 43v–44r; FSL Ms. V.b.280, 9v, 11v, 12v, 13v–14r, 16r, 22v–23v.
25. CUL Dd.2.11, Dd.5.78.3, Dd.9.33, and Nn.6.36. On the Holmes lutebooks, see Ian Harwood, "The Origins of the Cambridge Lute Manuscripts," *LSJ* 5 (1963): 32–48; Lyle Nordstrom, "The

Cambridge Consort Books," *JLSA* 5 (1972): 70–103; *LB*, 117–24. Holmes also copied a set of partbooks about the same time for mixed consort that also contain the works of Dowland (CUL Dd.3.18, Dd.5.20, Dd.5.21, Dd.14.24).
26. On differing views related to Holmes's motivations for collecting, see Julia Craig-McFeely, "Elizabethan and Jacobean Lute Manuscripts: Types, Characteristics and Compilation," *Études Anglaises* 73, no. 3 (2020): 375; and *LB*, 117.
27. Case, *Apologia Musices*. Case's treatise was dedicated to Sirs Henry Unton and William Hatton, both Oxford men. Dowland included a piece titled "Sir Henry Umpton's Funeral" in his consort collection *Lachrimae* (1604).
28. Harwood, "Origins of the Cambridge Lute Manuscripts," 3–6, 10–12.
29. Dowland also composed an almain for "Mrs. Clifton," found both in Holmes's third lute book and the Folger-Dowland manuscript and dated to the time after she was married in 1591 but before her husband gained his noble title in 1608. CUL Dd.9.33, f. 28v; FSL MS V.b.280, f. 23v.
30. Thomas Hoby was translator of the first English edition of Castiglione's *Book of the Courtier*, a tome that no doubt raised the value of lute playing. Bisham Abbey was the site of a very elaborate drama welcoming Queen Elizabeth on her 1592 progress. For estate descriptions, see Katherine Butler, "'By Instruments her Powers Appeare': Music and Authority in the Reign of Queen Elizabeth I," *Renaissance Quarterly* 65, no. 2 (2012): 369–71; and Bruce R. Smith, "Landscape with Figures: The Three Realms of Queen Elizabeth's Country-House Revels," *Renaissance Drama* ns 8 (1977): 67–68.
31. CUL Dd.5.78.3, ff. 43v–44r; *LB*, 122; *CLM*, 291.
32. Mistress White has not been identified, due to a lack of first name and the large number of people with the surname.
33. FSL MS. V.b.280. See John M. Ward, "The So-Called 'Dowland Lute Book' in the Folger Shakespeare Library," *JLSA* 9 (1976): 5–29; Gale, "John Dowland, Celebrity Lute Teacher," 205–18.
34. Julia Craig-McFeely, *English Lute Manuscripts and Scribes 1530–1630* (2000), http://www.ramesescats.co.uk/thesis/; Craig-McFeely, "Elizabethan and Jacobean Lute Manuscripts," 369–81; *LB*, 112.
35. Ward, "So-called 'Dowland Lute Book,'" 16–17.
36. Gale, "John Dowland, Celebrity Lute Teacher," 216.
37. Craig-McFeely, Appendix 5 in "English Lute Manuscripts and Scribes 1530–1630," https://www.ramesescats.co.uk/thesis/.
38. *LB*, 138.

Chapter 5

1. See *LB*, 102–4.
2. CL.
3. *FB*, note to the reader.
4. CL.
5. Wolfenbüttel, Niedersächsisches Landesarchiv, 17 III Alt, No. 64b, KR 7/1594–7/1595, f. 94v. Quoted in *NI*, 254.
6. Wolfgang Milde, "The Library at Wolfenbüttel, from 1550 to 1618," *The Modern Language Review* 66, no. 1 (1971): 110–11.
7. Eleven plays are recognized, but only ten were printed.
8. On the musical court of Duke Heinrich Julius, see *NI*. On the English comedians who performed throughout the German lands, including the duke's acting troupe, see George Oppitz-Trotman, *Stages of Loss: The English Comedians and Their Receptions* (Oxford: Oxford University Press, 2020).
9. Werner Flechsig, *Thomas Mancinus: Der Vorgänger von Praetorius im Wolfenbütteler Kapellmeisteramt mit neuen Beiträgen zur Geschichte der Wolfenbütteler Hofkapelle im 16. Jahrhundert* (Wolfenbüttel & Berlin: Georg Kallmeyer, 1933), 30. Cited in David Lasocki, "A Listing of Inventories and Purchases of Flutes, Recorders, Flageolets, and Tabor Pipes, 1388–1630," https://scholarworks.iu.edu/dspace/bitstream/handle/2022/323/utrecht.inventories.to1630.htm.
10. Michael Praetorius, *Terpsichore, Musarum Aoniarum* (Wolfenbüttel, 1613), nr. 157 "Courante" and nr. 300 "Galliarde."

11. The most comprehensive biography and works exploration of Howet is Godelieve Spiessens, "De Antwerpse luitcomponist Gregorius Huet alias Gregory Howet (Huy of Antwerpen, vóór 1560—Wolfenbüttel?, ca 1617)," *Revue belge de Musicologie/Belgisch Tijdschrift voor Muziekwetenschap* 57 (2003): 87–111. Also see *DM*, 94–96; and *NI*, 19–27, 211–44.
12. *NI*, 250–52.
13. BL Sloane 1021, f. 24. Noted in *NI*, 260; Spiessens, "Antwerpse luitcomponist Gregorius Huet," 101; and *JD*, 320.
14. *VLL*, G2r–v.
15. Adrian Denss, "Fantasia alia eiusdem," *Florilegivm omnes fere generis cantionvm svavissimarvm ad testvdinis tabvlatvram accomodatarvm, longe ivcvn. dissimvm.* (Cologne, 1594), R4v–S1r. Noted in *NI*, 268.
16. Spiessens, "Antwerpse luitcomponist Gregorius Huet," 100–102.
17. Wolfenbüttel, Niedersächsisches Landesarchiv, 17 III Alt, Nr. 64b, KR 7/1594–7/1595, f. 94v. Quoted in *NI*, 259. Wirth also notes a Wolfenbüttel payment to English musicians in January on f. 143v but contends they could have been made to any of the duke's actor-musicians.
18. The letter's author links the lutenists with the English acting troupe. Richard P. Wülcker, "Englische Schauspieler in Kassel," *Jahrbuch der deutscher Shakespeare-Gesellschaft* 14 (1879): 361.
19. Staatsarchiv Marburg, 4b, pack 46, No. 2. See Eckart Klessmann, "Die Deutschlandreisen John Dowlands," *Musica* 11 (1957): 13–15; and *JD*, 33–34.
20. Spiessens, "Antwerpse luitcomponist Gregorius Huet," 93.
21. CL.
22. Henry Peacham, *The Compleat Gentleman Fashioning him absolute in the most Necessary & Commendable Qualities concerning Minde or Bodie that may be required in a Noble Gentleman* (London, 1622), 99.
23. Among others, see Oppitz-Trotman, *Stages of Loss*, 125–26. Heinrich Julius was also a distant cousin of Elizabeth I, brother-in-law to James I and wife Anna, and brother-in-law to Christian IV.
24. *NI*, 257.
25. Claudia Knispel, "The International Character of Lute Music at the Court of Moritz, Landgrave of Hesse," *JLS* 36 (1996): 1.
26. See Richard Charteris, "English Music in the Library of Moritz, Landgrave of Hessen-Kassel, in 1613," *Chelys* 15 (1986): 33–37.
27. *VLL*, H2v; Kassel, Landesbibliothek und Murhardsche Bibliothek der Kassel, MS 4° mus. 108.1.
28. Christoph von Rommel, *Neuere Geschichte von Hessen* (Kassel: Perthes, 1837), 2:393; Horst Nieder, "The Kassel Baptism of 1596: Festivals and Politics at the Court of Landgrave Moritz of Hessen-Kassel," *Daphnis* 32 (2003): 120; *NI*, 259.
29. For examples, see Nieder, "Kassel Baptism of 1596"; Mara R. Wade, "Georg Engelhard von Loehneyss' *Della Cavalleria* (1609; 1624) and His Hamburg Tournament Pageant for King Christian IV of Denmark (1603)," *Daphnis* 32 (2003): 165–97.
30. Staatsarchiv Marburg 4b, no. 697. Quoted in Klessmann, "Deutschlandreisen John Dowlands," 13–14; and *JD*, 34.
31. *NI*, 260.
32. Staatsarchiv Marburg 4b, no. 697. An alternate translation is provided in *JD*, 34.
33. *FB*, note to reader.
34. FSL V.a.321, f. 53r.
35. Spiessens, "Antwerpse luitcomponist Gregorius Huet," 94.
36. FSL V.a.321, f. 22v, available at https://luna.folger.edu. Facsimile and transcription in A. R. Braunmuller, *A Seventeenth-Century Letterbook* (Newark: University of Delaware Press, 1983), 140–41.

Chapter 6

1. Thomas Coryat, *Coryats Crudities Hastily gobled vp in five Moneths trauells in France, Sauoy, Italy, Rhetia comonly called the Grisons country, Heluetia aliàs Switzerland, some parts of high Germany, and the Netherlands; Newly digested in the hungry aire of Odcombe in the County*

of Somerset, & now dispersed to the nourishment of the trauelling Members of this Kingdome (London, 1611).
2. Curtis Price, "Music, Style, and Society," in *The Early Baroque Era: From the Late 16th Century to the 1660s*, ed. Curtis Price (Englewood Cliffs, NJ: Prentice Hall, 1993), 4–5.
3. *JD*, 36.
4. Jeffrey Kurtzman, "Instruments, Instrument Makers, and Instrumentalists in the Second Half of the Sixteenth Century," in *A Companion to Music in Sixteenth-Century Venice*, ed. Katelijne Schiltz (Leiden: Brill, 2018), 292–320; Stefano Pio, *Viol and Lute Makers of Venice 1490–1630* (Venice: Venice Research, 2011); Klaus Wachsmann, James W. McKinnon, et al., "Lute," in *Grove Music Online*, https://www.oxfordmusiconline.com.
5. Henry Peacham, *Thalia's Banquet Furnished with an Hundred and Odde Dishes of Newly Deuised Epigrammes, Whereunto (Beside Many Worthy Friends) are Inuited all that Loue in Offensiue Mirth, and the Muses* (London, 1620), C8v.
6. Warneke, *Images of the Educational Traveller*, 3.
7. In Italy, only Naples was larger, reaching almost the population of Paris, which exceeded 200,000. While Venice lost population in the 1580s, London grew from approximately 115,000 to 185,000 residents between 1575 and 1600. Chandler Tertius, *Four Thousand Years of Urban Growth: An Historical Census* (Lewiston, NY: Edwin Mellen Press, 1987), 123, 188.
8. John Florio, *Florio His firste Fruites which yeelde familiar speech, merie Prouerbes, wittie Sentences, and golden sayings. Also a perfect Induction to the Italian, and English tongues, as in the Table appeareth. The like heretofore, neuer by any man published* (London, 1578), B3v. The same author's 1598 Italian-English dictionary has many entries associated with music and the lute. Florio was patronized by *Second Booke* dedicatee, the Countess of Bedford.
9. Coryat, *Coryats Crudities*, 158.
10. Jonathan Glixon, "Music at Parish, Monastic, and Nunnery Churches and at Confraternities," in *A Companion to Music in Sixteenth-Century Venice*, ed. Schiltz, 45.
11. John Izon, "Italian Musicians at the Tudor Court," *The Musical Quarterly* 44, no. 3 (1958): 334.
12. Denis Arnold, "Croce, Giovanni," in *Grove Music Online*, http://www.oxfordmusiconline.com. Some of these madrigals appeared in London with translated English words in the second *Musica Transalpina* (1597), including "Ove tra l'herb' ei fiori'" from *Trionfo di Dori* (1592), newly appearing as "Hard by a crystal fountain." This piece served as the inspiration for Thomas Morley's later *The Triumphes of Oriana* (1601), ending with these words: "Poi concordi seguir Ninfe e Pastori, Viva la bella Dori" (adapted as the final couplet in each *Triumphes* inclusion as "Then sang the shepherds and nymphs of Diana, Long live fair Oriana"). See Joseph Kerman, "Morley and 'The Triumphes of Oriana,'" *ML* 34, no. 3 (1593): 186–87. Dowland wrote a lute song with similar lyrics to the Croce text titled "By a fountain where I lay," published in the *Third Booke* (1603).
13. Peacham, *Compleat Gentleman*, 102.
14. On music at the Venetian confraternities, see Jonathan Glixon, *Honoring God and the City: Music at the Venetian Confraternities, 1260–1807* (Oxford: Oxford University Press, 2003), and Glixon, "Music at Parish, Monastic, and Nunnery Churches," 45–78.
15. Ellen Rosand, "Venice, 1580–1680," in *Early Baroque Era*, ed. Price, 84.
16. A theorbo is a lute with a longer neck and extended range. On San Rocco, see Coryat, *Coryats Crudities*, 251–53. Quoted in part in Rosand, "Venice, 1580–1680," 83; Glixon, *Honoring God and the City*, 157–58; Tim Carter, "The North Italian Courts," in *Early Baroque Era*, ed, Price, 42; and Bruce Smith, "Sounding Shakespeare's London: The Noisy Politics of Ceremonial Entries," in *Hearing the City in Early Modern Europe*, ed. Tess Knighton and Ascensión Manzuela-Anguita (Turnhout: Brepols, 2018), 103.
17. Jane A. Bernstein, *Print Culture and Music in Sixteenth-Century Venice* (New York: Oxford University Press, 2001), 9–27.
18. Brooks, *Courtly Song*, 263–64.
19. See Silvano Cavazza, "Praga e le Corti Tedesche all'Epoca di Alessandro Orologio," in *Alessandro Orologio (1551–1633) musico frivulano e il suo tempo: Atti del convegno internazionale di studi, Pordenone, Udine, S. Giorgio della Richinvelda, 15–17 ottobre 2004*, ed. Franco Colussi (Udine: Pizzicato, 2008), 52–54; and Franco Colussi, introduction to *Alessandro Orologio, Canzonette a Trè Voci* (Udine: Pizzacato, 1992), 4–12.
20. See Cynthia Klestinec, "A History of Anatomy Theatres in Sixteenth-Century Padua," *Journal of the History of Medicine and Allied Sciences* 59, no. 3 (2004): 375–412; and Klestinec, "Civility,

Comportment, and the Anatomy Theater: Girolamo Fabrici and His Medical Students in Renaissance Padua," *Renaissance Quarterly* 60, no. 2 (2007): 434–63.
21. Klestinec, "A History of Anatomy Theatres," 400, 407–8.
22. See Lorenzo Bianconi and Glenn Watkins, "Gesualdo, Carlo, Prince of Venosa, Count of Conza," in *Grove Music Online*, http://www.oxfordmusiconline.com.
23. Intriguingly, Cardinal Luigi d'Este, patron of Marenzio, was brother of Duke Alfonso of Ferrara. Dowland may have sought a connection to Marenzio while there.
24. See Anne Schnoebelen, "Bologna, 1580–1700," in *The Early Baroque Era*, ed. Price, 103.
25. CL. All uncited quotations following in this chapter are taken from the same source.
26. Thurston Dart, "Simone Molinaro's Lute-Book of 1599," *ML* 28, no. 3 (1947): 258–61. Gostena died in 1593.
27. "Dovrò dunque morire" and "Amarilli, mia bella," first published in *Le nuove musiche* (1601), *MB*, K2v–L2r.
28. Dowland received travel letters from John Scudamore to Nicholas Fitzherbert dated 7 July, for which he had waited more than a month.
29. John Walter Hill, "Florence: Musical Spectacle and Drama, 1570–1650," in *Early Baroque Era*, ed. Price, 121.
30. See Tim Carter, "Listening to Music in Early Modern Italy," in *Hearing the City in Early Modern Europe*, ed. Knighton and Manzuela-Anguita, 27–28.
31. Hill, "Florence," 130–35.
32. "And from thence [Venice] to Florence, where I played before the Duke and got great favors," CL.
33. *JD*, 36.
34. Dates based on correspondence written by Ferdinando and included in Florence, Archivio di Stato, *Mediceo del Principato*, vol. 289. In March and April, the duke was at times in Florence, and other times in Livorno, which is some eighty miles southwest, on the coast.
35. *FB*, f. A1r. Translated from Italian.
36. Florence, Archivio di Stato, *Mediceo del Principato*, vol. 289, f. 108.
37. Some previous scholarship has misidentified the priest as John Scudamore of Kentchurch, also in Herefordshire, rather than the one from Holme Lacy. The priest John was the son of Sir John Scudamore's first wife, Eleanor. Sir John was knighted in 1592, and he and his second wife, neé Mary Shelton, were valued members of Elizabeth's court, Mary serving in the queen's Privy Chamber for many years. See W. J. Tighe, "Courtiers and Politics in Elizabethan Herefordshire: Sir James Croft, His Friends and His Foes," *Historical Journal* 32, no. 2 (1989): 257–79; "Scudamore, John (c.1542–1623), of Holme Lacy, Herefs.," in *History of Parliament Online*, http://www.histparl.ac.uk/volume/1558-1603/member/scudamore-john-1542-1623; Warren Skidmore, "Holme Lacy, Herefordshire," in *Dore Abbey and John, Viscount Scudamore*, 8–10; and "Lady Mary Scudamore (c.1550–1603), Courtier," *Occasional Papers* 29, 1–25, http://www.skidmorefamilyhistory.com.
38. Tighe, "Courtiers and Politics," 264.
39. "He came but the day before to Florence, and I think they came all together," CL.
40. Scudamore returned to England in 1606, renounced his Catholicism, and was granted a pardon.
41. There is little information on Lord Grey prior to 1597. The only other English peer at the time with the surname Grey was Henry Grey, sixth Earl of Kent. Correspondence places him in England in the summer of 1595, handling affairs related to troops being sent to Ireland. Patrick, Lord Gray of Scotland spent a number of years in Italy, but returned to Scotland before 1595.
42. See J. J. N. McGurk, "Bodley, Sir Josias (c. 1550–1617), soldier and military engineer," in *Oxford Dictionary of National Biography*, https://www.oxforddnb.com.

Chapter 7

1. There is some irony in Cecil and the Privy Council's obsession with Spain's unrealized intent to invade England proper, as it was Spain's incursion into the German lands that ultimately affected Dowland's German host Moritz. In 1599 the landgrave led troops against forces invading the Lower Rhine District. Holger Th. Gräf, "Die Mauritianische Aussenpolitik 1592–1627," in *Moritz der Gelehrte: Ein Renaissancefürst in Europa*, ed. Heiner Borggrefe, Vera Lüpkes, and Hans Ottomeyer (Eurasburg: Edition Minerva, 1997), 102.

2. Knispel, "International Character of the Lute Music at the Court of Moritz," 1.
3. Edward Monings, *The Landgraue of Hessen his princelie receiuing of her Maiesties Embassador* (London, 1596), 21.
4. Ungerer, "French Lutenist Charles Tessier," 121.
5. Willem Schrickx, *The Foreign Envoys and Travelling Players in the Age of Shakespeare and Jonson* (Wetteren: Universa, 1986), 122–23. Original letter housed at Staatsarchiv Marburg, Bestand 4b 234. Browne was previously associated with the Wolfenbüttel troupe and traveled earlier with the Earl of Leicester. June Schlueter, "English Actors in Kassel, Germany, during Shakespeare's Time," *Medieval and Renaissance Drama in England* 10 (1998): 244–45.
6. Schlueter, "English Actors," 238–39.
7. See June Schlueter, "Celebrating Elizabeth's German Godchild: The Documentary Evidence," *Medieval and Renaissance Drama in England* 13 (2001): 57–81.
8. Elise Kruse, "'A Network of Honor and Obligation': Elizabeth as Godmother," in *Queens Matter in Early Modern Studies,* ed. Anna Riehl Bertolet (Cham, Switzerland: Palgrave Macmillan, 2018), 188. Also see Carole Levin, "All the Queen's Children: Elizabeth I and the Meanings of Motherhood," *Explorations in Renaissance Culture* 30, no. 1 (2004): 57–76.
9. Monings, *Landgraue of Hessen,* 2–13. Also documented by court historian Wilhelm Dilich in *Historische Breschreibung der Fürstlichen Kindtauff Fräwlein Elisabethen zu Hessen u. Welche im Augusto des 1596. Jahrs zu Cassel gehalten worden* (Kassel, 1598).
10. Some scholars have suggested that George Carey, newly Baron Hunsdon and soon to be Lord Chamberlain, was part of the group, but there is no evidence to support this claim. On 21 July, his father attested to him on his deathbed, so he was in England then. An internment and funeral took place at Westminster Abbey on 12 August. On 1 November, Carey took his father's position as Captain of the Gentlemen Pensioners.
11. Kassel, Landesbibliothek und Murhardsche Bibliothek, MS 4º mus. 108.1, ff. 64v–65r. See Claudia Knispel, "Die Intavolierungen der Dowlandschen Ayre 'Come Again' im Lautenbuch der Elisabeth von Hessen," *Concerto: Das Magazin für alte Musik* 6 (1989): 9–13.
12. Knispel, "International Character of the Lute Music at the Court of Moritz," 7.
13. Fourteen concordances of music by various composers are found between the Montbuysson manuscript and *Thesaurus Harmonicus* (1603) by Jean-Baptiste Besard, who visited Kassel in 1597, although the two Dowland concordances, based on "Lachrimae" and "Piper's Galliard" do not match. In the Kassel manuscript volume, "Pavana Dullande" (f. 92v) and "Galliarda Dullande" (ff. 94v–95r) look to be copied from Georg Leopold Fuhrmann's *Testudo Gallo-Germanica* (Nuremberg, 1615). Other Dowland pieces were copied by Georg Schimmelpfenning, including "Lachrimae" (f. 5r–v), "Can she excuse" (f. 2v), and one of the versions of "Come again," with an added Italian text (f. 32v). Knispel, "International Character of the Lute Music at the Court of Moritz," 10–11.
14. Samuel Robert Scargill-Bird, ed., *Calendar of the Manuscripts of the Most Hon. the Marquis of Salisbury* (London: HMSO, 1889), 3:424.
15. Mathew Lyons, "The gains doth seldom quit the charge: Henry Noel at the Court of Elizabeth I," blog accessed 18 March 2021, https://mathewlyons.co.uk/2011/10/11/the-gains-doth-seldom-quit-the-charge-henry-noel-at-the-court-of-elizabeth-i/.
16. Fuller, *History of the Worthies of England,* 137. Seems to be derived from William Burton, *The Description of Leicestershire* (London, 1622).
17. FSL V.a.321, ff. 52v–53r. The letter is marked 1 December, with no year specified. The year 1596 best suits Dowland's timeline. This letter and the one from Moritz were copied into a seventeenth-century letterbook by an uncertain collector. The manuscript may have belonged to dramatist George Chapman, who has a number of letters included. See Bertram Dobell, "Newly Discovered Documents of the Elizabethan and Jacobean Periods," *The Athenaeum* 3830 (1901): 369–70. On Noel, see David Greer, "'. . . Thou Court's Delight': Biographical Notes on Henry Noel," *LSJ* 17 (1975): 49–59; and *The History of Parliament: The House of Commons 1558–1603,* ed. P.W. Hasler (1981), https://www.historyofparliamentonline.org/volume/1558-1603/member/noel-henry-1597.
18. FSL V.a.321, f. 53r.
19. *VLL,* H2v.
20. Henry Peacham, *Minerua Britanna Or A Garden of Heroical Deuises, furnished, and adorned with Emblemes and Impresa's of sundry natures, Newly devised, moralized, and published* (London, 1612), 101. Quoted in Knispel, "International Character of the Lute Music at the Court of Moritz," 3.
21. FSL V.a.321, f. 53r. Copied in the same letterbook as the Noel correspondence.

22. "Here likewise buried ... Henry Noel, one of the Gentlemen Pensioners to Queen Elizabeth, who died on the twenty-sixth of February, anno [1597], both without any monuments or gravestones." H. K[eepe], *Monumenta Westmonasteriensia* (London, 1682), 172.
23. On the *Whole Booke of Psalmes*, see Beth Quitslund, *The Reformation in Rhyme: Sternhold, Hopkins, and the English Metrical Psalter, 1547–1603* (Aldershot: Ashgate, 2008), 193–273; and Samantha Arten, "'To be songe to the tune of [the] 25th psalme': Adapting *The Whole Booke of Psalmes* for Personal Devotion and Communal Singing," *Reformation* 27, no. 1 (2022): 65–84. Modern Edition: *The Whole Book of Psalms*, 2 vols., ed. Beth Quitslund and Nicholas Temperley (Tempe: Arizona Center for Renaissance and Medieval Studies, 2018).
24. *The Whole Booke of Psalmes with their Wonted Tunes, as they are song in Churches, composed into foure parts* (London, Thomas East, 1592). East's was not the first multi-voice version, but was the first that offered all voices in a single volume rather than as partbooks. Patent credit is assigned to Byrd, rather than Day.
25. See *JD*, 323–31.
26. *Whole Booke of Psalmes* (East, 1592), 84–87; *JD*, 325.
27. In addition to Psalm 38, Dowland's harmonization is also used for Psalms 47, 51, 53, 56, 60, 64, 71, 75, 80, 85, 86, 95, 98, 101, 106, 109, 114, 118, and "A Thanksgiving" prayer. In subsequent editions, it is added for Psalms 2, 10, 13, 17, 20, 26, 28, 32, 35, 38, 84, 138, and 142.
28. *Whole Booke of Psalmes* (East, 1592), 184–85.
29. *Foure score and seuen Psalmes of Dauid in Englishe mitre* (Geneva, 1560; London 1561).
30. New Haven, Yale University Music Library, Osborn fb7, f. 95r, c. 1600–1630.
31. Nicholas Temperley, "The Old Way of Singing," *MT* 120, no. 1641 (1979): 945.
32. Thomas Ravenscroft, *The Whole Booke of Psalmes: With the Hymnes Euangelicall, And Songs Spirituall. Composed into 4. parts by sundry Authors, to such seuerall Tunes, as haue beene, and are vsually sung in England, Scotland, Wales, Germany, Italy, France, and the Nether-Lands: Neuer as yet before in one volumne published* (London, 1621), A4r. On Ravenscroft's other sacred music, see Ian Payne, "The Sacred Music of Thomas Ravenscroft," *EM* 10, no. 3 (1982): 309–15.
33. *Whole Booke of Psalmes* (East, 1592), V2v–3r. The same tune is used for the tenor melody in a unique setting by John Farmer for Psalm 146.
34. University of Nottingham, Pw V 77–80. Noel also received musical tributes in printed songbooks by Thomas Morley ("Hark! Alleluia," *Canzonets or Litle Short Aers*, London, 1597) and Thomas Weelkes ("Noel, adieu thou court's delight," *Madrigals of 5. and 6. parts*, London, 1600). See K. Dawn Grapes, *With Mornefull Musique: Funeral Elegies in Early Modern England* (Woodbridge, UK: Boydell Press, 2018), 61–80.
35. Church of England, *The booke of Common prayer, and administration of the Sacraments, and other Rites and Ceremonies in the Church of England* (London, 1581), f. P7v.
36. Two four-part psalms in a nineteenth-century manuscript attribute harmonizations of Psalms 33 and 100 to Dowland, but no concordances of these settings contemporaneous to Dowland survive. St. Michael's, Tenbury, MS 722, ff. 34v–35. Noted in *JD*, 336.
37. Ravenscroft, *Whole Booke of Psalmes*, A4r–v.
38. See William Byrd, *Songs of Sundrie Natures (1589)*, ed. David Mateer (London: Stainer & Bell, 2004).
39. Orlando Lassus, *Psalmi Davidis poenitentiales* (Munich, 1584); Andrea Gabrieli, *Psalmi Davidici, qui Poenitentiales nuncupantur* (Venice, 1583).
40. Giovanni Croce, *Li sette sonetti penitentiali a 6* (Venice, 1596); *Septem psalmi pœnitentiales sex vocum* (Nuremburg, 1599); *Musica Sacra* (London, 1608). Croce omits the sixth penitential psalm, splitting the fifth into two parts. The chronological and geographical placement of these three editions approximate Dowland's own travel timeline.
41. Peacham, *Compleat Gentleman*, 102.
42. The penitential psalms were still used within many contexts related to death by Englanders of all faiths.
43. Dowland's setting of Psalm 143 includes two verses rather than one.
44. Detailed in Lynn Hulse, "Hardwick MS 29: A New Source for Jacobean Lutenists," *JLS* 26, no. 2 (1986): 64. Also see Keith Green, "Arbella, Oriana, and the Music of Michael Cavendish (1565–1628)," in *A Companion to the Cavendishes*, ed. Lisa Hopkins and Tom Rutter (Leeds: Arc Humanities Press, 2020), 35–47.
45. Lynn Hulse, "Apollo's Whirligig: William Cavendish, Duke of Newcastle and his Music Collection," *The Seventeenth Century* 9, no. 2 (1994): 219–21. Some scholars have suggested that the elder Cavendish was the anonymous translator of Nicholas Yonge's 1588 *Musica Transalpina*.

Chapter 8

1. William Byrd, *Psalmes, Sonets, & songes* (London, 1588); Nicholas Yonge, *Musica Transalpina* (London, 1588); William Byrd, *Songes of sundrie natures* (London, 1589); Thomas Watson, *The first sett, Of Italian Madrigalls Englished* (London, 1590); *Whole Booke of Psalmes* (East, 1592).
2. Teresa Ann Murray, "Thomas Morley and the Business of Music in Elizabethan England" (PhD Diss., University of Birmingham, 2010), 330–32.
3. Neither East's nor Short's prints were limited to musical volumes. In 1597, Short also printed books on other subjects, from military actions to devotional books, as well as a reprint of John Foxe's martyrology *Actes and Monuments*. In the later 1590s, he printed a number of early Shakespeare plays. See Akihiro Yamada, *Peter Short: An Elizabethan Printer* (Mie: Mie University Press, 2002).
4. Anthony Holborne, *The Cittharn Schoole* (London, 1597).
5. Short also printed the first sixteen songs in the cantus book of Morley's 1597 *Canzonets or Litle Short Aers to Five and Sixe Voices* with the cantus voice on the verso side of the folios with a lute tablature part facing. The final song in Morley's collection is an elegy to Dowland's friend Henry Noel.
6. Morley's treatise was entered in the Stationers' register in October 1596 but not printed until 1597. Thomas Morley, *A Plaine and Easie Introdvction to Practicall Mvsicke* (London, 1597); Morley, *Canzonets. Or Little Short Songs to Foure Voyces* (London, 1597).
7. *LB*, 266–67.
8. Jacques Moderne, *Le Parangon des Chansons* (Paris, 1538). On *Le Parangon*, see Samuel F. Pogue, *Jacques Moderne: Lyons Music Printer of the Sixteenth Century* (Geneva: Droz, 1969). Later prints of *Hortus musarum* and *Luculentum Theatrum Musicum* by Pierre Phalèse (Louvain, 1568) present lute duets in which the facing-page tablature for the second lute is printed upside down for across-the-table performance. Noted in Davitt Moroney, "Thomas Morley Portrayed," in *Thomas Morley's A Plaine and Easie Introduction to Practicall Musicke (London, 1597)*, vol. 3, ed. Jessie Ann Owens and John Milsom (forthcoming); Tessa Murray, "Peter Short and the Printing of Dowland's *First Booke of Songes*," *JLS* 53 (2013): 9; Holman, *Dowland: Lachrimae*, 8.
9. BL Add MS 31390. The handwritten title reads, "A booke of In nomines & other solfainge songes of v: vi: vii: & viii: p[ts] for voyces or Instrumentes." Add MS 4900 also features rotated parts. A much earlier Italian manuscript, Florence, Biblioteca Nazionale Central, MS Banco Rari 230, takes the form as well.
10. Arber, *Transcript of the Registers of the Company of Stationers*, 3:94.
11. *FB*, dedication.
12. William Barley, *A New Booke of Tabliture* (London, 1596).
13. On Barley, see Gerald D. Johnson, "William Barley, 'Publisher & Seller of Bookes,' 1591–1614," *The Library* s6 11, no. 1 (1989): 10–46; John M. Ward, "Barley's Songs Without Words," *LSJ* 12 (1970): 5–22; A. Lavin, "William Barley, Draper and Stationer," *Studies in Bibliography* 22 (1969): 214–23.
14. See David Greer, introduction to *Ayres for Four Voices* (London: Stainer and Bell, 2000), xxii–xxiii, 206–12; Certain spelling variants seem to indicate preferences of the compositor who set the type. Some lute parts were altered slightly after the 1603 print, but whether that was at Dowland's direction remains unknown.
15. On the cover image, see Moroney, "Thomas Morley Portrayed"; Rooley, "Time Stands Still," 444–60; Joseph M. Ortiz, *Broken Harmony: Shakespeare and the Politics of Music* (Ithaca: Cornell University Press, 2011), 106–8.
16. Thomas Fuller, *The Church-History of Britain from the Birth of Jesus Christ Until the Year M.DC.XLVIII* (London, 1655), 149. Noted in *JD*, 49.
17. See Kirsten Gibson, "The Order of the Book: Materiality, Narrative and Authorial Voice in John Dowland's *First Booke of Songes or Ayres*," *Renaissance Studies* 26, no. 1 (2012): 13–33.
18. See Chapter 6.
19. Luca Marenzio, *Madrigali a quattro voci* (Venice, 1585), 13. Discussed in Anthony Rooley, "New Light on John Dowland's Songs of Darkness," *EM* 11, no. 11 (1983): 6–8.
20. "Lady Hunsdon's allmande," also known as "Lady Hunsdon's puffe," is included in the Folger-Dowland Lutebook and signed by Dowland. FSL MS V.b.280, f. 22v. Concordances are found in eleven other contemporaneous lute manuscripts. *RG*, 18, 49–70.
21. At the time, Robert Johnson, John Johnson's son, was indentured at the Carey household. There is a chance then, that Dowland had some part in the younger lutenist's training.

22. Thomas Campion, *Thomæ Campiani Poemata. Ad Thamesin. Fragmentum Vmbræ. Liber Elegiarum. Liber Epigrammatum* (London, 1595). Translated from Latin.
23. *FB*, A1r. Translated from Latin.
24. For example, "If my complaints could passions move," "Can she excuse my wrongs," "Now, O now I needs must part," and "Awake, sweet love" are all based on galliards copied into Mathew Holmes's lute book prior to 1595 (CUL Dd.2.11, ff. 53r, 58r, 40v, 58r, 62v, 93r). Each also appears in arrangements in later instrumental sources, some with titles attached to specific individuals, such as "Captain Piper, his galliard," the "Earl of Essex galliard," the "Frog galliard," and simply "galliard." For concordances, see *RG*, 12–16.
25. Four of the texts in the *First Booke* were included in *England's Helicon* (1600), one of the most esteemed poetic miscellanies of the era. See David Greer, "Songbook Lyrics in *England's Helicon*," *English Studies* 74, no. 3 (1993): 236–45.
26. See J. W. Saunders, "The Stigma of Print: A Note on the Social Bases of Tudor Poetry," *Essays in Criticism* 1 (1951): 139–64; and Steven W. May, "Tudor Aristocrats and the Mythical 'Stigma of Print,'" *Renaissance Papers* 10 (1980): 11–18.
27. See *Selected Poems of Fulke Greville*, ed. Thom Gunn (Chicago: University of Chicago Press, 2009), 47, 81.
28. Gavin Alexander, "Martin Peerson and Greville's *Caelica*: From Lyric Sequence to Songbook," *Sidney Journal* 35, no. 1 (2017): 6.
29. The poem has been credited to others such as Walter Raleigh and William Shakespeare, as well as to Cumberland, sometimes with the title "To Cynthia." See E. H. Fellowes, *English Madrigal Verse*, 2nd ed. (London, 1950), 409; and Edward F. Rimbault, *Bibliotheca Marigaliana* (London: John Russell Smith, 1947), xi.
30. On this song and "Can she excuse my wrongs," see Jeremy Smith, "Music and the Cult of Elizabeth: The Politics of Panegyric and Sound," in *"Noyses, sounds, and sweet aires": Music in Early Modern England*, ed. Jessie Ann Owens (Washington, DC: Folger Shakespeare Library, 2006), 71–73; *JD*, 152–55, 226–29; Kirsten Gibson, "'So to the Wood Went I': Politicizing the Greenwood in Two Songs by John Dowland," *Journal of the Royal Musical Association* 132, no. 2 (2007): 221–51; and Lillian M. Ruff and D. Arthur Wilson, "The Madrigal, the Lute Song and Elizabethan Politics," *Past and Present* 44 (1969): 24–32.
31. See Chapter 3.
32. On Essex, see Paul E. J. Hammer, *The Polarisation of Elizabethan Politics: The Political Career of Robert Devereux, 2nd Earl of Essex, 1585–1597* (Cambridge: Cambridge University Press, 1999).
33. Gibson, "So to the Wood Went I," 229–30; Gibson, "John Dowland and the Elizabethan Courtier Poets," 239–53.
34. Gavin Alexander notes the song as an example of metrical stress used to adapt French song to English verse. Alexander, "The Elizabethan Lyric as Contrafactum: Robert Sidney's 'French Tune' Identified," *ML* 84, no. 3 (2003): 384. Also see *DM*, 136–39.
35. Nichols, *Progresses and Public Processions of Queen Elizabeth*, 2:346–47.
36. Nichols, *Progresses and Public Processions of Queen Elizabeth*, 2:346. Nichols's source was Bodleian Library, MS Ashmole 781. A modern edition with commentary listing concordant sources is available in Leah S. Marcus, Janel Mueller, and Mary Beth Rose, eds., *Elizabeth I: Collected Works* (Chicago: University of Chicago Press, 2000), 302–3. Also see Cristina Vallaro, "Elizabeth I as Poet: Some Notes on 'On Monsieur's Departure' and John Dowland's 'Now O Now I Needs Must Part,'" in *Elizabeth I in Writing: Language, Power and Representation in Early Modern England*, ed. Donatella Montini and Iolanda Plescia (Cham: Palgrave Macmillan, 2018), 109–26.
37. CUL Dd.2.11, ff. 40v, 53r, 93r.
38. Thomas Morley, *First Book of Consort Lessons made by Diuers Exquisite Authors, for Six Instruments to Play Together* (London, 1599). Other works in the volume include "Galliard Can shee Excuse," "Galliard to Captain Piper's pavan" and its corresponding pavan, and a version of Dowland's famous "Lacrimae Pauin."

Chapter 9

1. Edward Collard was granted a lutenist position in the English court in 1598. NA PRO AO 1/387/37. Cited in *DM*, 110n194.

2. DNA Rentemesterregnskaber, 1599–1600, f. 474v. Trans. Thomas Hatt Olsen in *DM*, 100.
3. Peter Hauge, "Dowland in Denmark 1598–1606: A Rediscovered Document," *JLS* 41 (2001): 13–14. 500 daler equaled approximately £170. Astrid Friis, and Kristof Glamann, *A History of Prices and Wages in Denmark 1660–1800* (London: Longmans, 1958), 1:3.
4. Peter Hauge, "John Dowland's Employment at the Royal Danish Court: Musician, Agent—and Spy?," in *Double Agents: Cultural and Political Brokerage in Early Modern Europe*, ed. Marika Keblusek and Badeloch Vera Noldus (Leiden: Brill, 2011), 198.
5. Peter Hauge, "Dowland and His Time in Copenhagen, 1598–1606," *EM* 41, no. 2 (2013): 192.
6. Angul Hammerich, *Musiken ved Christian den Fjerdes Hof: Et Bidrag til Dansk Musikhistorie* (Copenhagen: Wilhelm Hansen, 1892), 209.
7. Angul Hammerich, "Musical Relations between England and Denmark in the Seventeenth Century," *Sammelbände der Internationalen Musikgesellschaft* 13, no. 1 (1911): 118.
8. Hauge, "Dowland and His Time in Copenhagen," 192.
9. Hauge, "John Dowland's Employment," 198; DNA Rentemesterregnskab, 1608–1609, ff. 757v–758r. Trans. *DM*, 99.
10. Hauge, "John Dowland's Employment," 200.
11. NA SP 12/265, f. 206. Noted in Peter Hauge, "Was Dowland a Spy?" *EMH* 6 (2000): 10.
12. Hauge, "John Dowland's Employment," 200.
13. The most recent comprehensive biography of Christian IV is Steffen Heiberg, *Christian 4: En Europæisk Statsmand* (Copenhagen: Lindhardt og Ringhof, 2017), from which much information in this chapter on Christian's court and activities is mined. Also see Paul Douglas Lockhart, *Denmark, 1513–1660* (Oxford: Oxford University Press, 2007), 127–93. The seminal source on music in Christian IV's court is Hammerich, *Musiken ved Christian den Fjerdes Hof*. For a modern, updated overview, see Ole Kongsted, "Christian IV. und seine europäische Musikerschaft," in *Europa in Scandinavia: Kulturelle und soziale Dialoge in der frühen Neuzeit*, ed. Robert Bohn (Frankfurt am Main: Peter Lang, 1994), 115–26.
14. Arne Spohr, "'This Charming Invention Created by the King': Christian IV and His Invisible Music," *Danish Yearbook of Music* 39 (2012): 13.
15. Beate Agnes Schmidt, "Angels and the Muses of Zion: Michael Praetorius and Cultural Exchange between the Danish and German Lutheran Courts before the Thirty Years' War," in *Tracing the Jerusalem Code: The Chosen People, Christian Cultures in Early Modern Scandinavia (1536–ca. 1750)*, ed. Eivor Andersen Oftestad and Joar Haga (Berlin: De Gruyter, 2021), 393.
16. Hauge, "Dowland and His Time in Copenhagen," 190.
17. Peter Hauge, "Michael Praetorius's Connections to the Danish Court," in *Michael Praetorius: Vermittler europäischer Musiktraditionen um 1600*, ed. Susanne Rode-Breymann and Arne Spohr (Hildesheim: Olms, 2011), 40.
18. At its height in 1618, the musical entourage grew to at least seventy-seven members. Kongsted, "Christian IV," 122; Hammerich, "Musical Relations," 114–17. Hammerich compares these numbers to ninety-two musicians in Munich and 114 musicians in the English court.
19. Spohr, "This Charming Invention Created by the King," 32.
20. Bjarke Moe, "Italian Music at the Danish Court during the Reign of Christian IV: Presenting a Picture of Cultural Transformation," *Danish Yearbook of Musicology* 38 (2010–2011): 18; Hauge, "Michael Praetorius's Connections to the Danish Court," 39–42.
21. Thomas Heywood, *An Apology For Actors* (London, 1612). Cited in V. C. Ravn, "English Instrumentalists at the Danish Court in the Time of Shakespeare," *Sammelbände der Internationalen Musikgesellschaft* 7, no. 4 (1906): 555–56; and Hammerich, "Musical Relations," 114.
22. DNA Rentemesterregneskab, 1597–1598, afd. 19, 11 August 1597. Noted in Hammerich, *Musiken ved Christian den Fjerdes Hof*, 17; and Hauge, "John Dowland's Employment," 197.
23. Hauge, "Dowland and His Time in Copenhagen," 190.
24. Peter Hauge, "Et brev fra diplomaten Stephen Lesieur til Christian IV's lutenist John Dowland," *Magasin fra Det Kongelige Bibliotek* 15, no. 2 (March 2002): 3.
25. Berkeley Castle Archives, Berkeley Family Muniments, General series Bound Book 108, f. 196. Discussed in Michael J. Ashley, "Who Sent Dowland to Coventry in 1598?" *LN* 82 (2007): 17–20.
26. Susan Lewis Hammond, "Urban Music and Christian IV's Urban Agenda for Copenhagen," *Scadinavian Studies* 77, no. 3 (2005): 365; Heiberg, *Christian 4*, 86–88.
27. Ulrich Pfister, "Urban Population in Germany, 1500–1850," Center for Qualitative Economics, WWU Münster (2020), https://www.wiwi.uni-muenster.de/oeew/sites/oeew/files/CQE_paper/cqe_wp_90_2020.pdf.

28. Spohr, "This Charming Invention Created by the King," 33; Heiberg, *Christian 4*, 139.
29. Arne Keller, "Dowland on the Rocks, or Dowland and the Ship's Cat," *LN* 62 (2002): 20.
30. John Case, *The Praise of Mvsicke* (Oxford, 1586), 44.
31. Kongsted, "Christian IV. und seine europäische Musikerschaft," 119. Cited in Hammerich, *Musiken ved Christian den Fjerdes Hof*, 167.
32. Hammerich, *Musiken ved Christian den Fjerdes Hof*, 94–95; Spohr, "This Charming Invention Created by the King," 31.
33. Hammond, "Urban Music and Christian IV's Urban Agenda," 370–71.
34. DNA Bilag til Rentemesterregnskaber, 1600–1601 (Udg. konto no. 7[C.d.]). Trans. *DM*, 101–2. Poulton suggests this payment may have been for procuring items, but Ward strongly contends there is no reason to assume it was anything but a gift. *JD*, 56; *DM*, 102n184.
35. Heiberg, *Christian 4*, 150. Brahe left to work for the Holy Roman Emperor Rudolf II in 1599.
36. Hammerich, "Musical Relations," 116. Norcome returned to England and was appointed at Windsor Chapel but left in 1602 to work for the Governor of the Netherlands.
37. Hammond, "Urban Music and Christian IV's Urban Agenda," 371–77.
38. *SB*. For more details, see Chapter 10.
39. Trans. Hauge, "John Dowland's Employment," 204.
40. Hauge, "John Dowland's Employment," 205; Hauge, "Dowland and His Time in Copenhagen," 194.
41. Hauge, "Dowland and His Time in Copenhagen," 192. Information from DNA Rentemesterregnskab, 1599–1600, Udg. Afd. 19, 30 November 1600.
42. DNA Rentemesterregnskaber, 1599–1600, f. 474v, 476r–v; Rentemesterregnskab, 1600–1601, f. 529v, 530, 532v, 711. Trans. *DM*, 100–101.
43. DNA Rentemesterregnskab, 1601–1602, f. 711. Trans. *DM*, 102–3.
44. DNA Bilag til Rentemesterregnskaber, 1601–1602 (Udg. konto no. 7[C.d.]. Trans. *DM*, 103; Hauge, "John Dowland's Employment," 201; Hauge, "Dowland and His Time in Copenhagen," 194.
45. Hauge, "Dowland and His Time in Copenhagen," 194.
46. DNA D. Kanc. Sjæll. Tegn. no. 19, 1596–1604, f. 326v. Trans. *DM*, 103; Hauge, "John Dowland's Employment," 201; Hauge, "Dowland and His Time in Copenhagen," 194.
47. Heiberg, *Christian 4*, 132.
48. Spohr, "This Charming Invention Created by the King," 32.
49. DNA D. Kanc. Sjœll. Tegn. no. 19, 1596–1604, f. 379, 24 September 1602. Trans. *DM*, 103.
50. Hauge, "Dowland and His Time in Copenhagen," 194.
51. Hauge, "John Dowland's Employment," 203. The marriage never took place because Hans fell ill and died before the wedding.
52. Trans. Hauge, "John Dowland's Employment," 202. Original: DNA Rentemestserregnskab 1603–1604, afd. 23, 16 July 1603; D. Kanc. Sjæll. Tegn. no. 19, 1596–1604, f. 379, 24 September 1602. Also trans. *DM*, 103.
53. Hauge, "John Dowland's Employment," 203.

Chapter 10

1. The first notated musical dialogue seen in English print was William Byrd's "Who made thee Hob forsake the plough," *Songs of sundrie natures*. The dialogue form became a regular feature of songbooks in the generation following Dowland, such as those by William Lawes, and continued as models for Baroque ensemble numbers such as those by Henry Purcell.
2. Giles Farnaby, *Canzonets to Fowre Voyces, W*ith a Song of eight parts (London, 1598), A2v. The fourth poem was offered by Richard Alison, to whose 1599 *Psalmes* Dowland also contributed a commendatory verse.
3. The most comprehensive biography of Lucy Russell, Countess of Bedford, is Lesley Lawson, *Out of the Shadows: The Life of Lucy, Countess of Bedford* (London: Hambledon Continuum, 2007). Also see Barbara K. Lewalski, "Lucy, Countess of Bedford: Images of a Jacobean Courtier and Patroness," in *Politics of Discourse: The Literature and History of Seventeenth-Century England*, ed. Kevin Sharpe and Steven N. Zwicker (Berkeley: University of California Press, 1987), 52–77.
4. Oxford, Bodleian Library, MS Rawlinson Poet. 31, f. 39; MS Eng. Poet. F 9, ff. 122v–123v. Quoted in Jane Stevenson and Peter Davidson, eds., *Early Modern Women Poets (1520–1700)*:

An Anthology (Oxford: Oxford University Press, 2001), 131–32. Perhaps Dowland was not privy to the information that in 1600, the Russells were facing serious financial difficulties, so much so that an auditor was appointed to oversee all expenditures. Lawson, *Out of the Shadows*, 31–32.

5. Not to be confused with his famous nephew, Oliver Cromwell, who became Lord Protector of the Commonwealth in 1653. John Nichols, *A Short Genealogical View of the Family of Oliver Cromwell* (London: 1785), viii–ix, 4–5, 12; "Cromwell, Oliver (?1566–1655)," *History of Parliament Online*, http://www.historyofparliamentonline.org.
6. Andrew Thrush and John P. Ferris, eds., *History of Parliament: The House of Commons, 1604–1629* (Cambridge: Cambridge University Press, 2010), 3:774.
7. Shaw, *Knights of England*, 2:84–85.
8. On Essex, see Hammer, *Polarisation of Elizabethan Politics*.
9. "I saw my Lady weep" borrows thematic material from Alfonso Ferrabosco's "Donna se voi m'odiate," which was translated in *Musica Transalpina* (1588). Joan Wess, "Musica Transalpina, Parody, and the Emerging Jacobean Viol Fantasia," *VDGS Chelys: The Journal of the Viol de Gamba Society* 15 (1986): 5–8; Joseph Kerman, "Master Alfonso and the English Madrigal," *The Musical Quarterly* 38, no. 2 (1952): 232–33.
10. See Smith, "Music and the Cult of Elizabeth," 69; Rooley, "Time Stands Still," 446–48; Hannibal Hamlin, "Sobs for Sorrowful Souls: Versions of the Penitential Psalms for Domestic Devotion," in *Private and Domestic Devotion in Early Modern Britain*, ed. Alec Ryrie and Jessica Martin (New York: Routledge, 2012), 233.
11. Noted in Maynard, *Elizabethan Lyric Poetry*, 79n5.
12. Ruff and Wilson, "The Madrigal, the Lute Song and Elizabethan Politics," 38–39.
13. James Shapiro, *A Year in the Life of William Shakespeare: 1599* (New York: HarperCollins, 2005), 167. While the "O sweet woods" label might be read as an attribution to Holland as poet, the verse does not follow the style of most of his poetry. Holland, a Catholic, made his own journey to Rome.
14. Philip Sidney, *Syr P.S. His Astrophel and Stella Wherein the excellence of sweete Poesie is concluded. To the end of which are added, sundry other rare Sonnets of diuers Noble men and Gentlemen* (London, 1591), 80.
15. See Gibson, "So to the wood went I"; Ruff and Wilson, "The Madrigal, the Lute Song and Elizabethan Politics"; Lillian M. Ruff and D. Arthur Wilson, "Allusion to the Essex Downfall in Lute Song Lyrics," *JLS* 12 (1970): 31–36; Jeremy L. Smith, *Thomas East and Music Publishing in Renaissance England* (Oxford: Oxford University Press, 2003), 107–11.
16. Lawson, *Out of the Shadows*, 37–38.
17. On the Eastland-East litigation, see Margaret Dowling, "The Printing of John Dowland's Second Booke of Songs or Ayres," *The Library* 4s 12, no. 4 (March 1932): 365–80; Murray, *Thomas Morley*, 99–109; and Jeremy L. Smith, "The Hidden Editions of Thomas East," *Notes* 2s 53, no. 4 (June 1997): 1078–80. Original documents related to the case include NA KB 27/1364, REQ 2/202/63, 2/203/4, and C 2/Eliz/E1/64.
18. On Morley, printing, and the patent, see Murray, *Thomas Morley*, 85–97.
19. Arber, *Transcript of the Registers of the Company of Stationers*, 3:62.
20. NA C 2/Eliz/E1/64. Quoted in Dowling, "Printing of John Dowland's Second Booke," 376.
21. Arber, *Transcript of the Registers of the Company of Stationers*, 3:228.
22. Walter Raleigh, *A Report of the Truth of the Fight about the Iles of Açores, this last Sommer. Betwixt the Reuenge, one of her Maiesties Shippes, And an Armada of the King of Spaine* (London, 1591), C4r-v; John Smyth, *The Lives of the Berkeleys: Lords of the Honour, Castle, and Manor of Berkeley* (Gloucester: Bristol and Gloucestershire Archaeological Society, 1883), 2:402, 407; Richard L. Greaves, *Society and Religion in Elizabethan England* (Minneapolis: University of Minnesota Press, 1981), 187. Zouch was also dedicatee of *Emaricdulfe: Sonnets Written by E.C. Esquier* (London, 1595), A3r. Zouch is an interesting choice as dedicatee, for it seems he was perpetually deep in debt and unlikely to be able to finance print ventures. Richard S. Smith, "Sir Francis Willoughby's Ironworks," *Renaissance and Modern Studies* 11, no. 1 (1967): 115–30.
23. Berkeley Castle Archives, Berkeley Family Muniments, General series Bound Book 108, f. 196. Ashley, "Who Sent Dowland to Coventry?," 17–20.
24. Jan Broadway, *'No historie so meete': Gentry Culture and the Development of Local History in Elizabethan and Early Stuart England* (Manchester: Manchester University Press, 2006), 152.
25. Shaw, *Knights of England*, 1:153; 2:103.
26. See Gibson, "John Dowland and the Elizabethan Courtier Poets," 242–43; and Linda Shenk, "Essex's International Agenda in 1595 and his Device of the Indian Prince," in *Essex: The*

Cultural Impact of an Elizabethan Courtier, ed. Annaliese Connolly and Lisa Hopkins (Manchester: Manchester University Press, 2016), 81–98.
27. The text was possibly written by a Charles Reeves, who received his Oxford BA the same year as Dowland, identified as "Ch. Rives" in Oxford, Bodleian Library, Add. MS. 97, f. 18r and "Ch. R." in Philadelphia, Rosenbach Museum, Ms 186, f. 12r. James Lee Sanderson, *An Edition of an Early Seventeenth-Century Manuscript Collection of Poems (Rosenbach Ms. 186)* (PhD Diss, University of Pennsylvania, 1960), 102–5.
28. Essex's relation to Sidney is outlined earlier in this chapter, but he was also in contact with James, then King of Scotland. See Jeremy L. Smith, "Music and Late Elizabethan Politics: The Identities of Oriana and Diana," *Journal of the American Musicological Society* 58, no. 3 (2005): 507–10.
29. K. Dawn Grapes, "Italian Artistry, English Innovation: Thomas Watson's *Italian Madrigalls Englished* (1590)," *Mediaevalia* 39 (2018): 359.
30. See, for example, Alzada Tipton, "The Transformation of the Earl of Essex: Post-Execution Ballads and 'The Phoenix and the Turtle,'" *Studies in Philology* 99, no. 1 (2002): 57–80; Anthea Hume, "*Love's Martyr*, 'The Phoenix and the Turtle,' and the Aftermath of the Essex Rebellion," *The Review of English Studies* 40, no. 157 (1989): 48–71; William H. Matchett, *The Phoenix and the Turtle: Shakespeare's Poem and Chester's Loues Martyr* (The Hague: Mouton, 1965); Alexander B. Grosart, introduction to *Robert Chester's "Loves Martyr, or Rosalins Complaint" (1601)* (London: New Shakespeare Society, 1878). An alternate reading is found in James P. Bednarz, *Shakespeare and the Truth of Love: The Mystery of "The Phoenix and Turtle"* (Basingstoke: Palgrave MacMillan, 2012).
31. Linda Phyllis Austern notes that a parody of the song's refrain shows up later in Chapman's *The Widdowes Teares*. Austern, *Music in English Children's Drama of the Later Renaissance* (Philadelphia: Gordon and Breach, 1992), 53.
32. See Ross W. Duffin, "Framing a Ditty for Elizabeth: Thoughts on Music for the 1602 Summer Progress," *EMH* 39 (2020): 115–48.
33. Gibson, "John Dowland and the Elizabethan Courtier Poets," 246.

Chapter 11

1. On the humors, see Noga Arikha, *Passions and Tempers: A History of the Humors* (New York: Ecco, 2007).
2. Timothy Bright, *A Treatise of Melancholie. Containing the Causes thereof, & reasons of the strange effects it worketh in our minds and bodies: with the physicke cure, and spirituall consolation for such as haue thereto adioyned an afflicted conscience* (London, 1586), 1.
3. Robert Burton, *The Anatomy of Melancholy. What it is. With All the Kindes, Causes, Symptoms, Prognostickes, and Seuerall Cures of It* (Oxford, 1621). New editions were published in 1624, 1628, 1632, 1638, and 1651. On Burton, see Angus Gowland, *The Worlds of Renaissance Melancholy: Robert Burton in Context* (Cambridge: Cambridge University Press, 2006). On melancholy in the arts, see Kirsten Gibson, "Music, Melancholy, and Masculinity in Early Modern England," in *Masculinity and Western Musical Practice*, ed. Ian Biddle and Kirsten Gibson (London: Routledge, 2009), 41–66; and Lawrence Babb, "Melancholy and the Elizabethan Man of Letters," *Huntington Library Quarterly* 4, no. 3 (1941): 247–61.
4. For a detailed overview of Dowland's "Lachrimae" pavan, see Michael Gale and Tim Crawford, "John Dowland's 'Lachrimae' at Home and Abroad," *JLS* 44 (2004): 1–34.
5. CUL Add. 2764, Dd.2.11, Dd.5.78.3; BL Hirsch Ms. M.1353; Glasgow, University Library, Euing 25; London, Royal Academy of Music MS 601, MS 600; FSL Ms. V.b.280; Krakow, Biblioteka Jagiellońska, Mus.ant.pract. H 540; Kassel, Landesbibliothek und Murhardsche, Bibliothek der Stadt MS 4° mus 125/1–5; Stockholm, Musik- och teaterbiblioteket Tab no. 1; Cologne, Hochschule für Musik und Tanz, Ms R 242; Willey Park, Shropshire, Private collection, "Welde Lute Book."
6. Keyboard versions include those in BL Add MS 30485 and Royal Music 23.1.4. After 1604, seventeenth-century copies of Dowland's "Lachrimae" are found in more than fifty manuscripts and at least ten prints, for various instruments or voices, often arranged by the compiler or by other composers. See *RG*, 41–70.
7. Holman, *Dowland: Lachrimae*, 46–47.

8. John Bryan, "'*Full of Art*, and *Profundity*': The Five-Part Consort Pavan as a Medium for Sophisticated Musical Expression and Compositional Cross-Reference in Late Renaissance England," in *Networks of Music and Culture in the Late Sixteenth and Early Seventeenth Centuries*, ed. David J. Smith and Rachelle Taylor (Farnham: Ashgate, 2013), 192.
9. On Byrd's musical sequences, see Smith, "The Dilatory Space of *While that the sun*" 671–85.
10. John Coprario, *Fvneral Teares: For the death of the Right Honorable the Earle of Deuonshire* (London, 1606); Coprario, *Songs of Mourning Bewailing the vntimely death of Prince Henry* (London, 1613). The first two songs in *Songs of Mourning* clearly feature Dowland's tear motive in the opening phrases of the lute and bass, respectively.
11. See Peter Hauge, "Dowland's Seven Tears, or the Art of Concealing the Art," *Dansk Arbog for Musikforskning* 29 (2001): 9–36; Hauge, "John Dowland's Employment," 206–11; Holman, *Dowland: Lachrimae (1604)*, 36–60; David Pinto, "Dowland's Tears: Aspects of 'Lachrimae,'" *JLS* 37 (1997): 44–75; Alon Schab, "Dowland's *Lachrimae*: A Passionate Interpretation," *MT* 157, no. 1935 (2016): 17–35; Angela Voss, "'The Power of a Melancholy Humour': Divination and Divine Tears," in *Seeing with Different Eyes: Essays in Astrology and Divination*, ed. Patrick Currry and Angela Voss, (Cambridge: Cambridge Scholars Publishing, 2008), 143–72.
12. Burton was an Oxford academic and bibliophile who bequeathed some 2,000 books to the Bodleian library. Holbrook Jackson, introduction to *The Anatomy of Melancholy* (New York: New York Review Books, 2001), xix.
13. See for example, Maureen M. Meilke and Helen M. Payne, "From Lutheranism to Catholicism: The Faith of Anna of Denmark (1574–1619)," *Journal of Ecclesiastical History* 64, no. 1 (2013): 45–69; and Albert J. Loomie, "King James I's Catholic Consort," *Huntington Library Quarterly* 34, no. 4 (1971): 303–16.
14. For example, see David Pinto, "Dowland's True Tears," *JLS* 42 (2001): 9–15; and Schab, "Dowland's *Lachrimae*," 17–35.
15. CUL Dd.2.11, Dd.5.78.3; Glasgow University Library, Euing 25; BL Hirsch Ms. M.1353.
16. In a more roundabout exercise in connections, Unton's widow married George Shirley, who had previously been married to Frances, daughter of Henry Berkeley, and was thus brother-in-law by marriage to John Zouch. Shirley's son Henry married the daughter of Essex. Further, Berkeley's grandson George was the dedicatee of Burton's *Anatomie of Melancholie*.
17. Glasgow, University Library, Euing 25, f. 25r; Willey Park, Shropshire, Private collection "Welde Lute Book," f. 14v.
18. Fuller, *History of the Worthies of England*, 244. Note that Fuller made many errors in his biographical dictionary, so his characterization may not be faithful.
19. For instance, see Hopkinson Smith, "Francesco da Milano's Dance Music, and John Dowland's Character Portraits, a Pre-Concert Talk by Hopkinson Smith," *Lute News: The Lute Society Magazine* 89 (2009): 9–14.
20. The most comprehensive study of *Lachrimae* is Peter Holman, *Dowland: Lachrimae (1604)* (Oxford: Oxford University Press, 1999), which expounds upon much of the basic information provided in this chapter.
21. Thomas Morley. *The First Booke of Consort Lessons, made by diuers exquisite Authors, for Six Instruments to Play Together, the Treble Lute, the Pandora, the Cittern, the Base-Violl, the Flute & Treble-Violl* (London, 1599). Includes "Captaine Pipers Pauin," "Galliard to Captaine Pipers Pauin," "Galliard Can shee Excuse," "Lachrimæ Pavan," and "The Frog-Galliard."
22. Anthony Holborne, *Pauans, Galliards, Almains, and other short Æirs both graue, and light, in fiue parts, for Viols, Violins, or other Musicall Winde Instruments* (London, 1599).
23. CUL Dd.3.18, Dd.5.20, Dd.5.21, Dd.14.24.
24. Holman, *Dowland: Lachrimae*, 9.
25. This same configuration was used in *Intradae* (1597) by Orologio, the musician whom Dowland knew from his German travels. Holman, *Dowland: Lachrimae*, 19–20.
26. *LST*, A2r.
27. Holman, *Dowland: Lachrimae*, 19–22.
28. Arber, *Transcript of the Registers of the Company of Stationers*, 3:258.
29. Mark B. Bland, "John Windet and the Transformation of the Book Trade, 1584–1610," *Papers of the Bibliographical Society of America* 107, no. 2 (2013): 187. Bland misidentifies these two volumes as partbooks. Both were in tablebook format. Dowland's consort book was not the first printed by Windet with *Lachrimae* in the title. The printer helped produce the first volume of elegies to Philip Sidney, released on the day of his funeral in 1587: Alexander Neville, ed., *Academiae Cantabrigiensis Lachrymae Tumulo Nobilissimi Equitis, D. Philippi Sidneij Sacratæ Per Alexandrum Nevillum* (London, 1587).

Chapter 12

1. For details on Lesieur, Dowland, and the English-Danish conflict, see the following articles by Peter Hauge, cited in Chapter 9: "Et brev fra diplomaten Stephen Lesieur"; "Was Dowland a Spy?"; "Dowland in Denmark"; and "Dowland and His Time in Copenhagen." Lesieur's will is recorded in NA PROB 11/178/14.
2. FSL MS V.b.10, f. 17v; Hatfield House, CP 61/78. Cited in Tracey A. Sowerby, "'A memorial and a pledge of faith': Portraiture and Early Modern Diplomatic Culture," https://ora.ox.ac.uk/objects/uuid:c7487528-d4c9-4aaa-8324-8a5043808597/. Lord Zouche was a cousin of Sir John Zouch, for whom Dowland named a galliard in *Lachrimae* (1604). Francis Burton Harrison, "Footnotes on Some XVII Century Virginians. II. 'The Silver Falcon,'" *Virginia Magazine of History and Biography* 51, no. 1 (1943): 26.
3. Hauge, "John Dowland's Employment," 201–2. Elizabeth's letter is transcribed in Thomas Rymer, *Fœdera, Conventiones, Literæ, Et Cujuscunque Generis Acta Publica Inter Reges Angliæ, Et Alios quosvis Imperatores, Reges, Pontifices, Principes, vel Communitates*, ed. Robert Sanderson (London, 1727), 440–41.
4. Copenhagen, Royal Library, NKS1305, 2°, læg 5, 9 December 1602. Partially transcribed in Hauge, "Dowland and His Time in Copenhagen," 195–97, which also includes a facsimile of the letter.
5. See Hauge, "John Dowland's Employment," 194–95; and Ronald M. Meldrum, ed., *King James I of England to King Christian IV of Denmark: The Royal Correspondence of King James I of England, (VI of Scotland), to His Royal Brother-in-Law, King Christian IV of Denmark 1603–1625* (Sussex: Harvester Press, 1977), 4–5. For a larger study on international intelligence, see Ioanna Iordanou, *Venice's Secret Service: Organizing Intelligence in the Renaissance* (Oxford: Oxford University Press, 2019).
6. Hauge, "Dowland and His Time in Copenhagen," 197.
7. For instance, see Hauge, "Dowland's Seven Tears," 10–15.
8. Hauge, "Dowland in Denmark," 16–17; Hauge, "John Dowland's Employment," 206–9.
9. *LST*, A2r.
10. For example, Rowland Whyte was presented with a lifetime office and secured valuable leases. Millicent V. Hay, *The Life of Robert Sidney: Earl of Leicester (1563–1626)* (Washington, DC: Folger Books, 1984), 210–11.
11. Kenneth Sparr, "Some Unobserved Information about John Dowland, Thomas Campion, and Philip Rosseter," *JLS* 27 (1987): 35–37.
12. DNA Rentemesterregnskab, 1604–1605, f. 590v. Trans. *DM*, 104–5.
13. DNA Rentemesterregnskab, 1604–1605, f. 593r, 595r. Trans. *DM*, 105.
14. Heiberg, *Christian 4*, 179–97.
15. Hauge, "Dowland and His Time in Copenhagen," 198–99.
16. Francis Meres, *Palladis Tamia. Wits Treasvry Being the Second part of Wits Common wealth* (London, 1598), f. 288v. Thomas Campion, who wrote a Latin commendation in the *First Booke*, is included in Meres's comparable passage alluding to ancient and contemporary Latin poets, which precedes the section "On Music."
17. Richard Barnfield, *The Encomion of Lady Pecunia: Or the praise of Money* (London, 1598), E2r. In ensuing years, the poem was printed with the attribution "W.S.," which led scholars to misidentify the author as William Shakespeare. Barnfield's collection predated this credit. Barnfield was closely associated with premier poets of his day, including Thomas Watson and Francis Meres, the latter of whom in *Palladis* names "my friend Master *Richard Barnefielde*" as one of the best poets of pastorals. On Barnfield and his poem, see Richard Barnfield, *The Complete Poems*, ed. George Klawitter (Selinsgrove: Susquehanna University Press, 1990); Richard Barnfield, *Poems 1594–1598*, ed. Edward Arber (Westminster: Archibald Constable, 1896), xii; Jackson C. Boswell, "Spenser Allusions: In the Sixteenth and Seventeenth Centuries Addenda," *Studies in Philology* 109, no. 2 (2012): 361–62. Dowland followed a similar, if less lofty, scheme when providing his own commendatory verse for Richard Alison's *Psalmes* of 1599, beginning, "If Music's Art be Sacred and Divine." Alison, *The Psalmes of Dauid in Meter* (London, 1599), A3r.
18. Oxford, Bodleian Library, MS Douce 280, f. 8v. On Ramsey and Dowland, see Payne, *Almain in Britain*, 13–14.
19. MS Douce 280, f. 103v. Noted in *JD*, 61.
20. Guillaume de Salluste Du Bartas, *The Second Weeke or Childhood of the World*, trans. Joshua Sylvester (London, 1598), C8v; Du Bartas, *Du Bartas His Deuine Weekes & Workes*, trans. Joshua Sylvester (London, 1605), 308.

21. *The Retvrne from Pernassvs: Or the Scourge of Simony, Publiquely Acted by the Students in Saint Iohns Colledge in Cambridge* (London, 1606), H2r.
22. *LB*, 208.
23. *NI*, 266.
24. Hauge, "Dowland and His Time in Copenhagen," 199.
25. DNA D. Kanc. Sjæll. Reg. No. 15, 1605–1612, ff. 65v–66. Cited in *DM*, 105.
26. *SB*, A2v.

Chapter 13

1. Arber, *Transcript of the Registers of the Company of Stationers*, 3:400; John Dowland, *Andreas Ornithoparcvs His Micrologvs, Or Introdvction: Containing The Art of Singing* (London, 1609).
2. Johannes Rude, *Flores Musicæ* (Heidelberg, 1598), 2:91, 110. Rude references Luther in the opening remarks of his first volume, as Dowland does in *Micrologus*.
3. *VLL*, D1v.
4. BL Add. 27579, f. 75r.
5. George Kirbye used the melody from the Sternhold and Hopkins earlier editions in the tenor voice of his "Lord's Prayer" harmonization in East's 1592 *Whole Booke of Psalmes*, where the setting is also used for Psalms 112 and 127.
6. Solved by John M. Ward, *DM*, 85–86.
7. The title page of *Lachrimae* (1604) indicates volumes would be sold "at the author's house in Fetter Lane near Fleet Street," an indication repeated in *Micrologus*.
8. John Stow, *A Svrvay Of London. Contayning the Originall, Antiquity, Increase, Moderne estate, and description of that Citie, written in the yeare 1598* (London, 1598), 317.
9. Jacqueline Watson, "Ram Alley," https://mapoflondon.uvic.ca/RAMA1.htm; Harry Ford, "Fleet Street," https://mapoflondon.uvic.ca/FLEE6.htm; *Map of Early Modern London*, https://mapoflondon.uvic.ca.
10. *VLL*, E1r.
11. Peacham, *Minerua Britanna*, 74. This Henry Peacham was dubbed "The Younger" to distinguish himself from his father of the same name.
12. On Lee, see Chapter 3.
13. *VLL*, A2v.
14. Suzannah Lipscomb, *1536: The Year That Changed Henry VIII* (Oxford: Lion, 2009), 62–63; Keith Thomas, "Age and Authority in Early Modern England," *Proceedings of the British Academy* 62 (1976): 205–48.
15. Although Dowland joined the court of James I just prior to Henry Frederick's death, he is not included in the list of named musicians who participated in the Prince's funeral, so it is uncertain if he witnessed firsthand the events that consumed the entire kingdom.
16. Peacham, *Minerua Britanna*, 74.
17. Henry Hawkins, *Partheneia Sacra: Or the Mysterious and Delicious Garden of the Sacred Parthenes; Symbolically set forth and enriched with Pious Deuises and Emblemes for the entertainement of Deuout Soules* (London, 1633), 139. Quoted partially in Linda Phyllis Austern, "Nature, Culture, Myth and the Musician in Early Modern England," *Journal of the American Musicological Society* 51, no. 1 (1998): 36.
18. Peacham, *Minerua Britanna*, 101. Noted in Knispel, "International Character of Lute Music at the Court of Moritz," 3.
19. Noted in Ron Heisler, "The Forgotten English Roots of Rosicrucianism," *Hermetic Journal* (1992): 97–112.
20. Peacham, *Compleat Gentleman*, 101–2.
21. The dedication in Peacham's *The More the Merrier* (1608) is marked "from my lodging in Fetter Lane near unto Fleet Street," A2v. Cited in Alan R. Young, "Henry Peacham, Ben Jonson, and the Cult of Elizabeth—Oriana," *ML* 60, no. 3 (1979): 305.
22. Henry Peacham, *Graphice Or The Most Avncient And Excellent Art* (London, 1612), 131–32. Italian madrigal settings with Petrarch's "Zefiro" words in English translation include those of Giralamo Conversi in *Musica Transalpina* (Nicholas Yonge, 1588), Luca Marenzio in *Italian Madrigalls Englished* (Thomas Watson, 1590), and *Musica Transalpina: The Seconde Booke of Madrigalles* (Yonge, 1597). Alan R. Young suggested Peacham's song may have been performed

for James when he was staying with Sir Oliver Cromwell in 1603. Young, "Henry Peacham, Ben Jonson, and the Cult of Elizabeth-Oriana," *ML* 60, no. 3 (1979): 310–11.
23. BL Harleian MS 6855, art. 13.
24. Thomas Lodge, *A Learned Summary Upon the famous Poeme of William of Saluste Lord of Bartas* (London: John Grismand, 1621), 264. Lodge, a professional writer and doctor of Lincoln's Inn, was one of those Jacobean figures, like Case and Campion, who still practiced the philosophy of multi-various learning and application that was so greatly heralded during the Elizabethan era. See Alice Walker, "Studies in the Work of Thomas Lodge" (PhD Diss., University of London-Bedford College, 1925), 1.
25. Peacham, *Thalia's Banquet*, C8v.
26. Peacham, *Compleat Gentleman*, 198. Repeated in William Camden, *Remaines Concerning Britaine: Their Languages. Name. Surnames. Allusions. Anagrammes. Armories. Monies. Empreses. Apparel. Artillarie. Wise Speeches. Proverbs. Poesies. Epitaphs*, 5th ed. (London, 1636), 419. Dowland is also recognized as "doctor of music" in a 1623 state record that releases him and his fellow Musicians for the Lute from paying three Parliamentary subsidies. NA E179/70/134a.
27. G. S. Gordon, introduction to *Peacham's Compleat Gentleman 1634* (Oxford: Clarendon Press, 1906), x.
28. Peacham, *Compleat Gentleman*, 103.

Chapter 14

1. *MB*, A2v.
2. *VLL*, A2v.
3. Jean-Baptiste Besard, *Thesaurus Harmonicus Divini Lavrencini Romani, Nec non Praestantissimorvm Mvsicorvm* (Cologne, 1603). See Julia Sutton, "The Lute Instructions of Jean-Baptiste Besard," *Musical Quarterly* 51, no. 2 (1965): 345–62.
4. Dowland, *Micrologvs*, E1r.
5. *VLL*, D2r.
6. Ashbee et al., *Biographical Dictionary* 2:1686; *DM*, 110.
7. *LB*, 222–23.
8. *VLL*, H2v.
9. Heisler, "Forgotten English Roots of Rosicrucianism," 104.
10. Ben Jonson, *The Masque of Queenes Celebrated from the House of Fame* (London, 1609). Jonson knew Robert Sidney, the dedicatee of Robert Dowland's other 1610 volume, *A Musicall Banquet*, and wrote a poem "To Penhurst" about the Sidney estate. Both *Second Booke* dedicatee Lucy Russell, Countess of Bedford, and *Lachrimae* dedicatee Queen Anna participated in this masque. On the entertainment, see Richard Newton, "English Lute Music of the Golden Age," *Proceedings of the Musical Association* 65 (1938): 85; and Anne Daye, and Jeremy Barlow, "The Shock of the New: Ben Jonson's Antimasque of 1609," in *On Common Ground 4: Reconstruction and Re-creation in Dance Before 1850*, ed. David Parsons (Ingatestone, UK: Dolmetsch Historical Dance Society, 2003), 83–94.
11. Hay, *Life of Robert Sidney*, 144.
12. Hay, *Life of Robert Sidney*, 39.
13. CUL Dd.2.11, f. 52r. A second consort arrangement for viols was printed in Zacharias Füllsack and Christian Hildebrand, *Ausserlesener Paduanen und Galliarden Erster Theil* (Hamburg, 1607), nr. 18, with no title. It bears Dowland's name but was probably based on the *Lachrimae* version with added ornamentation, in an arrangement by someone else.
14. Gavin Alexander, "The Musical Sidneys," *Jonne Donne Journal* 25 (2006): 74–75.
15. See Alexander, "Musical Sidneys," 83–86; Gibson, "John Dowland and the Elizabethan Courtier Poets," 248–51; Brooks, "Tessier's Travels in Scotland and England," 185–94; Ward, "Tessier and the 'Essex Circle,'" 378–84; Ungerer, "French Lutenist Charles Tessier," 190–203.
16. Guillaume Tessier, *Primer Livre d'Airs tant François, Italien, qu'Espanol, reduitz en Musique, à 4. & 5. parties* (Paris, 1582), C2v. First identified in Edward Doughtie, "Sidney, Tessier, Batchelar, and *A Musicall Banquet*: Two Notes," *Renaissance News* 18 (1965): 123–26.
17. *SB*, B2v–C1r, D1v–2r. Anthony Rooley, "Dwelling In Darkness: Dowland's Dark Songs as Hermetic Pessimist Gnosis, and Could This Be 'Evidence' of the Esoteric 'School Of Night?,'" in *Music and Esotericism*, ed. Laurence Wuidar (Leiden: Brill, 2010), 81.

18. BL Add. MS 58435, f. 32r–34r. See Alexander, "Musical Sidneys," 72–76; Alexander, "Elizabethan Lyric as Contrafactum," 378–402; Hilton Kelliher and Katherine Duncan-Jones, "A Manuscript of Poems by Robert Sidney: Some Early Impressions," *British Library Journal* 1, no. 2 (1975): 107–44.

Chapter 15

1. *PS*, A2v. See Table 15.1 for a list of musical volumes featuring works by Dowland that were printed in the cities mentioned. While no Antwerp or Leipzig prints have been identified, the lutenist may have been referring to cities associated with the compilers of prints rather than their place of printing, such as Joachim van den Hove's *Florida* and *Delitiæ Musicæ* (Utrecht, 1601 and 1612, perhaps associated with Amsterdam) and Johannes Rude's two volumes of *Flores Mvsicæ* (Heidelberg, 1598, 1600, which may have been conflated with Leipzig). *DM*, 145–47.
2. See Lionel Pike, *Hexachords in Late-Renaissance Music* (Aldershot: Ashgate, 1998), 93–97.
3. Tobias Hume, *The First Part of Ayres, French, Pollish, and others together, some in Tabliture, and some in Pricke-Song* (London: 1605), B2v.
4. Arber, *Transcript of the Registers of the Company of Stationers*, 3:470.
5. *Poems Written by the Right Honorable William Earl of Pembroke, Lord Steward of his Majesties Houshold* (London, 1660), B3r.
6. For arguments on either side, see Steven W. May, "The Earl of Essex's Last Poem: Texts, Transmission, and Authorship," *Studies in Philology* 118, no. 4 (Fall 2021): 698–724; Hugh Gazzard, "Nicholas Breton, the Earl of Essex, and Elizabethan Penitential Poetry," *Studies in English Literature* 56 (2016): 23–44; and Edward Doughtie, "Nicholas Breton and Two Songs by Dowland," *Renaissance News* 17, no. 1 (1964): 1–3. Dowland likely took his three stanzas from a source featuring the sixty-three original six-line verses printed in the anonymous *The Passion of a Discontented Minde* (London, 1601). Identified in May, "Earl of Essex's Last Poem," 704.
7. Anthony Rooley, "1612—John Dowland and the Emblem Tradition." *EM* 41, no. 2 (2013): 279.
8. Nicholas Breton, *The Soules Harmony* (London, 1602), A4r.
9. See Chapter 3.
10. The classical characters Aeolus and Neptune, evoked in the lyrics of "Up merry mates," were popularly portrayed in a number of dramatic entertainments of the time, from Shakespeare's *The Tempest* to Beaumont's *The Maid's Tragedy*, which is tied to a wedding story.
11. Suggested in Edward Doughtie, *Lyrics from English Airs 1596–1622* (Cambridge: Harvard University Press, 1970), 618.
12. This is the dedication that led some early-twentieth-century scholars to believe Dowland was of Irish descent (see Chapter 1). No solid evidence supports this claim. Flood, "New Facts about John Dowland," 288–89.
13. "Cecil Papers: Miscellaneous 1607," in *Calendar of the Cecil Papers in Hatfield House: Volume 19, 1607*, ed. M. S. Giuseppi and D. McN. Lockie (London: HMSO, 1965), 124:84; *British History Online* (accessed 3 June 2022), http://www.british-history.ac.uk/cal-cecil-papers/vol19/pp397-521.
14. William Jewell, *The Golden Cabinet of true Treasure: Containing the summe of Morall Philosophie. Translated out of French & enlarged* (London, 1612), 118–19. Jewell's primary themes are virtue, honor, and pleasure, evidencing how common rhetoric might be used for different purposes.

Chapter 16

1. NA AO 1/389/49. Dowland's and court musicians' payments are detailed in Andrew Ashbee, *Records of English Court Music*, vols. 3 and 4 (London: Routledge, 2016).
2. Payment of 20 d. per day at 365 days/year equals £30 8s. 4d., plus £16 2s. 6d. for livery totals a yearly payment of £46 10s. 10d., the equivalent of approximately £9,000 in present day when adjusted for inflation.
3. *LB*, 209.

4. Ashbee, *Records of English Court Music*, 4:132–34.
5. Hammerich, "Musical Relations," 118. Christian IV had visited England once previously on an extended 1606 tour, during which Cecil hosted a two-day celebration at Theobalds, highlighted by a Ben Jonson entertainment. Heiberg, *Christian 4*, 141–42.
6. Middle Temple Archives, MT.7/GDE/3. Candlemas is celebrated 2 February. See John R. Elliott, Jr., "Finding Musicians in the Archives of the Inns of Court, 1446–1642," *Royal Musical Association Research Chronicle* 26 (1993): 53–54; and Priska Frank, "A New Dowland Document," *MT* 124 (1983): 15–16.
7. John Nichols, *The Progresses, Processions, and Magnificent Festivities, of King James the First* (London: J. B. Nichols, 1828), 2:567. Reprinted in W. P. Baildon, ed., *The Records of the Honourable Society of Lincoln's Inn: The Black Books* (London: Lincoln's Inn, 1898), 2:435.
8. Baildon, *Records of the Honourable Society of Lincoln's Inn*, 2:155–56.
9. On Ravenscroft, see Ross W. Duffin, *The Music Treatises of Thomas Ravenscroft: "Treatise of Practiall Musicke" and A Brief Discourse* (Farnham: Ashgate, 2014).
10. Thomas Ravenscroft, *A Briefe Discovrse of the True (but neglected) vse of Charact'ring the Degrees, by their Perfection, Imperfection, and Diminution in Measurable Musicke, against the Common Practise and Custome of these Times. Examples whereof are exprest in the Harmony of 4. Voyces, Concerning the Pleasure of 5. vsuall Recreations* (London, 1614).
11. Ravenscroft, *Whole Booke of Psalmes* (1621). Reprinted in 1633. See Chapter 7.
12. William Leighton, *The Teares or Lamentacions of a Sorrowfull Soule* (London, 1613). See David Greer, "Leighton, Sir William," in *Grove Music Online*; Richard Rastall, "Instructions for Performance in Sir William Leighton's *The Teares or Lamentacions of a Sorrowfull Soule* (1614)," *Early Music Performer* 21 (2007): 2–12.
13. William Leighton, *Teares or Lamentacions of a Sorrowfvll Sovle: Composed with Musicall Ayres and Songs, both for Voyces and diuers Instruments* (London, 1614), A2r.
14. "Broken" indicates a group of mixed instruments. This particular configuration was specified in Thomas Morley's *First Booke of Consort Lessons* (1599).
15. Leighton, *Teares Or Lamentations* (1613), 41.
16. Elias Mertel, *Hortus Musicalis Novus* (Strasbourg, 1615), 208–11, 226–28.
17. Poulton and Lam question the composership of one of these fantasias. *CLM*, 311.
18. Phillip Massinger, *The Maid of Honour. As it Hath Beene often Presented with good allowance at the Phœnix in Drurie-Lane, by the Queenes Majesties Servants* (London, 1632), B2v–B3r. On the play, see Cristina Paravano, "Italy in Philip Massinger's *The Maid of Honour*," *Ben Jonson Journal* 29, no. 1 (2022): 93.
19. Thomas Tomkins, *Songs of 3.4.5. and 6. parts* (London, 1622), Cantus B2r. See Bryan, "*Full of Art*, and *Profundity*," 195–98.
20. Francis Pilkington, *Second Set of Madrigals, and Pastorals, of 3.4.5. and 6. Parts; Apt for Violls and Voyces* (London, 1624), A2v.
21. C. F. Meyer, "Englische Komödianten am Hofe des Herzogs Philipp Julius von Pommern-Wolgast," *Jahrbuch der Deutschen Shakespeare-Gesellschaft* 38 (1902): 209.
22. NA LC 2/4/6. See Rimbault, *Old Cheque-Book*, 154–56; and Ashbee, *Records of English Court Music*, 3:1–3.
23. NA E 351/544; LMA P69/ANN.
24. BL Add MS 5750, f. 78; NA SO 3/8. The full text is printed in *JD*, 88–89, and Ashbee, *Records of English Court Music*, 3:16.
25. Michaelmas, observed on 29 September, was the traditional date when musicians received their yearly payment.
26. LMA P69/ANN.

Select Bibliography

This select bibliography is intended as an aid for those who wish to pursue more in-depth Dowland study. For this purpose, the list includes important sources directly related to Dowland and sources that were especially important in creating this biography. Citations are more comprehensively presented in individual chapter notes.

Primary Sources

Barley, William. *A New Booke of Tabliture, Containing sundrie easie and familiar Instructions, shewing howe to attaine to the knowledge, to guide and dispose thy hand to play on sundry Instruments, as the Lute, Orpharion, and Bandora: Together With diuers new Lessons to each of these Instruments*. London, 1596.

Barnfield, Richard. *The Encomion of Lady Pecunia: Or the praise of Money*. London, 1598.

Besard, Jean-Baptiste. *Thesaurus Harmonicus Divini Lavrencini Romani, Nec non Praestantissimorvm Mvsicorvm*. Cologne, 1603.

Campion, Thomas. *Thomæ Campiani Poemata Ad Thamesin. Fragmentum Vmbræ. Liber Elegiarum. Liber Epigrammatum*. London, 1595.

Case, John. *Apologia Musices Tam Vocalis Quam Instrumentalis et Mixtæ*. Oxford, 1588.

Dowland, John. *Andreas Ornithoparcvs His Micrologvs, Or Introdvction: Containing The Art of Singing*. London, 1609.

Dowland, John. *The First Booke of Songes or Ayres of fowre partes with Tableture for the Lute: So made that all the partes together, or either of them seuerally may be song to the Lute, Orpherian or Viol de gambo*. London, 1597.

Dowland, John. *Lachrimæ, Or Seaven Teares Figvred in Seaven Passionate Pauans, with diuers other Pauans, Galiards, and Almands, set forth for the Lute, Viols, or Violons, in fiue parts*. London, 1604.

Dowland, John. Letter to Robert Cecil, 10 November 1595. Hatfield House Archives, Cecil Papers, 172:91–93.

Dowland, John. *A Pilgrimes Solace. Wherein is contained Musicall Harmonie of 3. 4. and 5. parts, to be sung and plaid with the Lute and Viols*. London, 1612.

Dowland, John. *The Second Booke of Songs or Ayres, of 2. 4. and 5. parts: With Tableture for the Lute or Orpherian, with the Violl de Gamba*. London, 1600.

Dowland, John. *The Third and Last Booke of Songs or Aires. Newly composed to sing to the Lute, Orpharion, or viols, and a dialogue for a base and meane Lute with fiue voices to sing thereto*. London, 1603.

Dowland, Robert. *A Mvsicall Banqvet. Furnished with varietie of delicious Ayres, Collected out of the best Authors in English, French, Spanish and Italian*. London, 1610.

Dowland, Robert. *Varietie of Lute-Lessons: Viz. Fantasies, Pauins, Galliards, Almaines, Corantoes, and Volts: Selected out of the best approued Avthors, as well beyond the Seas as of our owne Country*. London, 1610.

Du Bartas, Guillaume de Salluste. *Du Bartas His Deuine Weekes & Workes*, trans. Joshua Sylvester. London, 1605.

Farnaby, Giles. *Canzonets to Fowre Voyces, with a Song of eight parts*. London, 1598.

Fuhrmann, Georg Leopold. *Testudo Gallo-Germanica*. Nuremberg, 1615.

Fuller, Thomas. *The History of the Worthies of England, Who for Parts and Learning have been eminent in the several Counties.* London, 1662.
Füllsack, Zacharias, and Christian Hildebrand. *Ausserlesener Paduanen und Galliarden Erster Theil.* Hamburg, 1607.
Le Roy, Adrian. *A briefe and plaine Instruction to set all Musicke of eight diuers tunes in Tableture for the Lute With a briefe Instruction how to play on the Lute by Tablature, to conduct and dispose thy Hand vnto the Lute, with certaine easie lessons for that purpose. And also a third Booke containing diuers new excellent tunes.* London, 1574.
Leighton, William. *The Teares or Lamentacions of a Sorrowfvll Sovle: Composed with Musicall Ayres and Songs, both for Voyces and diuers Instruments.* London, 1614.
Lodge, Thomas. *A Learned Summary Upon the famous Poeme of William of Saluste Lord of Bartas.* London, 1621.
Massinger, Phillip. *The Maid of Honour. As it Hath Beene often Presented with good allowance at the Phœnix in Drurie-Lane, by the Queenes Majesties Servants.* London, 1632.
Meres, Francis. *Palladis Tamia: Wits Treasvry Being the Second part of Wits Common wealth.* London, 1598.
Mertel, Elias. *Hortus Musicalis Novus.* Strasbourg, 1615.
Peacham, Henry. *The Compleat Gentleman Fashioning him absolute in the most Necessary & Commendable Qualities concerning Minde or Bodie that may be required in a Noble Gentleman.* London, 1622.
Peacham, Henry. *Minerua Britanna Or A Garden of Heroical Deuises, furnished, and adorned with Emblemes and Impresa's of sundry natures, Newly devised, moralized, and published.* London, 1612.
Peacham, Henry. *Thalia's Banquet: Furnished with an hundred and odde dishes of newly deuised Epigrammes, Whereunto (beside many worthy friends) are inuited all that loue in offensiue mirth, and the Muses.* London, 1620.
Pilkington, Francis. *The Second Set of Madrigals, and Pastorals, of 3. 4. 5. and 6. Parts Apt for Violls and Voyces.* London, 1624.
Praetorius, Michael. *Terpsichore, Musarum Aoniarum.* Wolfenbüttel, 1613.
Ravenscroft, Thomas, ed. *The Whole Booke of Psalmes: With the Hymnes Euangelicall, And Songs Spirituall. Composed into 4. parts by sundry Authors, to such seuerall Tunes, as haue beene, and are vsually sung in England, Scotland, Wales, Germany, Italy, France, and the Nether-Lands: Neuer as yet before in one volumne published. Also, 1. A briefe Abstract of the Prayse, Efficacie, and Vertue of the Psalmes. 2. That all Clarkes of Churches may know what Tune each proper Psalme may be sung to.* London, 1621.
Rude, Johannes. *Flores Musicae.* Heidelberg, 1598.
Speeches Delivered to Her Majestie This Last Progresse, at the Right Honorable the Lady Rvssels, at Bissam, the Right Honorable the Lorde Chandos at Sudley, at the Right Honorable the Lord Norris, at Ricorte. Oxford, 1592.
Sternhold, Thomas, and John Hopkins. *The Whole Booke of Psalmes with their Wonted Tunes, as they are song in Churches, composed into foure parts: all which are so placed that foure may sing,* collated and printed by Thomas East. London, 1592.
Tomkins, Thomas. *Songs of 3.4.5. and 6. parts.* London, 1622.
Wood, Anthony à. *Athenæ Oxonienses. An Exact history of All the Writers and Bishops Who have had their Educaton in The most ancient and famous University of Oxford.* London, 1691.

Secondary Sources

Alexander, Gavin. "The Elizabethan Lyric as Contrafactum: Robert Sidney's 'French Tune' Identified." *Music and Letters* 84, no. 3 (2003): 378–402.
Alexander, Gavin. "The Musical Sidneys." *John Donne Journal* 25 (2006): 65–106.
Arber, Edward, ed. *A Transcript of the Registers of the Company of Stationers of London, 1554–1640, A.D.* 3 vols. London: Privately Published, 1875–1876.
Ashbee, Andrew, ed. *Records of English Court Music.* Vols. 3 and 4. London: Routledge, 2016.

SELECT BIBLIOGRAPHY   255

Ashbee, Andrew, David Lasocki, Peter Holman, and Fiona Kisby. *A Biographical Dictionary of English Court Musicians 1485–1714*. 2 vols. Aldershot: Ashgate, 1998.
Brooks, Jeanice. *Courtly Song in Late Sixteenth-Century France*. Chicago: University of Chicago Press, 2000.
Bryan, John. "'*Full of Art*, and *Profundity*': The Five-Part Consort Pavan as a Medium for Sophisticated Musical Expression and Compositional Cross-Reference in Late Renaissance England." In *Networks of Music and Culture in the Late Sixteenth and Early Seventeenth Centuries*, edited by David J. Smith and Rachelle Taylor, 185–201. Farnham: Ashgate, 2013.
Gale, Michael. "John Dowland, Celebrity Lute Teacher." *Early Music* 41, no. 2 (2013): 205–18.
Gibson, Kirsten. "John Dowland and the Elizabethan Courtier Poets." *Early Music* 41, no. 2 (2013): 239–53.
Gibson, Kirsten. "'So to the Wood Went I': Politicizing the Greenwood in Two Songs by John Dowland." *Journal of the Royal Musical Association* 132, no. 2 (2007): 221–51.
Grapes, K. Dawn. *John Dowland: A Research and Information Guide*. New York: Routledge, 2020.
Hammerich, Angul. "Musical Relations between England and Denmark in the Seventeenth Century." *Sammelbände der Internationalen Musikgesellschaft* 13, no. 1 (1911): 114–19.
Hammerich, Angul. *Musiken ved Christian den Fjerdes Hof: Et Bidrag til Dansk Musikhistorie*. Copenhagen: Wilhelm Hansen, 1892.
Hammond, Susan Lewis. "Urban Music and Christian IV's Urban Agenda for Copenhagen." *Scandinavian Studies* 77, no. 3 (2005): 365–82.
Harris, David G. T. "Musical Education in Tudor Times (1485–1603)." *Proceedings of the Musical Association* 65 (1938–1939): 109–39.
Harwood, Ian. "The Origins of the Cambridge Lute Manuscripts." *Lute Society Journal* 5 (1963): 32–48.
Hauge, Peter. "Dowland and His Time in Copenhagen, 1598–1606." *Early Music* 41, no. 2 (2013): 189–203.
Hauge, Peter. "Dowland in Denmark 1598–1606: A Rediscovered Document." *The Lute: Journal of the Lute Society* 41 (2001): 1–27.
Hauge, Peter. "John Dowland's Employment at the Royal Danish Court: Musician, Agent—and Spy?" In *Double Agents: Cultural and Political Brokerage in Early Modern Europe*, edited by Marika Keblusek and Badeloch Vera Noldus, 194–212. Leiden: Brill, 2011.
Heiberg, Steffen. *Christian 4: En Europæisk Statsmand*. Copenhagen: Lindhardt og Ringhof, 2017.
Holman, Peter. *Dowland: Lachrimae (1604)*. Oxford: Oxford University Press, 1999.
Murray, Tessa. *Thomas Morley: Elizabethan Music Publisher*. Woodbridge, UK: Boydell Press, 2014.
Nichols, John. *The Progresses and Public Processions of Queen Elizabeth*. 3 vols. London: Nichols and Son, 1823.
Poulton, Diana. *John Dowland*. 2nd ed. Berkeley: University of California Press, 1982.
Poulton, Diana, and Basil Lam. *Collected Lute Music of John Dowland*. 3rd ed. London: Faber, 1981.
Price, Curtis, ed. *The Early Baroque Era: From the Late 16th Century to the 1660s*. Englewood Cliffs, NJ: Prentice Hall, 1993.
Rimbault, Edward F., ed. *The Old Cheque-Book, or Book of Remembrance, of the Chapel Royal from 1561 to 1744*. London: Camden Society, 1872.
Rooley, Anthony. "Time Stands Still: Devices and Designs, Allegory and Alliteration, Poetry and Music and a New Identification in an Old Portrait." *Early Music* 34, no. 3 (2006): 444–60.
Ruff, Lillian M., and D. Arthur Wilson. "The Madrigal, the Lute Song, and Elizabethan Politics." *Past and Present* 44 (1969): 3–51.
Schab, Alon. "Dowland's *Lachrimae*: A Passionate Interpretation." *The Musical Times* 157, no. 1935 (2016): 17–35.
Shaw, William A. *The Knights of England*. 2 vols. London: Sherratt and Hughes, 1906.

Smith, Jeremy. "Music and the Cult of Elizabeth: The Politics of Panegyric and Sound." In *"Noyses, sounds, and sweet aires": Music in Early Modern England*, edited by Jessie Ann Owens, 62–77. Washington, DC: Folger Shakespeare Library, 2006.

Spiessens, Godelieve. "De Antwerpse luitcomponist Gregorius Huet alias Gregory Howet (Huy of Antwerpen, vóór 1560–Wolfenbüttel?, *ca* 1617)." *Revue Belge de Musicologie/ Belgisch Tijdschrift voor Muziekwetenschap* 57 (2003): 87–111.

Spohr, Arne. "'This Charming Invention Created by the King': Christian IV and His Invisible Music." *Danish Yearbook of Music* 39 (2012): 13–33.

Spring, Matthew. *The Lute in Britain: A History of the Instrument and Its Music*. Oxford: Oxford University Press, 2001.

Ungerer, Gustav. "The French Lutenist Charles Tessier and the Essex Circle." *Renaissance Quarterly* 28, no. 2 (1975): 190–203.

Vallaro, Cristina. "Elizabeth I as Poet: Some Notes on 'On Monsieur's Departure' and John Dowland's 'Now O Now I Needs Must Part.'" In *Elizabeth I in Writing: Language, Power and Representation in Early Modern England*, edited by Donatella Montini and Iolanda Plescia, 109–26. Cham: Palgrave Macmillan, 2018.

Ward, John M. "A Dowland Miscellany." *Journal of the Lute Society of America* 10 (1977).

Ward, John M. "The So-Called 'Dowland Lute Book' in the Folger Shakespeare Library." *Journal of the Lute Society of America* 9 (1976): 5–29.

Ward, John M. "Tessier and the 'Essex Circle.'" *Renaissance Quarterly* 29, no. 3 (1976): 378–84.

Wirth, Sigrid. *Weil es ein Zierlich vnd lieblich ja Nobilitiert Instrument ist: Der Resonantzraum der Laute und musikalische Repräsentation am Wolfenbütteler Herzogshof 1580–1625.* Wiesbaden: Harrassowitz Verlag, 2017.

Wood, Anthony à. *Athenæ Oxonienses*. Vol. 2, edited by Philip Bliss. London, 1815.

Yates, Frances A. *The French Academies of the Sixteenth Century*. London: Warburg Institute, 1947.

General Index

For the benefit of digital users, indexed terms that span two pages (e.g., 52–53) may, on occasion, appear on only one of those pages.

Tables, figures, and music examples are indicated by an italic *t*, *f*, and *e* following the page number.

Académie de poésie et de musique/Académie du Palais, 11, 62–63
Accession Day, 21–25, 129, 132
Adams, Thomas, 132, 148–49, 163, 176, 177*t*, 203–4, 225
air de couer, 11, 13–15, 186–87
Alison, Richard, 243n.2, 247n.17
almain, 12, 13, 32, 35–36, 147, 181
Anna of Denmark, Queen of England, 7, 35, 130, 144, 148–50, 153–54, 156–58, 171, 177, 184–85, 187, 202, 225, 249n.10
apprenticeship, 6–8, 155, 158
Arbeau, Thoirot, *Orchesography*, 32–36
artistic persona, 89, 101–3, 145–46, 186, 192

Bacheler, Daniel, 7, 35, 180, 184–85
Baïf, Jean-Antoine, 11–13
Bailey, Friar, 65–66
ballads, 30–32, 35
Barley, William, 83–84, 87–88, 177*t*, 225
  New Booke of Tabliture, 87–88, 140, 176
Barnfield, Richard, 153–54, 156, 247n.17
Baxter, John, 116–17
Beaujoyeulx, Balthasar de, *Le Balet comique de la Royne*, 13–14
Berkeley, Henry, 96–97, 112, 132–33, 246n.16
Besard, Jean-Baptiste, 178, 225
  Thesaurus Harmonicus, 140, 165*t*, 189*t*
  in *Varietie of Lute-Lessons*, 178–79
Blount, Charles, Earl of Devonshire, 157, 186
Bodeck, Hans von, 154–55
Borchgrevinck, Melchior, 108, 112, 114–16
Brade, William, 108, 158–59
Breton, Nicholas, 194–98
Bright, Timothy, *Treatise of Melancholie*, 138
Burton, Robert, *Anatomie of Melancholie*, 138, 143, 246n.12, 246n.16
Byrd, William, 3–4, 6, 28, 39, 78–79, 83–86, 141, 156, 209–10

Caccini, Giulio, 62–63, 186–87
Campion, Edmund, 16–17, 27
Campion, Thomas, 93–94, 177, 211, 225, 247n.16
Carey, George, Lord Hunsdon, 7, 21, 39–40, 41, 88, 91–93, 96–97, 99, 132–33, 225, 240n.21
Case, John, 29, 33, 38–39, 114, 175
Cavendish, Charles, 80–82
Cavendish, William, Earl of Devonshire, 80–81, 239n.45
Cecil, Robert, 4, 18, 21, 39–40, 45–46, 53–54, 57–58, 70–71, 97, 108–9, 120, 135–36, 151–54, 163–64, 168–69, 169*f*, 171, 172–74, 181–82, 187, 199–200, 201, 225, 237n.1
  letter to, 4–5, 9, 18, 26–28, 45, 46, 53–54, 57–58, 61–68, 91, 152, 213–15, 229n.1
Cellarius, Johannes, 165–66
Christian IV, King of Denmark, 47, 50–52, 107–19, 110*f*, 132, 144–50, 151–55, 157–58, 163–66, 180, 202, 225, 251n.5
Clifford, George, Earl of Cumberland, 22, 94–96, 184–85
Clinton, Henry, Earl of Lincoln, 69–70, 232n.7
Cobham, Henry, 5, 8–18, 45–46, 55–57, 109, 225
Company of Stationers, 5, 19, 85–86, 91, 130–33, 148–49, 163, 168, 177*t*, 192
consort music, 3, 138, 141, 146–48, 183–84, 202–5
Coprario, John, 141–43, 149, 186, 211
Coryat, Thomas, 55–59
Croce, Giovanni, 58–60, 78–79, 91, 225
Cutting, Francis, 37, 87, 88, 108, 203

dances, 12–14, 30–37, 144–45, 147, 178–79, 184
Danyel, John, 37, 149
Darcy-Clifton, Katherine, 35–39, 180
Day, John, 73–74

Devereux, Robert, Earl of Essex, 7, 21, 36, 45, 57–58, 69, 94, 97–98, 124–37, 145, 157, 172–74, 180–82, 184–86, 194–95, 226, 246n.16
Dowland, John
  in Denmark, 103, 107–19, 123, 130–31, 148–49, 151–59, 165–66, 182
  First Booke, 4–6, 7, 9, 15, 19–23, 37, 39–41, 46, 52–53, 55, 57–59, 63–64, 70, 83–103, 115–16, 120–21, 128, 132–33, 145, 157, 174, 177*t*, 185–87, 200, 208
  in France, 6–20, 26–27, 30, 36, 45–46, 55–57, 59–60, 62–63, 69, 91, 98–99, 153, 181–82, 184–85
  in Germany, 18, 29, 45–54, 55–57, 68–82, 108–9, 179–82
  in Italy, 55–67
  Lachrimae (1604 print), 96–98, 115–16, 132–33, 138–50, 153–55, 177*t*, 200, 249n.10, 249n.13
  Micrologus, 143, 163–70, 176, 178–79, 187, 203–4
  Pilgrimes Solace, 3–55, 25, 37, 172, 177*t*, 188–201, 201, 203–5, 211–12
  religion, 16–17, 27–28, 45–46, 53–54, 57–58, 64–67, 68, 74–75, 108–9, 121, 130, 143–44, 157
  Second Booke, 23–24, 26, 36, 37, 88, 115–17, 120–31, 135–36, 139–40, 149–50, 154, 157, 177*t*, 186, 200, 249n.10
  Third Booke, 115–16, 120, 132–37, 148–50, 157, 177*t*, 185, 200, 211–12
Dowland, Mrs., 26, 49, 66–67, 109, 116–17, 120–21, 130–31, 152, 181–82
Dowland, Robert, 18, 26–27, 41, 48, 149, 171, 176–82, 184–85, 187, 203, 210, 226
  Musicall Banquet, 24–27, 37, 62, 125–28, 141–43, 176, 177*t*, 181–87, 249n.10
  Varietie of Lute Lessons, 3, 33, 35, 37, 39, 48, 50, 72, 98, 165–66, 170–74, 176–81, 177*t*, 186–87
Dudley, Robert, Duke of Leicester, 10, 47, 99, 111–12, 124–25, 128–29

East, Thomas, 73–74, 78–79, 83–84, 130–31, 177*t*, 226
  Whole Booke of Psalmes, 73–75, 79–80, 83, 165–66, 248n.5
Eastland, George, 116, 120–21, 123–24, 130–31, 177*t*, 226
Elisabeth of Hesse, 37, 69–71, 164*t*
Elizabeth I, Queen of England, 4, 10–11, 14–18, 21–26, 28–29, 35, 37, 45, 58, 69–72, 76–77, 82, 83, 92–101, 107–8, 124–25, 128–37, 151–54, 170–71, 178–83, 201, 226
  as Cynthia, 94–97, 101–2, 133–36, 153–54
  entertainments, 22–23, 25–26, 94, 133–37, 185, 198–200
  persona, 22, 96–97, 135–37, 145–46

fantasias/fancies, 30–31, 36–37, 40, 48, 62, 179–80, 207–8
Farnaby, Giles, 194
  Canzonets, 120
Ferdinando I de' Medici, Duke, 63–64
Ferrabosco, Alfonso, 180, 185–86
Fetter Lane, 148–49, 166–68, 168*f*, 174, 248n.7
Florio, John, 58, 236n.8
Francis, Duke of Anjou, 10–11, 18, 98–101
Fuller, Thomas, 4–5, 70–71, 89, 146, 246n.18
Füllsack Zacharias, and Christian Hildebrand, *Ausserlesener Paduanen und Galliarden*, 165*t*, 189*t*, 249n.13

galliard, 13, 19, 32–37, 62, 180, 188
Gerle, Hans, *Tabulatur auff die Laudten*, 3, 178–79, 229n.1
Gesualdo, Carlo, 61
Greaves, Thomas, 149
Greville, Fulke, 99
  Caelica, 94–96
Grey, Thomas, Baron Grey of Wilton, 65, 237n.41

Hales, Robert, 22–23, 29, 184–85, 201–2, 226
Heinrich Julius, Duke of Brunswick-Lüneburg, 45–53, 57–58, 69–70, 108–11, 158–59, 164, 179–80, 210, 226
Henri III, King of France, 9, 11–13, 15, 98–99
Herbert, Mary Sidney, Countess of Pembroke, 184–85, 192–93
Holborne, Anthony, 120, 180, 184–85, 226
  Cittharn Schoole, 84, 120
  Pavans, Galliards, Almains, 32, 146–47
Holland, Hugh, 120, 129, 244n.13
Holmes, Mathew, 31–32, 36, 38–42, 38*t*, 101, 132–33, 139, 145, 147, 180, 183–84, 226
Hove, Joachim van den, *Delitiae Musicae* and *Florida*, 140, 165*t*, 250n.1
Howard, Theophilus, Lord Walden, 191–92, 199, 201, 226
Howard, Thomas, Earl of Suffolk, 191, 201
Howet, Gregory, 46, 48–53, 154–55, 164–65, 179–80, 207–8, 226
Hume, Tobias, 190–93

GENERAL INDEX 259

Inns of Court, 21, 156, 168, 202–3
intelligence activities, 10–11, 16–18, 45–46, 68, 109, 151–53

James I, King of England, 94, 130, 132–33, 135, 149–54, 156–57, 163, 171, 174, 177–79, 183, 187, 201, 210, 226, 248n.15
Johnson, John, 28–29, 37, 39, 41, 45, 53, 71, 107, 187, 226, 240n.21
Johnson, Robert, 7, 37, 157–58, 201–3, 240n.21
Jones, Robert, 88, 149, 183, 226
Jonson, Ben, 120–21, 181, 249n.10, 251n.5

Laiton, Lady, 37, 41
Le Roy, Adrian, 9, 14–15, 35–36, 227
  Airs de cour miz sur le luth 13
  A Briefe and Plaine Instruction, 8, 14–15, 35–36, 88, 176
  Premier Livre de Tabulature, 35–36
Lee, Henry, 21–25, 96–97, 128, 170–71, 184, 185, 227
Leighton, William, *Tears or Lamentacions*, 112, 204–7, 227
Lesieur, Stephen, 151–54, 227
Lilliat, John, 23–24
lutes, 8, 13, 59, 61, 87, 132, 147, 165–66, 170, 190
  in English court, 28–29, 157–58, 163, 178–79, 187, 201–2, 210
  instruction, 5–6, 8, 190
  makers, 57, 60
  music, 30

madrigals, 59–63, 83–84, 91, 211
manuscripts, 37–39, 88–89
  Elisabeth von Hessen, 37, 50, 70, 164*t*
  Euing lute book, 38*t*, 145
  Folger Dowland lutebook, 29, 38*t*, 40–41, 240n.20
  Holmes lute and consort books, 31–32, 36, 38–41, 38*t*, 42, 101, 132–33, 139, 145, 147, 180, 241n.24
  Noel partbooks, 79–82
Marenzio, Luca, 55, 57–58, 60, 62–66, 91, 174, 227
Mason, Mathias, 29, 178–79, 187, 237n.23
masques, 94, 181, 191, 199, 202–3, 249n.10
Massinger, Philip, *The Maid of Honour*, 208
melancholy, 26, 87, 101–2, 125–28, 138–43, 146, 150, 172, 186, 195, 200
Meres, Francis, *Palladis Tamia*, 155–56, 175, 247n.16, 247n.17
Merson, Simon, 187, 201–2

Mertel, Elias, *Hortus Musicalis*, 165*t*, 207–8
Moderne, Jacques, *Le Parangon des Chansons*, 60, 85–86
Molinaro, Simon, 60, 62
Monings, Edward, 69–70
Monson, Thomas, 177, 180, 227
Montbuysson, Victor de, 70, 164*t*
Morgan, Nicholas, 16–17
Moritz, Landgrave of Hesse, 26, 37, 46, 49–53, 57–60, 69–73, 103, 107–9, 111, 113–14, 172–74, 179–80, 227, 237n.1, 238n.17
Morley, Thomas, 6, 21, 28, 39, 75–76, 83–86, 91, 130–31, 156, 175, 177*t*, 180, 209–10, 211, 227
  Canzonets or Litle Short Aers to Five and Sixe Voices, 91–93
  First Booke of Consort Lessons, 101, 140, 146–47, 246n.21, 251n.14
  A Plaine and Easie Introduction to Practicall Musicke, 84–86, 89
Morris, Richard, 16–17
Morris, Thomas, 16–17
Munday, Anthony, 39
  A Banquet of Daintie Conceits, 19, 29
music education, 5–8, 20–21, 40–41, 170, 189–90

Nielsen, Hans, 114–16, 154–55, 158
Noel, Henry, 53–54, 64–65, 70–73, 78–82, 92–93, 99, 108–9, 124, 141–43, 145, 191, 227, 238n.17
Norris, Mrs., 21, 37

O'Reilly, Charles, 117–18, 151–52
Ornithoparcus, 164, 170, 178–79
Orologio, Alessandro, 46, 49, 57–58, 60, 68, 111–12, 227, 246n.25
Orpheus, 93, 94, 156, 179–81
Oxford University, degree from, 19–21, 27–29, 39–40, 45, 89, 103, 132, 168–69, 180, 203–4

pavans, 12, 13, 32–33, 35–36, 62, 141
Peacham, Henry, 49–50, 57–5959, 72, 78–79, 170–75, 181, 210, 227
  Compleat Gentleman, 49–50, 59, 78–79, 171, 172–75
  Minerva Britanna, 72, 170–74, 173*f*, 175
  Thalia's Banquet, 57, 174
Pedersøn, Mogen, 114, 115–16
Peele, George, 153–54
  Polyhymnia, 22–23
penitential psalms, 78–79, 141–44

Pilkington, Francis, 37, 208–10, 211
plague, 4, 9, 14, 58, 154
poetry, 11, 15, 94–96, 98, 101–2, 123–24, 129–30, 132–33, 156, 184–85
Praetorius, Michael, 47–48, 165*t*
print culture, 73, 83–89, 115–16, 130–31, 147, 148–49
   choirbook format, 73–74, 84–85
   partbook format, 85, 147
   tablebook format, 85*f*, 85–87, 147

Ravenscroft, Thomas, 149, 227
   A Briefe Discourse, 203–4
   Whole Booke of Psalmes, 75–76, 78, 204
religion, 3–4, 10–11, 13–18, 28, 64–67, 79, 82, 108–9, 141–43
Rich, Penelope Devereux, 37, 130, 141–43, 180, 184–85
Rosseter, Philip, 88, 157–58, 177, 201–2, 203, 228
Rude, Johannes, *Flores Musicae*, 140, 164–65, 165*t*, 248n.2, 250n.1
Russell, Edward, Earl of Bedford, 120–21, 130
Russell, Elizabeth, 25, 36–40, 228
Russell, Lucy, Countess of Bedford, 120–24, 130–31, 154, 228, 249n.10

Sandon, Henry, 117–18, 151–52
Schütz, Heinrich, 57
Scudamore, John, 64–66, 228, 237n.37
Segar, William, 22–23, 232n.11
Short, Peter, 84–86, 88, 120, 132, 177*t*, 228, 240n.3
Sidney, Philip, 18, 27, 128–30, 135, 184–86

Sidney, Robert, 18, 20, 21, 26–27, 108–9, 124, 136, 154, 181–87, 182*f*, 192–93, 228, 249n.10
Snodham, Thomas, 176, 177*t*
social hierarchy, 7–8, 19–20, 36–37
Stafford, Edward, 17–18, 228
Sudeley Castle, 25, 198–99
Swart, Willem, 140, 165*t*, 189*t*
Sylvester, Joshua, 157

Talbot, Jane, Lady Shrewsbury, 81–82
Tessier, Charles, 14, 69, 84, 185, 228
Tessier, Guillaume, 14–15, 184–87
   Premier Livre d'Airs, 14–15, 185–87
Tomkins, Thomas, 75–76, 208
travel considerations, 9, 45–46, 55–58

Unton, Henry, 124, 145–46, 246n.16

Vaux, Mrs., 37, 230n.9
Verstigan, Richard, 16–17

Walsingham, Francis, 7, 10–18, 64, 98–99, 151
Watson, Thomas, 18, 133, 247n.17
   Italian Madrigalls Englished, 83, 135
Whole Booke of Psalmes, 27, 73–77, 78, 79–80, 83, 108–9, 165–66, 204, 248n.5
Whythorne, Thomas, 21
Windet, John, 148–49, 177*t*

Yonge, Nicholas, *Musica Transalpina I and II*, 83–84, 86–87, 91, 185–86

Zouch, John, 132–33, 145, 228, 244n.22, 246n.16

Index of Dowland's Works

For the benefit of digital users, indexed terms that span two pages (e.g., 52–53) may, on occasion, appear on only one of those pages.

Tables, figures, and music examples are indicated by an italic *t*, *f*, and *e* following the page number.

This index includes titles mentioned in text only. For a more complete listing of Dowland works, see Appendix C.

All ye whom love or fortune hath betrayed, 95*t*, 101–2
Awake sweet love, thou art returned. *See* K. Darcy's galliard
Away with these self-loving lads, 94–96, 95*t*, 101–2

Behold a wonder here, 133–35, 134*t*
Bucton, his galliard. *See* Susanna galliard
Burst forth my tears, 95*t*, 101–2

Can she excuse my wrongs. *See* Earl of Essex galliard
Candish (Captain), his galliard, 36–37
Case's Pavan (Dr.), 33, 38–39
Cease these false sports, 193*t*, 199
Clifton's almain (Lady), 41
Clifton's spirit (Lady). *See* Darcy's spirit
Collier (Thomas), his galliard, 145
Come again, sweet love doth now invite, 70, 95*t*, 101–2
Come when I call, or tarry 'til I come, 134*t*, 137

Daphne was not so chaste as she was changing, 134*t*, 135
Darcy's galliard (K.), 35–36, 38–39, 95*t*, 241n.24
Darcy's spirit (K.), 38–39, 101–2, 180
Disdain me still, that I may ever love, 192–93, 193*t*
Dowland's adieu for Master Oliver Cromwell, 121, 126*t*

Earl of Essex galliard, 36, 87, 95*t*, 97–98, 101, 128, 145, 184–85, 200, 241n.24, 246n.21

Far from triumphing court, 24–25, 185–86
Farewell (fantasia), 30–31, 40, 172–74
Fleetwood's pavan (Bridget), 164–65

Flow my tears. *See* Lachrimae (theme and composition)
Forlorn Hope Fancy, 30–31
Fortune my foe, 31–32, 87
Frog galliard. *See* Now, o now I needs must part
From silent night, true register of moans, 193–95, 199–200
Fuga, 165–66

Galliard for two to play upon one lute, 92–93, 95*t*
Galliard to *Lachrimae*, 35, 193*t*, 200
Go crystal tears, 95*t*, 101–2
Go from my window, 87
Go nightly cares, the enemy to rest, 193–94, 193*t*
Griffith (Nicholas), his galliard, 145

An heart that's broken and contrite, 205–6
His golden locks Time hath to silver turned, 22–24, 95*t*, 96–97, 170–71, 185–86
Hoby (Giles), his galliard, 145
Hunsdon's allemande/puffe (Lady), 41, 240n.20

I saw my lady weep, 120, 125–29, 126*t*, 244n.9
I shame at mine unworthiness, 206–7
If floods of tears could cleanse my follies past, 126*t*, 129–30
If my complaints could passions move. *See* Piper's galliard
If that a sinner's sighs be angels' food, 196
In darkness let me dwell, 125–28, 141–43, 185–86
In this trembling shadow, 193*t*, 195–96
It was a time when silly bees could speak, 134*t*, 136–37

King of Denmark's galliard, 144, 145

Lachrimae (theme and composition), 33, 36, 40, 87–88, 101–2, 124–28, 126t, 138, 139–41, 146, 149–50, 164–66, 178, 186, 196, 208, 246n.10, 246n.21
Lady, if you so spite me, 185–86
Laiton's almain (Lady), 41
Langton's pavan (John), 33, 144, 180
Lasso vita, mia, mi fa morire, 189–90, 193t, 193–94
Loth to depart, 31–32
Love those beams that breed, 193t, 200

Me, me, and none but me, 134t, 135
Mignarda. *See* Shall I strive
Monson (Thomas), his galliard, 180
Monson (Thomas), his pavan, 180
Mourn, mourn, day with darkness fled, 125–28, 126t, 186
My heart and tongue were twins, 25, 193t, 198–200
My thoughts are winged with hopes, 36, 94–97, 95t, 132–33, 145

Nichol's (Mrs.) almain, 145
Noel (Henry), his galliard. *See* Shall I strive
Noell (Mr.), his funerall Psalmes, 73, 78–82, 141–43
Now, O now I needs must part, 36, 95t, 98–101, 241n.24, 246n.21

O sweet woods, the delight of solitariness, 120, 126t, 128–29, 200

Piper's galliard (Captain), 36, 95t, 145, 238n.13, 241n.24, 246n.21
Piper's pavan (Captain), 87, 246n.21
Praise blindness eyes, for seeing is deceit, 126t, 128, 129
Praise God upon the lute and viol, 121

Queen Elizabeth's Galliard. *See* Darcy's galliard
Queen's galliard, 35

Rich's galliard (Lady), 184–85

Russell's pavan (Lady), 36–40

Say Love, if ever thou didst find, 134t, 135–36
Semper Dowland, semper dolens, 144–46, 148f
Shall I strive with words to move, 36, 145, 193t, 200
Shall I sue, shall I seek for grace, 126t, 200
Sidney's galliard (Robert). *See* Susanna galliard
Smith's almain, 36–37, 41, 181
Sorrow stay, lend true repentant tears, 125–28, 126t
Souch's galliard. *See* My thoughts are winged with hopes
Stay Time awhile thy flying, 193–94, 193t, 200
Susanna galliard, 145, 183–84
Sweet stay awhile, why will you rise, 193t, 199–200

Time stands still, 134t, 136
Time's eldest son, 23–24, 126t, 128

Umpton's (Sir Henry) funerall, 144–46
Unquiet thoughts, 87–88, 95t
Up merry mates, to Neptune's praise, 193t, 198–99

Vaux's galliard (Mrs.), 230n.9
Vaux's jig (Mrs.), 230n.9

Walsingham, 31–32, 35
Welcome black night, 193t, 199
Were every thought an eye, 193t, 193–94
What if a day, 41
When Phoebus first did Daphne love, 134t, 135–36
Where sin sore wounding, 193t, 197–98
Whitehead (George), his almand, 145
White's nothing (Mrs.), 38–40
Whoever thinks or hopes of love for love, 94–96, 95t
Whole Booke psalms and prayers, 73–78, 79–80, 80f
Winter's jump (Mrs.), 41, 47–48, 87
Would my conceit that first enforced my woe, 91, 95t

www.ingramcontent.com/pod-product-compliance
Ingram Content Group UK Ltd.
Pitfield, Milton Keynes, MK11 3LW, UK
UKHW020847120326
468925UK00006B/80